PRAGMATIST TRUTH IN THE POST-TRUTH AGE

It is commonly believed that populist politics and social media pose a serious threat to our concept of truth. Philosophical pragmatists, who are typically thought to regard truth as merely that which is "helpful" for us to believe, are sometimes blamed for providing the theoretical basis for the phenomenon of "post-truth". In this book, Sami Pihlström develops a pragmatist account of truth and truth-seeking based on the ideas of William James, and defends a thoroughly pragmatist view of humanism which gives space for a sincere search for truth. By elaborating on James's pragmatism and the "will to believe" strategy in the philosophy of religion, Pihlström argues for a Kantian-inspired transcendental articulation of pragmatism that recognizes irreducible normativity as a constitutive feature of our practices of pursuing the truth. James himself thereby emerges as a deeply Kantian thinker.

SAMI PIHLSTRÖM is Professor of Philosophy of Religion at the University of Helsinki.

PRAGMATIST TRUTH IN THE POST-TRUTH AGE

Sincerity, Normativity, and Humanism

SAMI PIHLSTRÖM

University of Helsinki

CAMBRIDGE
UNIVERSITY PRESS

CAMBRIDGE
UNIVERSITY PRESS

Shaftesbury Road, Cambridge CB2 8EA, United Kingdom

One Liberty Plaza, 20th Floor, New York, NY 10006, USA

477 Williamstown Road, Port Melbourne, VIC 3207, Australia

314–321, 3rd Floor, Plot 3, Splendor Forum, Jasola District Centre, New Delhi – 110025, India

103 Penang Road, #05–06/07, Visioncrest Commercial, Singapore 238467

Cambridge University Press is part of Cambridge University Press & Assessment,
a department of the University of Cambridge.

We share the University's mission to contribute to society through the pursuit of
education, learning and research at the highest international levels of excellence.

www.cambridge.org
Information on this title: www.cambridge.org/9781009048347

DOI: 10.1017/9781009047142

First published 2021
First paperback edition 2024

A catalogue record for this publication is available from the British Library

Library of Congress Cataloging-in-Publication data
NAMES: Pihlström, Sami, author.
TITLE: Pragmatist truth in the post-truth age : sincerity, normativity, and humanism / Sami
Pihlström, University of Helsinki.
DESCRIPTION: Cambridge, United Kingdon ; New York, NY, USA : Cambridge University
Press, 2021. | Includes bibliographical references and index.
IDENTIFIERS: LCCN 2021022815 (print) | LCCN 2021022816 (ebook) | ISBN 9781316517703
(hardback) | ISBN 9781009048347 (paperback) | ISBN 9781009047142 (ebook)
SUBJECTS: LCSH: Pragmatism. | Truth. | BISAC: RELIGION / Philosophy
CLASSIFICATION: LCC B832 .P545 2021 (print) | LCC B832 (ebook) | DDC 144/.3–dc23
LC record available at https://lccn.loc.gov/2021022815
LC ebook record available at https://lccn.loc.gov/2021022816

ISBN   978-1-316-51770-3   Hardback
ISBN   978-1-009-04834-7   Paperback

What happened to the truth is not recorded.

Julian Barnes, *Flaubert's Parrot*

Contents

Acknowledgments

In a sense, I have been writing this book for a long time, presumably ever since I defended my doctoral thesis on the problem of realism in the tradition of pragmatism a quarter of a century ago, in 1996. Since then I have published several monographs, many of which examine topics relevant to the present undertaking, such as transcendental pragmatism and philosophical anthropology (Pihlström 1998, 2003, 2016), pragmatist ethics (Pihlström 2005, 2011a), pragmatist metaphysics (Pihlström 2009), pragmatist philosophy of religion inspired by William James (Pihlström 2008a, 2013, 2020a), as well as our need to address the evil and suffering we see around us in the world we live in (Pihlström 2014a, 2020a; Kivistö and Pihlström 2016). Only in this volume, however, do these prima facie diverse philosophical topics come together, and only here do I think I have been able to weave them into (what I hope to be) a coherent whole.

Some of the chapters of this book have a background in articles or conference papers originally written separately over the past couple of years. All the material from which the volume emerges has, however, been significantly expanded and thoroughly rewritten, and insofar as any copyrighted material is used, the appropriate permissions have been obtained.

Some sections of Chapter 1 are partly based on an essay published in the open access journal *Pragmatism Today*, the twentieth anniversary issue of the Central European Pragmatist Forum (2021), invited by the special issue editors Armen Marsoobian and Lyubov Bugaeva. Chapter 3 partly draws on a paper titled "Kantian Transcendental Pessimism and Jamesian Empirical Meliorism," published in another open access journal, *Contextos Kantianos*, vol. 11 (2020), a special issue featuring Finnish contributions to Kant scholarship (thanks to Hemmo Laiho for the invitation). A brief and early version of Chapter 5 appears in *Acta Philosophica Fennica*, vol. 96, in a collection of essays titled *Normativity*, based on the 2019 Entretiens of Institut International de Philosophie (I.I.P.), edited by Ilkka

Niiniluoto and myself (© Societas Philosophica Fennica, 2020). Chapter 6 combines some elements of two open access papers published in 2020: "Meaning Agnosticism and Pragmatism" appears in *Religions*, vol. 11 (a special issue on agnosticism – thanks to Francis Jonbäck for inviting my contribution), and "Theodicy by Other Means?" in *Cosmos and History*, vol. 17. In addition, short fragments of some small pieces of my work have been used in appropriate contexts. These include my reviews of Naoko Saito's *American Philosophy in Translation* (*Metaphilosophy*, vol. 51, 2020; © Metaphilosophy LLC and John Wiley & Sons Ltd.) and of Logi Gunnarsson's *Vernunft und Temperament* (*William James Studies*, Fall 2020), and my brief essay, "Advancing Pragmatist Humanism," in *Esperienza, contingenza, valori: Saggi in onore di Rosa M. Calcaterra*, edited by Guido Baggio et al. (Quodlibet, 2020).

Some conference presentations and guest talks whose audiences have played a role in the critical development of these chapters should also be mentioned. Parts of Chapter 1 were presented in the memorial conference in honor of Rein Vihalemm at the University of Tartu, Estonia, in August 2019 (thanks are due to Endla Löhkivi for the invitation), and as an online visiting lecture at the École Normale Supérieure in Paris, hosted by Mathias Girel, in November 2020; an early Finnish version was presented in a seminar on truth and the "post-truth" era at the University of Helsinki in November 2018. Chapter 2 was partly presented in a workshop organized by the Academy of Finland Centre of Excellence, *Reason and Religious Recognition*, at the University of Helsinki, in September 2019, in collaboration with Naoko Saito (Kyoto University). Chapter 3 was partly presented as a guest lecture related to my visiting position at the École Normale Supérieure in December 2019. (That visit, kindly organized by Mathias Girel and originally planned as a context for the presentation of many of the early versions of the book chapters, was unfortunately disrupted due to various reasons, including the 2019 strikes in France and then the COVID-19 pandemic.)

Various parts of Chapter 4 have been presented at a number of institutions and conferences: a conference on epistemic vices at Leiden University, The Netherlands (January 2018); Jagiellonian University, Cracow, Poland (March 2018 – thanks to Adam Dyrda for hosting my visit); the Department of Philosophy at the University of Tartu, Estonia (May 2018 – thanks to Roomet Jakapi); the World Congress of Philosophy in Beijing, China (August 2018); the "Science Days" at the University of Helsinki (January 2019); a workshop on "The Will to Believe" and medieval philosophy at the Faculty of Theology, University of Helsinki

(February 2019 – thanks to Nicholas Faucher); and a session of the "Comprehensive Worldviews" group at FEST in Heidelberg, Germany (August 2019 – thanks to Matthias Jung and Magnus Schlette, in particular). Chapter 5, furthermore, in a sense goes back to my early inquiries into pragmatist philosophical anthropology and pragmatist accounts of normativity in the 1990s, or even to my earliest interest, as a student, in the philosophical issues of "human nature" that Heikki Kannisto – one of my undergraduate teachers – was at that point working on. More recently, I have discussed its material on a number of occasions, including two symposia at the Helsinki Collegium for Advanced Studies in May–June 2019, as well as the I.I.P. Entretiens at the University of Helsinki in August 2019. My warm thanks go to all the I.I.P. conference participants who commented on that paper, including Pascal Engel, Camilla Serck-Hansen, Dagfinn Føllesdal, and Martin Kusch.

I would also like to thank the entire academic community of the Faculty of Theology at the University of Helsinki for an inspiring scholarly context within which this book has emerged – and especially for the friendly way in which I have been welcomed by my colleagues as Professor of Philosophy of Religion with no theological background whatsoever. In particular, the Academy of Finland Centre of Excellence *Reason and Religious Recognition* hosted by the Faculty of Theology in 2014–2019 was an important context for my work over the past few years. Warm thanks are due to its director, Risto Saarinen, for his continuous support for serious scholarship in philosophy and theology.

In addition to the individuals already mentioned earlier, I am grateful to a number of friends and colleagues whose constructive criticism at various stages has made a difference to how I think about the topics of this undertaking: Hanne Appelqvist, Mats Bergman, Hasok Chang, Vincent Colapietro, Dirk-Martin Grube, Logi Gunnarsson, Martin Gustafsson, Leila Haaparanta, Sara Heinämaa, David Hildebrand, Ana Honnacker, Jukka Kekkonen, Jonathan Knowles, Simo Knuuttila, Timo Koistinen, Heikki J. Koskinen, Sandra Laugier, Aki Petteri Lehtinen, Sarin Marchetti, the late Joseph Margolis, Torjus Midtgarden, Ilkka Niiniluoto, Martha Nussbaum, Isto Peltomäki, Wayne Proudfoot, Panu-Matti Pöykkö, Henrik Rydenfelt, John Ryder, Chris Skowroński, Lauri Snellman, Friedrich Stadler, Emil Višňovský, Kathleen Wallace, Niels Weidtmann, Kenneth R. Westphal, Oliver Wiertz, Ulf Zackariasson – as well as, above all, Sari Kivistö, with whom some of the ideas of Chapter 6, in particular, have originally been developed and whose support is implicitly manifested on every page of the book.

I would also like to most warmly acknowledge two highly perceptive critical readers of the manuscript who anonymously proposed a great number of revisions. I have tried to take all their suggestions into consideration, insofar as it has been possible to do so within a single volume, but the responsibility for any errors and obscurities that remain in the book is of course mine. Sincere thanks are also due to Hilary Gaskin for guiding me through the publishing process at Cambridge University Press.

Finally, regarding different versions of humanism in particular, as well as my sincere hope that we might some day live in a world not haunted by the "post-truth" worries that largely set the context for this inquiry, I would also like to acknowledge my continuous conversation with my feminist and environmentalist daughters Meeri and Katri.

Introduction

The so-called pragmatist conception of truth, along with various brands of postmodern relativism and irrationalism, might be claimed to have been one of the background factors enabling the emergence of the notorious "post-factual" or "post-truth" era we seem to be witnessing today. We know very well that many people, including leading politicians, deliberately lie or at least blur the truth in pursuing their own selfish interests. In particular, some social media users tend to distort truth to the extent that one may wonder whether we have started to create a pseudo-reality of "alternative facts" no longer answerable to any independent reality external to human beings' contingent interests. Truth itself seems to be under attack in different ways: there are people who spread lies as well as people who just do not care for truth, nor for the pursuit of truth, in their public or private pronouncements. (See, e.g., McIntyre 2018.) To be sure, we have always had our private fantasies disconnected from a shared reality of objective truth, but we now seem to be living in a world where dis- and misinformation can spread with alarming speed. It is unclear whether our traditional ways of responding to such concerns about truth are sufficient. The concept of truth may have landed in new kinds of danger, and we need to rethink how to defend it. It is through pragmatism that I propose such a rethinking should proceed.

However, for us philosophers, it may, and should, come as a shock that pragmatists – among many other theorists, including postmodernists, poststructuralists, and deconstructionists – may not be innocent for the turn of events just described. In this book, I argue that pragmatist philosophers should indeed be self-critically concerned about a potentially problematic slippery slope from the idea that (in William James's words) "truth is only the expedient in our way of thinking" to the downgrading and fragmentation of truth in populist (e.g., Donald Trump's and many others') politics of power. However, I also argue that the tradition of pragmatism provides us with considerable intellectual and ethical resources to enrich and deepen our critical thinking in the interest of finding a place to stop on such a slippery slope, in a way that honors the diversity of our sincere individual pursuits of truth in the plurality of our social practices. In order to deal with truth today, we need *more* pragmatism, not less.

Accordingly, this book is a critical inquiry into how pragmatists should approach the concept of truth and the practices of pursuing the truth, avoiding threatening vulgarizations of pragmatism. I cannot offer any cultural or political diagnosis of the "post-truth era", though; my discussion will remain at a philosophical level. Nor will I keep my explorations strictly focused on the concept of truth itself but will inquire into the complex interrelations between a number of philosophical concepts surrounding it. I will argue that, while pragmatism itself must, for pragmatic reasons, be subjected to thoroughgoing self-criticism, this does not mean that pragmatism ought to be abandoned (in favor of, say, metaphysical realism and its traditional correspondence-theoretical account of truth). On the contrary, pragmatism prevails at the meta-level by being, arguably, the most critically self-reflective philosophical approach to truth and the practices of inquiry. Our pragmatist investigations of these matters should combine themes from general ethics and metaphysics as well as the philosophy of religion and, ultimately, metaphilosophy. I will in this volume examine pragmatist truth in its ethical and existential dimensions, in particular, by exploring pragmatist philosophy of religion as an area of inquiry where our commitment to truth and truthfulness matters deeply to us.

My main argument can, I suppose, be summarized as follows.[1] We seem to be living in a cultural situation that has endangered the concept of truth itself. However, when considering philosophical ways of defending the concept of truth, we also need to recognize discourses and practices within which it may, at least prima facie, seem to be difficult to apply this concept. Thus, for example, when resisting populist politicians' distorting claims, outright lies, and other violations of truth, we have to do so in a manner that is also able to make sense of people's *sincere* ethical, political, religious, and other "*weltanschaulichen*"[2] beliefs. It is not at all obvious how exactly (or if at all) the concept of truth *can* be applied to all such beliefs, let alone how to determine whether our beliefs are true or false, but a pragmatist account of the pursuit of truth as a value-directed human practice should at

---

[1] For this formulation, I am indebted to one of the anonymous reviewers of my book manuscript.

[2] I find myself often resorting to the use of this German word (which William James also occasionally used), because there does not seem to be any exact English equivalent. ("Worldview-related" might work, but it sounds clumsy to me.)

least aim at accommodating the ethical norm of individual sincerity in seeking the truth within a diversity of normative contexts shaping our lives. I will suggest that the pragmatist conception of truth enables us to defend the fundamental role played by the concept of truth – and thus to firmly resist, for example, populist rhetoric that does not seem to properly acknowledge that concept at all – while also enabling us to remain committed to the pursuit of truth in areas of culture, such as religion, that cannot easily be accounted for in terms of any traditional realistic (e.g., correspondence) theory of truth. Thus, I will argue that the concept of truth must itself be understood as contextually practice-laden: it is a structural element of our thoroughly normatively organized habitual action in the world we live in, always challenging us to sincere individual (and hence also irreducibly ethical) commitment.

In this manner, I hope to contribute to the critical discussion that the pragmatist tradition has, since its initiation, sought to advance, that is, the on-going examination of our need to both inquire into the way things are independently of our human contingencies and reflect on our own exist-ential depths, which provide us all with unique and distinctive perspectives on viewing the ways the world is independently of those perspectives.

***

I have chosen to investigate these topics by dividing the book into six main chapters. After this introduction briefly explaining the outline of the volume, the first two chapters specifically deal with *the notion of truth in the context of pragmatist articulations of diversity and pluralism.*

In Chapter 1, "James's Children? The Pragmatist Conception of Truth and the Slippery Slope to 'Post-Truth'", I directly take up the question of whether James's account of truth, as articulated in *Pragmatism: A New Name for Some Old Ways of Thinking* (1907) and other major works, leads, first, to the radical neopragmatism espoused by Richard Rorty (especially in his *Contingency, Irony, and Solidarity*, 1989) and, secondly, to the more radical and much more problematic "pragmatism" we may perceive at work in current "post-truth" populist politics dramatically exemplified not only by, say, the Trump presidency and the Brexit process in the UK but also by political developments in various European countries. I argue that pragmatism can accommodate a contextualizing meta-level pluralism con-cerning the "truth" about truth itself and thus counter the realistic criti-cism that claims such a slippery slope to be inevitable. Realism, then, is to be maintained within pragmatism itself. A critical integration of the pragmatist concepts of truth and truthfulness will, however, be needed for this purpose.

In Chapter 2, "Religious Truth and Pluralism from a Pragmatist Point of View", I apply the general Jamesian pragmatist considerations about truth to a more specific yet potentially extremely wide-ranging issue, the pluralism and diversity of religious and more generally existential outlooks in contemporary societies. Pragmatism, especially in its Jamesian variety, can and should honor what Hannah Arendt called our "natality", that is, our individual and irreplaceable capacity of beginning things anew, of spontaneously creating novelties into the world. By combining Jamesian pragmatic pluralism with an Arendtian concern with the political – and more generally ethical and existential – significance of the pursuit of truth and truthfulness, we can demonstrate the considerable relevance of pragmatism in the confusing times we are living in.

Chapter 3, "Around or through Kant? Kantian Transcendental Pessimism and Jamesian Empirical Meliorism", continues the exploration of the legacy of Jamesian pragmatism by returning to what we may call *the Kantian background of pragmatism*. In a sense, this chapter poses the question "*why* pursue the truth?", suggesting that our commitment to truth-seeking is constitutively embedded in our ethical commitment to ameliorating the human condition. I argue that while James himself thought we ought to go "round" instead of going "through" Kant, this is a serious mistake and distorts the pragmatist's philosophical self-understanding, especially when it comes to inquiring into fundamental issues of human life, ethics, and value. In addition to briefly demonstrating why, and how, pragmatists can employ Kantian-styled transcendental argumentation (or, more broadly, transcendental reflection) as a philosophical method,[3] I will offer a critical comparison of Kant's transcendental philosophy and James's pragmatism by focusing on their shared philosophical anthropology, especially their pessimistic conception of the human being (in an ethical as well as epistemic sense), which however gives rise to a kind of meliorism (to use James's favorite term) about the possibility of always making things better with no guarantee of success. This combination of pessimism and meliorism, again, has both ethical and religious significance.

James's philosophical anthropology is further studied in Chapter 4, "The Will to Believe and Holistic Pragmatism", which focuses on his

---

[3] This is a topic I have explored in a series of works since the late 1990s. See, for example, Pihlström 2003, 2004, 2009, 2013, 2016, 2020a.

"will to believe" argument and the underlying holism emphasizing the "whole man [*sic*]" in us, sharply critical of narrow rationalism and "vicious intellectualism", yet never sacrificing the critical stance of inquiry. This chapter asks *how* we ought to pursue the truth, suggesting that a Jamesian will to believe strategy may be needed in personal existential situations of human life (both religiously relevant and secular). I interpret and further develop these Jamesian ideas in terms of what Morton White, a somewhat neglected twentieth-century pragmatist, called *holistic pragmatism*. The combination of holistic pragmatism and the will to believe idea will also enable us to further illuminate the pragmatist entanglement of the epistemic and the ethical, as well as the (Arendtian) emphasis on individual natality and the significance of our personal vocations in contexts of social habituality. A will to believe leap is, arguably, needed for us to be what or who we are, but at the same time the pragmatist constantly needs to deal with the actual or potential tensions between concrete existential decisions and continuous habits of action. By willing to believe, we may also pursue the truth in our individual way.

The kind of individual diversity of ethical, existential, and religious outlooks defended in the context of largely Jamesian pragmatism needs, however, a shared human framework of values and norms. Chapter 5, "How Is Normativity Possible? A Holistic-Pragmatist Perspective", investigates the very possibility of normativity from a pragmatist perspective, asking *how it is possible* to (individually or collectively) pursue the truth and drawing attention to the irreducibly normative contexts of inquiry and, more generally, of the human form of life. Such normative contexts are necessary for pursuing both truth and truthfulness in any epistemic and ethical matters. The chapter criticizes attempts to ground normativity in mere psychological or social facts or processes, such as our contingent acts of recognition, and further examines what it means, from a pragmatist point of view, for us to be genuinely *committed* to normativity within our human practices. This applies to the norms of the epistemic pursuit of truth as much as it applies to ethical and political normativity and existential truthfulness. In relation to this issue, the very structure of what we know as the human form of life is at stake, and the Jamesian pragmatist approaches it in terms of our irreducibly ethical commitment to living a life colored by genuine existential concern. Ultimately this yields a defense of *pragmatist humanism* in contrast to attempts to reduce humanity and humanly distinctive normativity to something non-human and non-normative.

6 Introduction

Chapter 6, "Pragmatic Agnosticism – Meaning, Truth, and Suffering", the final substantial chapter of the book, returns to pragmatist philosophy of religion and the "will to believe" discussion by suggesting that even though James claimed agnosticism to collapse (pragmatically) to atheism, there is actually a sense in which the pragmatist, especially the pragmatist humanist as characterized in Chapter 5, may plausibly develop a sophisticated form of agnosticism, especially regarding the meaningfulness of religious language. Even though we should advocate a pragmatic pursuit of truth and truthfulness in the "post-truth" era, we must not uncritically assume that all our discourses, especially religious discourses, always are truth-apt and cognitively meaningful. In particular, this chapter investigates a special issue in which the will to believe strategy may be inefficient: *religious meaning agnosticism*. I argue that agnosticism is crucial for avoiding the "post-truth" situation, as it enables us to maintain a critical distance to too easy truth-claims and hence to *care for* our pursuit of truth itself (both at the "first-order" epistemic level and at the meta-level concerned with the meaningfulness of what we are trying to say). In this sense, agnosticism at the meta-level is an element of the pragmatic pursuit of truthfulness and the critical avoidance of self-deception and insincerity. In addition to the application of agnosticism to the issue concerning the truth-aptness of religious language (cf. also Chapter 2), the chapter examines the controversy between "theodicist" and "antitheodicist" responses to the problem of evil and suffering from a pragmatically agnostic perspective.[4]

The conclusion briefly summarizes the main argument of the book in terms of what I like to call "transcendental humanism" in pragmatism, reminding pragmatism scholars that it is, indeed, primarily William James whom we may regard as a (transcendental) humanist among the classical pragmatists, defending the irreducible value of the individual human perspective on the world – in contrast to Peircean emphasis on continuity (synechism) and Deweyan transactional naturalism. The concluding remarks thus also show how pragmatism must embrace humanism as a necessary condition for the possibility of our not only being committed to the pursuit of truth but (transcendentally formulated) our even being able to ask the question about whether any normative truth-pursuit is possible in the first place.

---

[4] This is another theme I have explored in a series of (relatively recent) works: see Pihlström 2013, 2014a, 2020a, 2020c; Kivistö and Pihlström 2016.

These six main chapters are thus sandwiched between this introduction and a brief conclusion summarizing the key findings in terms of holistic pragmatism and transcendental humanism.

***

It should be noted that this book is not a thoroughgoing historical investigation of James's (or anyone else's) pragmatist philosophy or what I am calling Jamesian pragmatism, not even of James's conception of truth; rather, it attempts to follow a Jamesian-*inspired* pragmatist line of argument focusing on such key concepts as truth, normativity, belief, sincerity, and individuality – concepts that receive a distinctively pragmatist and humanist flavor when subjected to the kind of Jamesian interpretation and articulation that I will sketch and defend. The book, I hope, does not merely make a novel contribution to our understanding of James's pragmatism and its philosophical significance today. It also examines how some of the fundamental issues concerning the pursuit of truth especially in ethical, existential, and religious (or generally *weltanschaulichen*) contexts ought to be reconsidered when we take seriously the worry that some philosophical ideas – including pragmatism itself – might threaten to take us down the slippery slope leading to "post-truth" and irresponsible irrationalism.

I hope my book may therefore be of interest not only to scholars of pragmatism but to anyone seriously reflecting on what it means to be genuinely committed to the pursuit of truth and to the normative contexts enabling such commitments in our contemporary societies. Even so, I can offer no analysis of the current post-truth situation itself. That would be a task for more general cultural philosophy, media commentary, and/or political theory. I will try to be sufficiently sensitive to the ways in which issues concerning the pursuit of truth arise in non-academic contexts, including political and religious contexts, while confining my own discussion to an academic philosophical examination.

There is a sense in which my project in this book cuts across a number of philosophical sub-disciplines. To a certain degree, my discussion falls within general epistemology and metaphysics, pragmatistically conceived, as I will be investigating our ability to pursue the truth in various areas of human life. Some of my most important case studies (e.g., the extended discussions of religious diversity and Jamesian "will to believe" in Chapters 2 and 4, as well as the exploration of meaning agnosticism in Chapter 6) are drawn from (pragmatist) philosophy of religion, however, so the book could also be categorized as primarily belonging to the philosophy of religion. On the other hand, the more general examinations of our com-mitment to the pursuit of truth (and the very concept of truth) and of the normative structure of human forms of life (see Chapters 1 and 5) are by no means restricted to the philosophy of religion. Along with the Kantian-cum-Jamesian philosophical anthropology articulated in Chapter 3, they could be regarded as philosophical attempts to understand the human form of life in its basic conceptual and normative features. Perhaps the best overall category for my pragmatist elaborations is thus something like "critical philosophical reflection on the human condition". Working under this very general and inevitably vague rubric, my argument may occasionally seem to take somewhat complicated detours, but I am trying to carve out a recognizable path – an essentially Jamesian path incorporat-ing Kantian transcendental insights – through the philosophical discus-sions I comment on, showing why I think we have good reasons to walk that path when considering what exactly to do with the concept of truth (and related concepts) that we possess.

Even if the end point of that path is something relatively obvious – we must continue to seriously and responsibly use the concept of truth, and we ought to carefully reflect on the practices within which we do so – I believe the philosophical route to that point is worth following. Philosophical reflection, arguably, is not valuable primarily for the results it yields but for the intellectual, and hopefully ethical, progress during the process leading toward those results. Furthermore, someone might ask (as one of the anonymous reviewers of my manuscript did) why exactly I need James, among the pragmatists, for the philosophical path I am proposing to tread. At least some of my views on why the pursuit of truth matters to us in our lives could perhaps be more easily defended by employing Charles S. Peirce's or John Dewey's pragmatism, rather than James's. My brief response to this question is that James is needed precisely because his version of pragmatism takes the ethically, religiously, and existentially problematic character of what we may call "the human condition" more seriously than any other version of pragmatism I am familiar with. While I certainly do not wish to neglect the other key pragmatists or neopragma-tists (cf., e.g., Pihlström 2015), I vitally need James for this particular inquiry because of his sensitivity to existential concerns, his openness to a certain kind of melancholy and even the tragic dimension of human life, including his commitment to what I have called his "antitheodicism" (see Chapter 6, as well as Kivistö and Pihlström 2016; Pihlström 2020a). My longer response will become available only throughout this entire book, as

I hope to show how we can actually do some philosophical work by employing broadly Jamesian ideas in my selected areas of discussion.

It is unfortunately impossible to acknowledge all relevant scholarship on the topic of my research in a single book. Pragmatism, including Jamesian pragmatism, has of course been investigated voluminously in earlier philosophical literature.[5] So has, obviously, the concept of truth, and so have many other concepts that are central in my inquiry, such as normativity and truthfulness or sincerity. However, I suppose this book is distinctive in its attempt to develop precisely the kind of argument that I am planning to formulate, focusing on the constitutive (transcendental) entanglement of truth, sincerity, and humanism in pragmatism – in the context of what I hope to be a timely analysis of pragmatist truth in the unfortunate "post-truth" era. Clearly, some of the recent contributions to James scholarship and broader pragmatism scholarship will be taken into account in specific contexts in the chapters that follow, and some critical dialogue with other interpreters will be included, but the main aim of this undertaking is not to secure the final scholarly truth about what James (or anyone else) actually thought but to investigate what we can and should pragmatically do with the notions he (and others) developed. In addition to being broadly Jamesian, this book finds inspiration in, for example, White's holistic pragmatism and even Rorty's neopragmatism, as well as many other philosophical ideas that have hardly been brought into contact with each other previously, such as Arendt's analysis of natality and early analytic philosophy of religion. I also offer excursions to, as well as some critical dialogue with, a number of contemporary philosophers whose views are relevant to either my interpretation of pragmatism or the overall position I seek to develop. These philosophers include, among others, Richard Bernstein, Rosa Calcaterra, Logi Gunnarsson, Martha Nussbaum, and Naoko Saito. Their very different voices, I think, enrich our picture of pragmatist diversity.[6]

Let me also note that, as pragmatists are strongly divided in their responses to Kant's critical or transcendental philosophy as a historical background of the pragmatist tradition, my approach is presumably rather controversial in emphasizing the need to integrate Jamesian pragmatist insights with Kantian critical ones. One key reason why I also need a strong

---

[5] For more extensive use of both primary and secondary literature on pragmatism in some of my earlier work, see, for example, Pihlström 2003, 2008a, 2009, 2013, 2015, 2016, 2017, 2020a.

[6] Thus, my methodology could be described as a two-way movement from highly general explorations (e.g., on Jamesian truth) to zoomings into specific analyses or interpretations (e.g., Calcaterra's reading of James on freedom in comparison to G. H. von Wright's views) and back again.

Kantian "voice" for my argument in this book is that I find it natural to construe the dependence of both facts and truths on the normative practices of our pursuit(s) of truth in a (quasi-)Kantian sense. More precisely, pragmatist explorations of, for example, the constitutive dependence of the objects of inquiry on the practices of inquiry ought to be understood in this Kantian meaning: the objects of inquiry are dependent on the practices of inquiry, instead of existing "ready-made" prior to inquiry, not in the causal or factual sense that our human practices would directly "produce" them but in the transcendental sense that it is only in the context of a certain practice of inquiry that certain (kinds of) objects become possible as objects for us in the first place.

Accordingly, our purpose-driven practices provide contextually necessary (transcendental) conditions for the possibility of the kinds of entities postulated within them. Roughly, our social participation in shared practices – or in what Ludwig Wittgenstein called the human "form of life" – takes the role of the traditional Kantian transcendental self in the process of world-constitution. The objects of truth-pursuing inquiry are only possible within value-laden, normatively structured practices of inquiry, analogously to the way in which the objects of human cognition are, according to Kant, necessarily constituted by the constitutive transcendental features of the human cognitive faculty (i.e., space and time as forms of pure intuition, and the categories, or the pure concepts of the understanding).

This is not to suggest that a Kantian transcendental articulation of pragmatism could be uncritically assumed. On the contrary, within our pragmatist examination of truth, post-truth, and the pursuit of truth it will be vitally important to consider critically how far this form of pragmatism is able to function as a comprehensive philosophy of the human condition (see also, e.g., several essays in Skowroński and Pihlström 2019, some of them highly critical of any Kantian account of pragmatism). The choice to integrate Kantian critical philosophy with pragmatism should itself be regarded as a relatively controversial philosophical hypothesis to be tested by its success in formulating a plausible overall – holistic – pragmatist position. *If* a comprehensive account of our practices of pursuing the truth, normativity, and individual sincerity can be based on transcendental pragmatism, this will yield an important meta-level (pragmatic) argument for the plausibility of such pragmatism. Furthermore, my comprehensive account of pragmatism as a critical fallibilist and pluralist reconceptualization of Kantian transcendental idealism, and of transcendental philosophy more generally, cannot be developed in a single book. I have devoted a number of earlier publications to this topic, and while I do try to explain, especially in Chapter 3, why an integration of Jamesian and Kantian perspectives is important for my overall project in this volume, for a full-scale argumentation for this general position the reader is referred to some of my earlier work (e.g., Pihlström 2003, 2009, 2020a).

It can, finally, be easily noticed that I am, throughout the volume, defending a pragmatist (as well as Kantian) form of *humanism*. It is precisely humanism that ultimately motivates my discussions of sincerity, individualism, and even the pursuit of truth. This is not, however, "secular humanism" attacking religious thinking (though my humanism is certainly *not* non-secular – or religious – for that matter) but a humanism affirming the irreducibility of our normatively structured human form of life. Humanism as a commitment, on the one hand, to such a shared normative context enabling us to engage in any meaningful activity – be it epistemic, ethical, or anything else – and, on the other hand, to the quest for individual existential reflection offers a double-aspect view of our existence and practices. These two dimensions of our life, shared practices and individual commitments, are constitutively reciprocally contained in each other, because individual sincerity arguably partly constitutes the normativity defining the structures of our lives, while no individual sincerity is possible independently of the trans-individual normative frameworks within which it is a task or a duty for us to be, or become, epistemically as well as ethico-existentially sincere. I find this a Kantian transcendental rearticulation of what pragmatists may always have meant by insisting that we inevitably live as individuals-in-communities.

It is for this reason that we need a thoroughly developed pragmatist approach to truth, entangling, again constitutively, objective truth with individual ethico-existential truthfulness. Or so I will argue in what follows.

CHAPTER I

James's Children?
The Pragmatist Conception of Truth and the Slippery Slope to "Post-Truth"

Together with a group of Finnish colleagues, I have since 1999 been involved in writing and revising a series of philosophy textbooks for high-school students, published by a Finnish publishing house specializing in textbooks and nonfiction. In an introductory volume published in 2005, we included a brief discussion of "the pragmatist theory of truth" in the context of a more general exploration of the concept of truth. As textbooks usually, our books also include plenty of pictures, hopefully keeping their young readers alert. For the truth-theoretical section, we decided to use a photograph of Donald Trump, picturing him with his bestseller, *How to Get Rich* (2004). In those years, Trump was not at all well known in my home country Finland, although he was already at that point a famous celebrity in the United States. I cannot remember who decided to use the picture in the book; I certainly had no idea whatsoever who this guy in the photograph was, and I had never heard of him before. The point of the photograph was obvious: by using it we asked our prospective readers whether the sentences of Trump's books are true if they make their author (or, possibly, their reader) rich and if they in that sense pragmatically "work." Getting rich would then be their concrete "cash value."

1.1 Vulgar Pragmatism?

Little, of course, did we know. I could never have imagined that I would write another book – this book – seriously asking whether there is a slippery slope leading from William James (one of my favorite philosophers) all the way down to Donald Trump, and even beyond, but this is precisely what I am now doing. One might argue that if Trump is a pragmatist, he is certainly a most *vulgar* pragmatist.[1] Susan Haack

---

[1] During Barack Obama's presidency, there was serious scholarly discussion (including a special session at the Society for the Advancement of American Philosophy and a thematic issue of the journal

(1995) once called Richard Rorty's pragmatism "vulgar," contrasting it with Peircean pragmatism, in particular (see also Haack 1998), but it should be obvious that there can be no serious comparison between pragmatist intellectuals like Rorty (no matter how controversial their views might be) and truly vulgar "pragmatists" like Trump – many of whose pronouncements are not only false but degrading, insulting, full of hate, and a continuous threat not just to global economy but also to world peace. After the US 2020 Elections, there is reason to hope that the chaos caused by the disgraceful Trump presidency will be over as soon as possible (and that any possible readers of this book in the coming years need not worry about it anymore, though they will then undoubtedly have many new things to worry about), but I do believe that we must seriously consider how exactly pragmatism is related to the kind of attitude to truth and reality that we find him, and his supporters, exemplifying. The worry that there might indeed be something like a slippery slope from James – via Rorty – to Trump is to be taken seriously: Are post-factualists "James's children," and if so, in what sense exactly?[2]

There is no need to describe even in general terms the ways in which Trump and his supporters, like many other populists in many other countries, on the one hand deliberately lie in order to advance their own pursuits, and on the other hand just do not seem to care about the distinction between truth and falsehood at all – or seem to care about it only in the crudest possible "pragmatic" sense of having their own interests served.[3] We all know very well how Trump's disrespect for truth was

---

Contemporary Pragmatism) on "Obama's pragmatism," that is, on how Obama's background at the University of Chicago might have exposed him to pragmatist influences that could have played a role in his thinking about law and politics, among other things. In Trump's era, an analogous talk about his "pragmatism" would be a dark joke, comparable perhaps to Mussolini's well-known admiration of James.

[2] The allusion here, as any historian of pragmatism easily recognizes, is to Murphey's (1968) characterization of the classical Cambridge pragmatists as "Kant's children" – a view that I largely share (see Chapter 3). Note that the reason I am focusing on James and Rorty in this chapter is practical: it is in the work of these two pragmatists that the threat of a "slippery slope" is the most striking. Other pragmatist contributions to debates on the concept of truth, including, say, Peirce's or (in contemporary pragmatism) Robert Brandom's, would not as obviously lead to such problems. On the other hand, I am definitely not committed to the picture of there being two clearly distinguishable pragmatisms, the Peircean realistic one and the more relativist or subjectivist one starting from James's alleged misreading of Peirce (see Mounce 1997); I find the pragmatist tradition much more complicated – and also more unified (cf., e.g., Pihlström 2008a, 2008b, 2015, 2017).

[3] My aim in this chapter or this book is not to analyze in detail whether, or in what sense exactly, Trump's or other populists' disregard for truth is a form of "bullshit" in Harry Frankfurt's (2005) famous terms (see also, for further elaborations of this concept, several essays in Hardcastle and Reisch 2006). From the point of view of vulgar pragmatism, both deliberate lying (which obviously entails caring about the truth) and "bullshitting" (which involves a disrespect and unconcern for

consistently manifested[4] in his actions and public statements as president, including his incredible flow of tweets. In an extremely crude sense of pragmatism, those speech acts openly loathsome of truth and of the commitment to pursue the truth may have been pragmatically "true," as they did bring Trump to his powerful position.[5] They indeed pragmatically "worked" for him – but they certainly do not seem to work from the point of view of those suffering from the political and economic catastrophes of his presidency. In this situation, many people disillusioned by recent political developments talk about "post-factualism" and the "post-truth era," and if there is any individual who can act as a face for this cultural situation, it is presumably Trump (surrounded, of course, by an alarming number of leaders of major countries all over the world who share the willingness to sacrifice truth in the interest of greed and power). The slight re-emergence of the recognition of the value of science, knowledge, and truth due to the COVID-19 pandemic in 2020 might have changed this situation a bit, but I am afraid we just need to wait for a while to see, once again, brutal political attempts to opportunistically use a crisis like the pandemic for selfish and/or narrowly nationalist purposes.

Ironically, on the page next to the one with Trump's picture in our 2005 textbook, we placed a picture of a Soviet citizen reading the newspaper *Pravda* (meaning "truth"). Every statement contained in the pages of that official newspaper of the Communist Party of the Soviet Union had passed the strict censorship of the Soviet authorities. There was just one official truth available: the view the Party held. Our situation today, with the Soviet Union fortunately long gone (along with most – though not all – cruel communist administrations), is quite different: in Trump's era, there

---

truth, caring only for the impression one makes on one's audience) could be seen as serving (at least short-term) "pragmatic goals" or interests. For insightful recent critical analyses of "post-truth," see McIntyre 2018 and Haack 2019.

[4] Even this is incoherent or a bad joke: one needs the concept of truth to be consistent at anything, including one's disrespect for truth. Moreover, as Haack (2019) argues, the concept of objective truth is needed for dismissals of truth.

[5] Moreover, Trump of course perversely uses the notion of truth, as well as related notions like "fake news," always suggesting that what he says is true and what his opponents say is false. For some illustrative picks from among thousands of possible examples, see www.theguardian.com/books/2018/jul/14/the-death-of-truth-how-we-gave-up-on-facts-and-ended-up-with-trump and https://edition.cnn.com/2018/07/25/politics/donald-trump-vfw-unreality/index.html. On the latter occasion, Trump is reported to have urged his supporters: "Stick with us. Don't believe the crap you see from these people, the fake news. ... What you're seeing and what you're reading is not what's happening." It is of course a traditional populist strategy to claim that only the populist leader has a privileged access to what is "really" happening, including what the mystified "people" really thinks or hopes. Trump consistently continued his truth-denialism when insisting in November 2020 that he had "won" the presidential election he clearly lost.

seem to be no shared truth (or shared falsity) available at all but just a confusing rhapsody of self-serving tweets. Nonetheless, we might be in an equally serious danger of losing contact with truth and reality.

I will now ask whether the pragmatists are in some ways guilty of this development. The two main figures I will focus on in this chapter are, unsurprisingly, James and Rorty. There is no point in offering any close reading of their well-known views here,[6] but I will explore them in the context of the worries many of us share regarding the truth-degrading populists in our confusing political world today.

1.2 William James on Truth

It needs to be emphasized that, far from leading to radical relativism or political opportunism, James's (as well as Dewey's) pragmatism functions as a link between acknowledging the crucial relevance of the concept of truth, on the one hand, and emphasizing individual diversity and spontaneity, on the other.[7] It is through Jamesian pragmatism that we can bring the notion of truth itself to bear on the analysis of human experiential plurality and unique individuality (see also, e.g., Cormier 2001; Capps 2019). This requires, however, that we not only maintain that there is a plurality of truths, or that truths may be relativized to a plurality of practice-laden human perspectives of inquiry, but seriously try to understand and reconceptualize the concept of truth itself from a Jamesian pragmatist perspective. *Pragmatic pluralism* in a Jamesian style insists that our individual perspectives and commitments to truth-seeking matter to what truth is or means for us. This is clear in James: truth is always *truth-for-someone-in-particular*, an individual person, a human being actively pursuing truth both generally and in, for

---

[6] Indeed, neither this chapter nor this book as a whole aims at any kind of thoroughgoing exposition of the pragmatist conception of truth or its historical development. See, for example, Misak 2013 for a comprehensive historical account of pragmatism, including its conceptions of truth and inquiry in particular. Rather, I will explore issues related to pragmatism and truth in order to be able to investigate a number of philosophical topics that motivate our paying due attention to pragmatism and truth, that is, individuality, sincerity, meliorism, religious diversity, as well as religious and "existential" life. One of the best recent examinations of the pragmatist conception of truth is Capps 2019.

[7] The main sources for James's views here are, of course, *Pragmatism* and *The Meaning of Truth* (James 1975 [1907] and 1978 [1909], respectively). My take on James does not directly follow any single commentator's interpretation, but I am generally profoundly indebted to Hilary and Ruth Anna Putnam's readings of James (as well as the other classical pragmatists) on truth (see Putnam and Putnam 2017, especially chapters 8–9, 11–12).

example, their existential, ethical, or religious lives; it is not abstract or antecedently existing *truth-in-general*.[8]

The pragmatist theory of truth is far from uncontroversial, as anyone who ever read undergraduate textbooks on truth knows. We may, however, approach it in terms of the distinction between *truth* and *truthfulness* (very interestingly analyzed in Williams 2002). These are clearly different notions, but they are also connected. One may pursue truthfulness without thereby having true beliefs; one can be truthful also when one is mistaken, insofar as one sincerely seeks to believe truths and avoid falsehoods and also honestly seeks to tell the truth whenever possible (and whenever the truth to be told is relevant). Clearly, whatever one's theory of truth is, one should in some way distinguish between truth and truthfulness.

On the other hand, certain accounts of truth, such as the pragmatist one, may be more promising than some others in articulating the intimate relation between those two concepts. We might say that this distinction is "softened" in James's pragmatist conception of truth, which rather explicitly turns truth into a *value* to be pursued in individual and social life rather than mind- and value-independent objective propositional truth corresponding to facts that are just "there" no matter how we as truth-seekers (or truth-tellers) engage with or relate ourselves to them. In pragmatism, the concept of truth is not primarily conceptualized or investigated as an objective and static relation obtaining between our thoughts or statements, on the one hand, and something external to those thoughts and statements, on the other – namely, a relation obtaining independently of us and our practices of inquiry – but as a processual and practice-laden engagement with the world we live in, inherently connected with valuational, especially ethical, concepts such as sincerity and truthfulness that are used to evaluate our processes of inquiry. Truth in the Jamesian sense is, hence, richer and broader than mere propositional truth precisely because it incorporates truthfulness – a normative *commitment* to truth inherent in our practices of seeking and telling the truth – as a dimension of the notion of truth itself.

Truth, then, is a normative property of our practices of thought and inquiry in a wide sense and in this way something that our practice-embedded life

---

[8] This, clearly, does not mean that truth would be *idiosyncratic* to an individual (thanks are due to an anonymous reviewer for the recommendation to emphasize this important point). Rather, James makes clear throughout his discussions of truth (e.g., James 1975 [1907], 1978 [1909]) that while human beings create "ideas" and give them meaning – that is, truth does not "antecedently" exist in a divine or Hegelian "absolute" mind – when we do "make truths" in this sense, they also have an objective, or at least intersubjective, claim to recognition. We could rephrase this by saying that we place our claims to truth into a normative practice of pursuing the truth. There is no truth, and no truth-claims, in the absence of a *practice* expecting sincere commitment from its practitioners.

with the concepts we naturally and habitually employ involves, not merely a formal semantic property of statements or a metaphysical property of propositions that could be detached from that context of life practices. Its normativity is, moreover, both epistemic and ethical.[9] James's pragmatic conception of truth hence crucially accommodates truthfulness, as truth belongs to the ethical field of interhuman relations of mutual dependence and acknowledgment. Truth is an element of this "being with others" (to borrow a Heideggerian term out of context), while being inherently linked with our deeply individual ways of living our own unique lives, too. It also incorporates an acknowledgment of at least potential if not always actual inner truth (and truthfulness) of others' experiences.[10]

Jamesian pragmatic truth is, furthermore, inextricably entangled with our individual existential concerns; therefore, it is indistinguishable from James's general *individualism* (see, e.g., Pawelski 2007). Individuals' responses to their existential life-challenges vary considerably, and any ethically, politically, existentially, or religiously relevant conception of truth must in some sense appreciate this temperamental[11] variability – without succumbing to the temptations of uncritical subjectivism or relativism, though. Now, if we for ethical reasons do wish to take seriously the Jamesian approach to individual diversity (see also Chapter 2), as I think we should, then we must pay attention to what he says about the "plasticity" of truth and about truth being a "species of good" in Lecture II of *Pragmatism*:

> Truth independent; truth that we *find* merely; truth no longer malleable to human need; truth incorrigible, in a word; such truth exists indeed super-abundantly – or is supposed to exist by rationalistically minded thinkers; but then it means only the dead heart of the living tree, and its being there means

---

[9] This understanding of both truth(fulness) and normativity generally as both theoretical (epistemic and/or metaphysical) and practical (ethical) will be a guiding thought to be developed throughout this volume in slightly different contexts. See Chapter 5 for the concept of normativity specifically.

[10] This particularly concerns others' experiences of suffering (cf. Kivistö and Pihlström 2016, chapter 5; Pihlström 2008a, 2020a). Only irresponsible metaphysical speculation about, say, "theodicies" leads us to postulate a false transcendent meaningfulness for such experiences. My "antitheodicist" reading of James is very closely connected with my understanding of his conception of truth and truthfulness, but this is a large topic that must be set aside in this chapter (see, however, Chapter 6).

[11] James's (1975 [1907], Lecture I) account of individual philosophical temperaments should, I think, be understood in close entanglement with his notion of truth. There is no way of completely disentangling the temperamental aspects from our practices of pursuing the truth. Yet, while truth for James is to a certain degree relative to individual (temperament-laden) goals and interests, such goals and interests must be set by an autonomous subject, rather than externally forced upon us; hence, the notions of sincerity and freedom will also turn out to be crucial for a Jamesian investigation of the pursuit of truth (see also Chapter 4). I am grateful to Alexander Klein for a brief but important exchange on this point.

only that truth also has its paleontology and its "prescription," and may
grow stiff with years of veteran service and petrified in men's regard by sheer
antiquity. But how plastic even the oldest truths nevertheless really are has
been vividly shown in our day by the transformation of logical and mathematical ideas, a transformation which seems even to be invading physics.
(James 1975 [1907], 37)

> … truth is *one species of good*, and not, as is usually supposed, a category
> distinct from good, and co-ordinate with it. *The true is the name of whatever
> proves itself to be good in the way of belief, and good, too, for definite, assignable
> reasons.* (James 1975 [1907], 42)

Another famous Jamesian formulation (in Lecture VI) relevant here is this:

> Pragmatism, on the other hand [in contrast to other accounts of truth], asks
> its usual question. "Grant an idea or belief to be true," it says, "what
> concrete difference will its being true make in anyone's actual life? How
> will the truth be realized? What experiences will be different from those
> which would obtain if the belief were false? What, in short, is the truth's
> cash-value in experiential terms?"
>
> The moment pragmatism asks this question, it sees the answer: *true ideas
> are those that we can assimilate, validate, corroborate and verify; false ideas are
> those that we cannot.* That is the practical difference it makes to us to have
> true ideas; that, therefore, is the meaning of truth, for it is all that truth is
> known-as. This thesis is what I have to defend. The truth of an idea is not
> a stagnant property inherent in it. Truth *happens* to an idea. It *becomes* true,
> is *made* true by events. Its verity is in fact an event, a process: the process
> namely of its verifying itself, its veri-*fication*. Its validity is the process of its
> valid-*ation*. (James 1975 [1907], 97)

Note how easy it is to interpret such ideas in the "vulgar" way. One might
think that truth "happens" to an idea when that idea leads to useful or
satisfactory results in one's life – such as one's becoming rich and powerful,
for instance. However, it should be obvious that, no matter how careless
James's formulations were, such crude pragmatism was never even close to
his own view. He is unclear and controversial, to be sure, but he is certainly
not recommending that we just replace truth with our subjective wishful
thinking or political and economic pursuit of power.[12]

---

[12] Note also that James is here speaking about the potential consequences of our ideas or beliefs
(actually) "being true," not about the consequences of their being believed to be true. The passage
just quoted is therefore one of the more realistic formulations of the pragmatic conception of truth
by James, even presupposing his commitment to something like (a minimalist version of) the
correspondence theory truth. Generally, however, James is presumably less clear than Peirce in
formulating his pragmatism as a principle concerning not just the consequences of the truth of our
ideas but of those ideas being believed or entertained by us (cf. Pihlström 2015). But he is certainly

Several outstanding James scholars have already shown how nuanced James's view on truth is – also in the political sphere – so I only need to cite a few readings to emphasize this point. For example, in his discussion of James's theory of truth, which I find highly pertinent to these concerns, Jose Medina (2010) defends Jamesian pluralism in a politically relevant manner (cf. also Pihlström 2013, chapter 4). In ethics and politics, Medina tells us, we can never reach an "absolute" conception of what is universally best for human beings and societies, but different suggestions, opinions, experiential perspectives, and interests must have their say – that is, must be acknowledged as (at least potentially) truthful. A conception of political solidarity can, then, be grounded in Jamesian ideas about truth. James maintains not only pluralism and individualism but also (on Medina's reading) a *relational* conception of individual identities: nothing exists in a self-sustained manner but everything that there is finds its place in reality only as part(s) of networks of mutual interdependence. Such a metaphysics of diversity and relationality needs, furthermore, something like the concept of acknowledgment: we must sincerely (which is not to say uncritically) respond to even those perspectives on life that we find alien or even repulsive, though this is much more easily said than done. While James's pluralism and relationalism are, according to Medina, elements of a metaphysical view according to which everything must be understood in relation to other things, in terms of ubiquitous relationality, they are irreducibly ethical and political ideas, applying even to the reality of the (epistemic, ethical, political) self.

It is precisely in this context that we should, according to Medina, appreciate James's theory of truth. True beliefs are, as James says, "good to live by"; when maintaining a belief, any belief, we are responsible for its consequences in our lives, and in those of others. The pragmatic "theory" of truth – which should not be called a "theory," in order to avoid seeing it as a rival to, say, the "correspondence theory" – invokes not only, say, the satisfactory or agreeable consequences of true beliefs but also ethical ideas such as solidarity and justice in terms of which the functionality of our beliefs ought to be measured. Therefore, we may say that truth (in the pragmatic sense), truthfulness, and the acknowledgment of otherness are conceptually tied to each other in James's pragmatism. One cannot genuinely pursue truth in the Jamesian sense unless one also acknowledges, or at least truthfully seeks to acknowledge, others' perspectives on reality –

---

not as careless as he has standardly been taken to be among his critics. Even James's informal pronouncements on truth are usually carefully considered.

indeed, the uniqueness of such individual perspectives, and their potentially opening up genuine novelties. If we take this articulation of Jamesian
pragmatic truth seriously, then we can immediately see how vulgar
a "Trumpist" version of pragmatism is. Trump's views may in some
sense be "satisfactory" or "agreeable" for him and his opportunistic (or
cynical and disillusioned) supporters, but they can hardly be said to truly
acknowledge other perspectives on the world, let alone to honor any
commitment to pursuing the truth independently of personal or political
benefit. The Jamesian pragmatist may also say that there is no *sincerity* in
vulgar pragmatism at all – and hence no truth, either.

The pragmatist account of truth is insightfully connected with James's
moral philosophy by Sarin Marchetti (2015, 33), one of the most perceptive
recent commentators of James. It is easy for us to agree with his general
claim that pragmatism as a philosophical method also incorporates
a fundamentally ethical intention based on a conception of ethics as self-
transformation and self-cultivation.[13] He maintains that James is not primarily advancing a theory of truth but "using pragmatism to unstiffen our
views on truth and put them to work" (Marchetti 2015, 169). We are invited
to rethink the meaning of truth "in our lives," and James is therefore offering
us a "genealogical phenomenology" of this concept (Marchetti 2015, 177).[14]
Truth is something that processually functions in our ethical world-
engagement, not a static relation between our beliefs (which are not static,
either, but dynamically developing habits of action) and an allegedly independent external world. The concept of truth is also interestingly entangled
with James's important but often neglected metaphor of *blindness*: "We are

---

[13] In addition to being an application of the "pragmatic method," we might say that in a sense the
Jamesian approach to *metaphysics* is an application of the pragmatist conception of truth. On James
(1975 [1907]) as engaging in a pragmatically shaped metaphysical inquiry (rather than rejecting
metaphysics altogether), see, for example, Pihlström 2009, 2013. Our ideas expressed or expressible
by means of concepts like substance, God, freedom, and so on – our metaphysical views and
commitments – are pragmatically "true" or "false" insofar as they put us in touch with ethically
significant experiences. The truth of a metaphysical view can be assessed by means of the pragmatic
criterion of its ability to open us to what James (1979 [1897]) called "the cries of the wounded" (see
also Kivistö and Pihlström 2016, chapter 5). It is right here, in a pragmatist ethically structured
metaphysics, that truth, in James's memorable phrase, "happens to an idea."

[14] Pragmatism, James maintains (according to Marchetti), "transforms the absolutely empty notion of
correspondence in a rich and active relationship between our truths and the way in which we can
entertain them and thus engage the world" (Marchetti 2015, 184). For a non-empty correspondence
theory, see, however, for example, Niiniluoto (1999). Certainly the pragmatist must *not* ridicule the
correspondence theory of truth by claiming, for example, that it requires a one-to-one correspondence between our propositions or beliefs and facts obtaining in the world (as if those facts had
already been pre-organized into a propositional structure); there are much more sophisticated
versions of the correspondence theory available, including Niiniluoto's.

morally blind when we fail to see how the sources of truth are nested in the very meaning those experiences have for those who have them . . ." – and the most serious blindness is our losing touch "with the meaning of our own truths and experiences." (Marchetti 2015, 202, 205)[15]

In a more recent paper, Marchetti persuasively argues that James, who is not conventionally read as a political thinker, stands in an original manner in the tradition of liberal thought, largely due to his conception of the self "as contingent and mobile" (Marchetti 2019, 193). According to James, we live in a world of risk and uncertainty, and understanding human freedom as an ethically and politically (and not merely metaphysically) loaded concept is a practical necessity in this situation. Marchetti goes as far as to claim that James's "entire philosophical vision" can be regarded as "a positive response to chance, possibility, and probability" (Marchetti 2019, 197). I find this suggestion compatible with my own proposal to view James's pragmatism as framed by an "antitheodicist" attitude to evil and suffering as something contingent (i.e., avoidable) to be fought against, never to be just accepted as a necessary element of a deterministic universe (see Chapter 6). I find it extremely important for our understanding of James's pragmatism to insist, with Marchetti, that the Jamesian conception of "freedom as self-transformation" offers us no metaphysical grounding for morality but on the contrary reminds us that our moral reactions to the world we live in contribute to (re)shaping our reality into whatever structure it may take (Marchetti 2019, 200).[16] Therefore, the concept of truth, as pragmatically construed, is also inseparably linked with our duty to view the world taking seriously the contingencies of evil and suffering we find around us (cf. also Pihlström 2020a, as well as Chapter 6).

Marchetti's remarks on James can also be read as a warning against tendencies to overlook the thoroughly ethical character of the concept of *freedom*. From the perspective of (Marchetti's) James, it makes little sense to try to settle the metaphysics of freedom independently of the – often painful – ethical employment of freedom (see also Chapter 4). The Jamesian pragmatist pursuit of truth is *never* a pursuit of pure metaphysical truth in abstraction of ethical concerns about how to live in this world.[17]

---

[15] As Marchetti notes, James sees the "possibility of overcoming" such blindness as a "transformation of the self" (Marchetti 2015, 206). The relevant reference here is James 1962 [1899]; see also Pihlström 2019b, 2020a, as well as Chapter 2.

[16] This notion of freedom also challenges some of the received ideas of liberal thought and thus helps to rethink the very tradition of liberalism, as Marchetti (2019) suggests.

[17] Incidentally, we may note that (Jamesian) pragmatism is interestingly analogous to Wittgensteinian philosophy in this respect. From both standpoints, it would be extremely problematic or even absurd to suggest that our practices of moral responsibility and deliberation would be dependent on

The scholars I have briefly cited (Medina and Marchetti) are of course only individual voices among many. They nevertheless help us appreciate a certain approach to Jamesian truth that is inherently ethical. I have tried to capture this basic idea by using the concept of truthfulness, but that is obviously only one possible concept that can be employed here. Regarding the active union of truth and ethics, I find myself mostly in agreement with Medina's and Marchetti's readings (without going into any more detail here).[18] However, we will now have to move on to the worry that James's pragmatist account of truth might be easily developed into a direction that turns problematic, especially in our "post-truth" era.

1.3   Rorty (on Orwell) on Truth

Rorty is famous for advocating a version of pragmatism that endorses *ethnocentrism* ("we have to start from where we are," acknowledging our historical contingency) and *antirepresentationalism* (which rejects any representational relations between language and reality, claiming that the traditional problems of realism and skepticism, among others, only arise in the context of representationalism). Here we cannot deal with the complex development of Rorty's pragmatism, or even its approach to truth, since his early work in the 1960s and 1970s to his late proposals to replace systematic philosophy by "cultural politics".[19] I will merely focus on a specific strand of Rorty's pragmatism, relevant to the worries about

---

our (purely) theoretical beliefs about, say, the metaphysics of free will that would be allegedly independent of ethics. Clearly, free will is a notion that is absolutely crucial for ethics – only free actions can be morally evaluated – but this does not mean that we would or even could *first* settle the epistemological and metaphysical issues concerning free will in order to *then* turn to ethical considerations (see Chapter 4). On the contrary, I entirely agree with Timo Koistinen (2019) and Wittgensteinians like D. Z. Phillips that our moral practices involve notions such as the freedom of the will in a *constitutive* sense. However, I would be prepared to take the crucial step of understanding such constitutivity in a Kantian-inspired transcendental sense, without sacrificing its pragmatic character, though (cf. Chapter 3).

[18] See Pihlström 2008a, 2013 for my more comprehensive discussions of James's pragmatism and its conception of truth especially in metaphysics and the philosophy of religion.

[19] I have written critically on Rorty from early on (see, e.g., Pihlström 1996, 1998), so here I will confine myself to a brief discussion of truth in the context of his remarks on Orwell. (For my later criticisms of Rorty, see Pihlström 2013; Kivistö and Pihlström 2016.) This book is not a scholarly study on Rorty, and therefore Rorty's views, as formulated in his Orwell essay, only function here as a placeholder for a position somewhere in between James and Trump (and his emphasis on the significance of Orwell's O'Brien refers to the horror we may expect awaiting us, beyond Trump, at the end of the slippery slope I am imagining). For Rorty's earlier formulations of pragmatism as an account of truth characterized as what our "cultural peers" let us say, see Rorty 1979; for his antirepresentationalist understanding of pragmatism, see Rorty 1991; for his denial that truth can be usefully considered an aim of inquiry, see Rorty 1998; and for philosophy as cultural politics, see Rorty 2007. It is also important to note that other neopragmatists, most prominently Hilary Putnam, have defended

post-factualism and the pragmatist's potential "slippery slope" raised in this chapter. As was suggested earlier (and as other James commentators like Marchetti have emphasized), the concept of truth, far from being restricted to the oft-ridiculed "pragmatist theory of truth," is fundamentally important in pragmatist moral thought in general. It is in this context that we will now expand our horizon from James's pragmatism to Rorty's neopragmatism and especially to Rorty's treatment of George Orwell.

While discussions of Orwell's *Nineteen Eighty-Four* (1949) have often primarily dealt with Winston, the main protagonist of the novel, Rorty's treatment of *Nineteen Eighty-Four* finds O'Brien, the Party torturer, the most important character of the novel.[20] In his essay on Orwell, "The Last Intellectual in Europe" (in Rorty 1989), Rorty rejects the standard realistic reading of *Nineteen Eighty-Four*, according to which the novel defends an objective notion of truth in the context of a penetrating moral critique of the horrible and humiliating way in which Winston is made to believe that two plus two equals five. Consistently with his well-known position (if it can be regarded as a philosophical "position" at all), Rorty denies that "there are any plain moral facts out there in the world, [. . .] any truths independent of language, [or] any neutral ground on which to stand and argue that either torture or kindness are preferable to the other" (Rorty 1989, 173). Orwell's significance lies in a novel redescription of what is possible: he convinced us that "nothing in the nature of truth, or man [*sic*], or history" will block the conceivable scenario that "the same developments which had made human equality technically possible might make endless slavery possible" (Rorty 1989, 175). Hence, O'Brien, the "Party intellectual," is Orwell's key invention, and Orwell, crucially, offers no answer to O'Brien's position: "He does not view O'Brien as crazy, misguided, seduced by a mistaken theory, or blind to the moral facts. He simply views him as *dangerous* and as *possible*." (Rorty 1989, 176)

While O'Brien is, of course, an extreme character, it may not be too far-fetched to speculate that today people may increasingly recognize the thoroughgoing contingency of our form of life by recognizing, alarmingly, that things could, even in stable Western democracies, turn really bad

conceptions of truth very different from Rorty's; Putnam, in particular, has consistently emphasized – even across the numerous changes in his views on realism and truth over the decades – that truth is an irreducibly normative notion we cannot deflate in Rorty's manner (see, e.g., Putnam 1981, 1990; for some of his late reflections on truth and realism, see Putnam 2016, especially chapters 1 and 4). (See also, again, Misak 2013 for highly relevant historical comparisons.)

[20] My discussion here partly relies on the chapter on James, Rorty, and Orwell in Kivistö and Pihlström 2016, chapter 5.

really rapidly. Whether O'Brien is possible or not (and in what sense), there are certainly possible and extremely dangerous scenarios that might imaginably change our lives into truly Orwellian-like dystopic directions. The rise of "post-truth" populist politics, the inability of world leaders to come up with any clear and sufficiently efficient strategies to combat the deepening environmental crisis, and unexpected threats such as the COVID-19 pandemic in 2020 may all have increased our awareness of the precariousness of our cultural situation.

The key idea we should arrive at by contemplating the Orwellian situation, according to Rorty, is that truth as such does not matter: "[. . .] what matters is your ability to talk to other people about what seems to you true, not what is in fact true".[21] In *Nineteen Eighty-Four*, Winston's self is destroyed as he is made to believe that two plus two equals five – and to utter, "Do it to Julia!", when faced with his worst fear, the rats. Rorty points out that this is something that Winston "could not utter sincerely and still be able to put himself back together" (Rorty 1989, 179). The notion of *sincerity* is highly central here, as it obviously establishes a link to the key idea of truthfulness that I above claimed to find at the heart of James's account of truth.

Maintaining a basic distinction between truth and falsity – a distinction not messed up by any vulgarization of the pragmatist account of truth – is, however, necessary for the concepts of sincerity and truthfulness to function. Insofar as Rorty's pragmatism carries Jamesian pragmatism into a certain extreme, we will be left wondering whether there is any way to stop on the slippery slope arguably leading from James to Rorty (and eventually bringing in, with horror, first post-factualists like Trump and then Orwell's O'Brien). Reality must still be contrasted with unreality, while truth and truthfulness must be opposed not only to falsity but also to lying and self-deception, as well as other kinds of loss of sincerity that may follow from the collapse of the truth vs. falsity distinction itself. What we find here is, as we might say, the problem of realism in its existential dimensions. This is, arguably, the core *pragmatic meaning* of the problem of realism and truth, and therefore the very possibility of ethical truthfulness is a key pragmatist issue to be dealt with in any critical examination of the Jamesian-Rortyan engagement with truth. While pragmatists have had very interesting things to say about realism and truth in the more conventional areas of this discussion, including, for example, scientific realism and

---

[21] This is followed by the well-known Rortyan one-liner, "If we take care of freedom, truth can take care of itself." (Rorty 1989, 176)

moral realism, the full-blown pragmatic significance of realism and truth is brought into the focus only when we approach the matter in this Orwellian context rightly emphasized by Rorty.[22]

By destroying Winston's capacity for sincerely uttering something and still being able to "put himself back together," O'Brien leads us to imagine the possibility of evil that renders truthfulness itself impossible. Our problem now is that this will then collapse the Jamesian pragmatist conception of truth as well, given that it starts from a kind of pragmatic softening of the notion of objective truth culminating in the "truth happens to an idea" view that we may find characteristic of James's ethically grounded metaphysics of truth, and his pragmatism generally, as inherited by Rorty.[23]

While James only resisted certain metaphysically realistic forms of metaphysics, especially Hegelian monistic absolute idealism (and corresponding metaphysical realisms), without thereby abandoning metaphysics altogether (see Pihlström 2008a, 2009, 2015), Rorty's reading of Orwell is deeply grounded in his rejection of *all* forms of metaphysics. According to Rorty, Orwell is urging us that "whether our future rulers are more like O'Brien or more like J. S. Mill does not depend [. . .] on deep facts about human nature" or on any "large necessary truths about human nature and its relation to truth and justice" but on "a lot of small contingent facts" (Rorty 1989, 187–188). Now, this is hard to deny; various minor contingent facts have enormous influence on how our world and societies develop. We should certainly join Rorty in maintaining that our form of life does not

---

[22] On (pragmatic) realism in religion and theology, see Pihlström 2020a, especially chapters 1–2.

[23] Let me again note that I am certainly not saying that either James's or Rorty's view would entail a rejection of truth such as Trump's. I am, rather, emphasizing the (pragmatist's) self-critical worry that such a slippery slope might be opened up. This is particularly relevant not so much in the political area (where populists are busily constructing their lies and "alternative facts") but in the highly personal area of religious and existential commitments. The Jamesian pragmatist needs to analyze the kind of sincerity we must attach to our pursuit of truth in this context – this, indeed, is what this entire book is all about – and while my discussion of Rorty here is relatively brief, I am convinced that the Rortyan deflated understanding of truth is normatively insufficient to account for such sincerity. Certainly (and here I am again responding to an anonymous reviewer's highly relevant comment) Rorty denies objective truth only in the sense that there is according to him (see, e.g., Rorty 1989, 4–7) no truth antecedent to, or beyond, the human life with language within which we formulate all truths (as well as falsehoods). Rorty would obviously be in favor of truthfulness and sincerity just as James would, and he never denies that there is an external world of objects "out there" about which we can make true or false statements. (See, e.g., his 1986 essay, "Pragmatism, Davidson, and Truth," in Rorty 1991.) The problem is whether, given what he says about the relation between freedom and truth in the Orwell essay, in particular, he is in the end entitled to all these, or any, genuinely normative claims about the role played by the concept of truth in our practices. For a detailed critical engagement with Rorty's responsibility for "post-truth" politics that I find supportive of my criticism, see Forstenzer 2018.

depend on "big" metaphysical Truths or Facts but is constantly shaped by "small" historical contingencies. This is also a very important message of Rortyan *ironism*: our firmest moral commitments, our "final vocabularies," are historically contingent, and we ought to fully acknowledge this contingency even when resolutely defending such final vocabularies, including, say, the idea of universal human rights.[24] But the worry is that if we give up (even pragmatically rearticulated) objective truth entirely, we will end up giving up the very possibility of sincerity, too, and that is something we need for resisting the future of all possible O'Briens' Newspeak seeking to justify not merely lies but also evil, suffering, and torture.

It is, indeed, one thing to accept, reasonably, historical contingency and to reject any unpragmatic overblown metaphysics of "deep facts about human nature"; it is quite another thing to give up even a minimal pragmatic sense of objective truth required not only for truthfulness and sincerity but for their very possibility (and, hence, for the possibility of insincerity as well, because insincerity is possible only insofar as sincerity is possible, and vice versa), that is, the very possibility of keeping in touch with "the meaning of our own truths and experiences" (quoting Marchetti's apt phrase again). The fact that this discussion rapidly rises onto a meta-level invoking the conditions for the *possibility* of, among other things, individual sincerity can be regarded as a preliminary reason for considering pragmatism from a Kantian transcendental point of view – a suggestion I will get back to in the later chapters.

I want to emphasize that I am not claiming Rorty (or James) to maintain, in any straightforward sense, an erroneous conception of truth (or facts, or history). However, if Rorty is right in his comments on truth (whatever it means to say this, given the alarming disappearance, in his neopragmatism, of the distinction between being right and being regarded as being right by one's cultural peers),[25] then we may be in a bigger trouble regarding the place of truth in our lives than we may have naively believed. We may lack not only political but also sufficient philosophical resources for dealing with people like Trump. Jamesian pragmatism seems to take

---

[24] One problem for Rorty is how such an "oughtness" can ever take off the ground, if the contingent development of our practices is ultimately reducible to mere causal clashes of uses of vocabularies in historico-political contexts. See Chapter 5 for my attempt to view the normativity of our social practices as irreducible. I am not saying that Rorty necessarily has to deal with this problem insofar as he just bites the bullet and makes no claim to this type of "oughtness" at all, merely proposing his "ironism" about final vocabularies as a replacement for any (explicit or implicit) remnant of metaphysics that more strongly normative views may still be committed to.

[25] I am not here even speculating on what exactly it could mean to say that Rorty's statements (about, e.g., truth) are "true".

the correct, indeed vital, step toward integrating the ethically and existentially normative notion of truthfulness into the pragmatist account of truth itself, as we briefly saw. However, insofar as this kind of pragmatism develops into something like Rorty's neopragmatism, which lets the notion of truth drop out as unimportant, the end result is not only an insightful emphasis on historical contingency[26] but also the possible fragmentation of truthfulness itself, which seems to depend on a relatively robust distinction between truth and falsity. What this shows is a quasi-Rortyan point: Orwell is more important, and O'Brien more dangerous, than we might have thought; and so is, arguably, someone like Trump. Therefore, furthermore, Rorty's version of pragmatism as an intermediary stage between James and full-blow post-factualism is also more important than many pragmatism scholars might want to admit. Paradoxically, precisely due to the insightfulness of his claims, Rorty in effect deprives us of the linguistic, literary, and philosophical resources that we might have seen Orwell as equipping us with.

This criticism of Rorty comes close to James Conant's (2000) in my view devastating attack on Rorty's reading of Orwell.[27] According to Conant, Rorty is committed to (or even obsessed by) the same philosophical prejudices as his metaphysically realist[28] opponents in claiming that notions such as objectivity, facts, or historical truth are not in the focus of Orwell's worries. Conant argues that Rorty fails to see that there is an "ordinary"[29] way of using these and related concepts that need not be construed either metaphysically realistically or antirealistically (or in a Rortyan deflated manner); hence, "when our intellectual options are

---

[26] As well as the role of literature in showing us fascinating, and dangerous, contingent possibilities (see also the other relevant essays in Rorty 1989; cf. Conant 2000).

[27] See also Rorty 2000. Conant's essay is one of the best critical discussions of Rorty's project in general, by no means restricted to the interpretation of *Nineteen Eighty-Four* – yet, as it focuses on that book and Rorty's reading of it, it does show us something about the fundamental philosophical relevance of Orwell's novel. (My criticism of Rorty is, implicitly, a qualified criticism of Jamesian pragmatism, too, though *not at all* a proposal to give it up but to carefully rethink its lasting value, being aware of its potential problems.)

[28] When speaking of *metaphysical realism* in this book, I primarily mean something like what Putnam (1981) meant in characterizing metaphysical realism as the combination of the theses that there is a "ready-made" world of mind- and discourse-independent objects and properties, that there is, at least in principle, a single complete truth about the way that world "absolutely" is, and that truth is to be defined as a non-epistemic relation of correspondence between linguistic items and the items of the mind-independent world our language-use refers to. For critical discussion, see, in addition to Putnam's seminal writings (e.g., 1981, 1990, 1994, 2016), Pihlström 2009.

[29] The significance of the concept of "the ordinary" would deserve a more comprehensive treatment in relation to both Jamesian and Rortyan pragmatism. See, for example, Saito 2019 (to be briefly discussed in Chapter 2).

confined to a forced choice between Realist and Rortian theses [. . .] we are unable to recover the thoughts Orwell sought to express [. . .]" (Conant 2000, 279–280). Conant obviously does not dispute Rorty's (or Orwell's) emphasis on historical contingency, but he argues that in a perfectly ordinary sense, "the demise of 'the possibility of truth'" could still be an extremely scary scenario (Conant 2000, 285–286). In Conant's view, Orwell's novel is primarily "about the possibility of a state of affairs in which the concept of objective truth has faded as far out of someone's world as it conceivably can" (Conant 2000, 297),[30] and therefore it is directly relevant to our concerns here.[31]

Conant contests in a thoroughgoing manner Rorty's deflated reading of O'Brien's character as someone who *simply* enjoys torturing Winston and seeks to "break him" for no particular reason (see Conant 2000, especially 290). Truth and truthfulness do, he maintains, occupy a central place in Orwell's analysis of what is really frightening in totalitarianism; in this way, the debate between Rorty and Conant on these notions in the context of *Nineteen Eighty-Four* directly continues the general pragmatist elaborations on truth and truthfulness.[32] O'Brien's "unqualified denial of the idea that (what Orwell calls) 'the concept of objective truth' has application to the past" (Conant 2000, 308) can be directly applied to Jamesian sincerity and

---

[30] He also says the novel "is perhaps as close as we can come to contemplating in imagination the implications of the adoption of a resolutely Rortian conception of objectivity (i.e., a conception in which the concept of objectivity is exhausted by that of solidarity)" (Conant 2000, 307). This formulation is perhaps better than the one quoted in the main text above as it avoids involving the notion of a state of affairs which might itself be regarded as a remnant of old "Realist" metaphysics.

[31] Among the innumerable critical discussions of Rorty's pragmatism, I would, in addition to Conant's criticisms, like to recommend Dirk-Martin Grube's (2019) recent essay. If Grube is correct, the Rortyan attempt to replace the realism vs. antirealism debate by the one between representationalism and antirepresentationalism, allegedly moving beyond the realism issue in neopragmatism, is mere rhetoric. I also agree with Grube that Rortyan neopragmatists need to choose between antirealism and naturalism, as they cannot get both (Grube 2019, 95) – but then again I am not entirely convinced that Grube's own discussion does justice to Rorty's in many ways complex overall position, either. Some of the undeniably simplistic rhetoric that Rorty uses may serve genuinely philosophical goals, after all. While I agree with Grube's dictum that "*[w]e pragmatists relativize without succumbing to relativism*" (Grube 2019, 96, original emphasis), I also believe that Rorty's ironism emphasizing the historical contingency of our final vocabularies is something that pragma-tists (of any kind) ought to take seriously even when not following Rorty into "ethnocentrism," or any other neopragmatists into what is more often called relativism.

[32] Note how different Orwell's views on totalitarianism, at least on Conant's reading, are from Hannah Arendt's well-known ideas, in which the concentration camp is the epitomization of totalitarianism. (See Arendt 1976 [1951].) For Orwell, such atrocities are peripheral; hostility to truthfulness is the "really frightening" thing. (Conant 2000, 295.) While Rorty charges Conant of confusing truth with truthfulness (Rorty 2000, 347), Conant perceives that the "capacity of individuals to assess the truth of claims on their own" threatens "the absolute hegemony of the Party over their minds" (Conant 2000, 299).

truthfulness. It must be possible for the Jamesian pragmatist to argue that O'Brien has given up any ethical commitment to truthfulness through his arbitrary reduction of truth to the opinion of the Party. But then, *pace* Rorty, freedom and the availability of the concept of objective truth are inseparable:

> What [Orwell's] novel aims to make manifest is that if reality control and doublethink were ever to be practiced on a systematic scale, the possibility of an individual speaking the truth and the possibility of an individual controlling her own mind would begin simultaneously to fade out of the world. The preservation of freedom and the preservation of truth represent a single indivisible task for Orwell – a task common to literature and politics. (Conant 2000, 310.)

No matter how exactly we should interpret Orwell and Rorty, this is a fundamentally important link between freedom and truth, a link also needed to make sense of the very idea of truthfulness in its pragmatist meaning. In particular, the preservation of individual freedom and truth – the task Conant argues is shared by literature and politics – is inseparably intertwined with the need to fight against "the corruption of language," which corrupts our concepts and, thus, thought itself (Conant 2000, 313). This inseparability of freedom and truth also indicates how important it is to examine the pragmatist conception of truth in relation to individuals' existential pursuits, as we will do in the later chapters.

Even so, in the interest of being fair to Rorty, we can still try to understand the situation in Rortyan terms. Rorty, famously, rejects the very idea of our being responsible or answerable to any non-human objective reality – traditionally presupposed, he believes, in realist accounts of truth – and emphasizes that we can only be answerable to human audiences.[33] This could be analyzed as a relation of acknowledgment: we acknowledge human audiences as our potential rational critics in a way we cannot acknowledge any non-human reality, thereby also acknowledging a shared normative form of life (cf. Chapter 5). Thus formulated, Rorty is not very far from Jamesian truthfulness, which involves the continuous challenge of acknowledging others' perspectives on the world. However, part of our response to a (relevant) audience is a response to an audience (at least potentially) sincerely using the concepts of objective reality and truth. We have to recognize the relevance of those concepts by recognizing the

---

[33] This theme runs through Rorty's entire thought (cf. Rorty 1991, 1998, 2007), but *Contingency, Irony and Solidarity*, the book containing the Orwell essay, is one of its best articulations. Our answerability to other human beings merely, instead of any non-human remnant of God, is the core of Rorty's "deep humanism" (see Bernstein 2010, chapter 9; cf. Višňovský 2020).

relevant audience. This is a case of what has been called "mediated recognition" (cf. Koskinen 2017, 2019): we recognize the normatively binding status of the concepts of objective reality and truth by recognizing the appropriate audience(s) and our responsibility or answerability toward it/them. We thus derivatively acknowledge objective reality itself by being answerable, and recognizing ourselves as being answerable, to an audience (e.g., our potential rational critics) that might challenge our views on reality or our entitlement to the truth we claim to possess. Rorty's well-known rhetoric emphasizing our answerability to other human beings in contrast to our answerability to an imagined deity or the realist's mind- and language-independent "world" is simplistic and misleading, because it is precisely by being answerable to other human beings that we indicate our sharing a normative form of life with them in a shared world – or, in brief, our sharing a common world.

Now, one major problem here – to recapitulate our worries once more – is that our relevant audience could change in an Orwellian manner. The *use* and (thus) meaning (recalling the broadly pragmatist and Wittgensteinian idea that "meaning is use")[34] of the concept of objective truth could even be destroyed. Then the kind of mediated recognition alluded to here would no longer work. In some sense there would no longer be any audience we would be responsible to anymore. And there would then be no views to have on anything anymore. Rational thought would collapse. In other words, we can recognize each other as using the concept of an objective reality (and a related concept of truth), and thereby acknowledge each other and ourselves as being normatively – truthfully – committed to pursuing objective truth about reality – but only until O'Brien gets us. Then that commitment collapses, and so does our acknowledgment of each other as genuine users of the notion of truth. So does, then, our commitment to sincerity and truthfulness, which are needed for any moral and political seriousness. All this reminds us that our pursuing the truth, as well as our merely thinking, takes place in a contingent and precarious world whose structures may unpredictably and uncontrollably change – even beyond recognition.

Rorty, then, seems to be right in reminding us about how dangerous O'Brien is – and, thus, about how fragile our life with truth is. But for this same reason he is wrong about the idea that defending freedom would be sufficient for defending truth. It is certainly necessary but hardly sufficient. In particular, *negative freedom* from external constraints is not enough:

---

[34] The best-known *locus* of this is Wittgenstein 1953, I, §23.

what is needed is *positive freedom* and the responsibility that goes together with such freedom, hence sincere commitment to truth-seeking, something that the Jamesian integration of truth with truthfulness takes some steps toward articulating. There certainly is a kind of unrestricted (negative) freedom in American politics, for instance, but truth apparently has not been able to "take care of itself".[35] Moreover, Rorty (1989, 188) himself needs to use the concept of truth – and related concepts such as the ones of fact and reality – when telling us that "[w]hat our future rulers will be like will not be determined by any large necessary truths about human nature and its relation to truth and justice, but by a lot of small contingent facts".

Interestingly, Rorty also maintains the following: "If we are ironic enough about our final vocabularies, and curious enough about everyone else's, we do not have to worry about whether we are in direct contact with moral reality, or whether we are blinded by ideology, or whether we are being weakly 'relativistic.'" (Rorty 1989, 176–177.) This is, indeed, a very big "if". We do need to worry about these matters because we can never be sure that we are, or will remain, able to be "ironic enough" and "curious enough" – indeed, precisely because of the kind of contingency and precariousness Rorty himself brilliantly analyzes.[36] These attitudes themselves require a commitment to truthfulness; they are inherently normative attitudes that presuppose a comprehensive context of genuine epistemic and ethical commitments. Our need to maintain a pragmatic conception of truth more realistic than Rorty's can thus be seen to be based on Jamesian pragmatic reasons. Moreover, this need emerges as a result of our taking seriously a crucial Rortyan lesson about the fundamental contingency of even our most basic conceptual commitments. It is precisely due to the fragility of truth – the possibility that O'Brien might arrive, as Orwell warns us, destroying our ability of distinguishing between truth and falsity – that we must cherish our Jamesian capacities of responding, with ethical sincerity and truthfulness, to others' perspectives along with our own continuous commitment to pursuing the truth. The most important moral we must draw from our reading of Rorty is the seriousness – the sincerity – we should attach to our realization of such

---

[35] For an insightful historically based political argument for the view that without taking care of truth (and truthfulness), we will slide down the "road to unfreedom," see Snyder 2018. We may view Snyder's discussion as an extended attempt to show that the Rortyan conception of truth is wrong: taking care of freedom presupposes taking care of truth.

[36] This Rortyan pragmatist analysis of our natural and historical contingency can be traced back to, for example, Dewey's pragmatic naturalism emphasizing similar themes (see especially Dewey 1986 [1929], chapter 4, titled "Nature as Precarious and Stable").

contingency and fragility constitutive of the human condition. We need not agree with Rorty's analysis of truth and freedom in order to incorporate this moral into our (more Jamesian) pragmatism.[37]

1.4 Reflexivity, Pluralism, and Critical Philosophy

In order to further emphasize the political significance of the issue of truth, let me, before concluding this chapter, very briefly compare these pragmatist elaborations on our need to be committed to the pursuit of truth – and the related integration of truth and truthfulness – to Hannah Arendt's views on truth (and Richard Bernstein's useful reading of Arendt), especially as they are articulated in Arendt's "Truth and Politics," an essay originally published in 1967 (see Arendt 2003).[38]

Arendt not only offered us an analysis of totalitarianism of lasting relevance and an equally lasting defense of human spontaneity in its ethical and political dimensions but also an ever more timely account of the significance of the concept of truth. In "Truth and Politics," she carefully examines the often antagonistic relation between truthfulness and political action, drawing attention to deliberate lying as a political force – and one may argue that her views are, for well-known reasons, even more relevant today than they were half a century ago (see also Bernstein 2018, 67–83). She reminds us that while truth itself is "powerless," it is also *irreplaceable*; political force, persuasion, or violence cannot substitute it, and "[t]o look upon politics from the perspective of truth [...] means to take one's stand outside the political realm," from "the standpoint of the truthteller" (Arendt 2003, 570). This kind of *critical distance* necessary for an adequate understanding of the relation between truth and politics requires the age-old project of "disinterested pursuit of truth" (Arendt 2003, 573). It is, of course, this very project that the populist culture of "post-truth" raising into power people like Trump seeks to suppress.

---

[37] I believe my analysis is congenial with Haack's (2019) – albeit slightly more friendly to Rorty than hers – in the sense of acknowledging that we inevitably need an objective concept of truth insofar as the post-truth phenomena of lies, half-truths, misleading and unwarranted claims, and various other forms of unconcern for truth that we witness everywhere around us are to be so much as possible. This could be rephrased as a pragmatic transcendental argument (which Haack does not do): even in order for it to be possible for us to violate the norms of truth(fulness), truth itself is necessarily required as an element of our discursive practices. What I have tried to argue here is that there is no reason why the kind of truth needed here could not be Jamesian pragmatic truth, appropriately interpreted.

[38] A slightly more comprehensive comparison between Arendt and Jamesian pragmatism will be postponed to Chapter 2.

Now, is such disinterestedness available in pragmatism? Isn't pragmatism, especially the Jamesian version of pragmatism we are preoccupied with here (let alone the Rortyan one), inevitably "interest-driven," and doesn't its individualism therefore open the doors for political manipulation and disrespect for truth? Why, more generally, is the concept of truth important for a sound appreciation of pragmatic pluralism and human diversity, after all (see also Chapter 2), and why exactly should we aim at a pragmatist articulation of this concept in the first place?

A key to this issue is *reflexivity*: pragmatism – better than other philosophical approaches, I believe – is able to acknowledge the meta-level "interests" guiding our pursuit of disinterestedness itself. We pragmatically *need* a concept of truth *not* serving any particular need or interest – or, perhaps better, a concept of truth only, or primarily, serving the need or interest of maximal disinterestedness. This is compatible with maintaining that we pragmatically need a deep pluralism (but not shallow relativism) about truth. The reflection we are engaging in here, with the help of Arendt as well as James and Rorty, is in a crucial sense internal to pragmatism. We are asking what kind of purposes our different philosophical conceptualizations of truth, including the traditional realist (correspondence) one and the more comprehensive pragmatist one, are able to serve. In this sense, Jamesian pragmatism, I would like to suggest, "wins" at the meta-level. Its potential collapse to Trumpist populism or O'Brien's destruction of truth is definitely a threat to be taken very seriously – especially if one is willing to take seriously Rorty's ways of developing Jamesian and Deweyan pragmatism – but there is no reason to believe that a slide down the slippery slope is unavoidable. By drawing attention to the continuous meta-level critical (and self-critical) inquiry into our own commitments, and the truthful commitment to ameliorating our practices of truth (in science, ethics, politics, and everywhere else as well), we should be able to stop that slide. But where exactly it can be stopped is a question that needs to be asked again and again in varying historical and cultural contexts.

One important aspect of pragmatic pluralism about truth is that very different human discourses and/or practices can indeed be taken to be "truth-apt" in the sense of engaging with truth and seeking truths about the ways things are (as seen from the perspectives of those discourses or practices). For example, the pragmatic pluralist should not, in my view, claim that "moral truths" are only second-rate in relation to, or derivative from, more fundamental scientific truths about the natural world. Nor should the pragmatic pluralist maintain that the truths we pursue in, say, humanistic scholarship concerning history, religion, or literature are second-rate in comparison to the truth of natural-scientific theories. There can be genuine and full-blown truth available in all these areas as much as there is in the sciences,[39] but the concept of truth need not function exactly in the same way within all those very different practices. Moral truths, for instance, can be quite as genuine, as "really true" as scientific truths, or truths about the everyday world around us. The pragmatist point here is a contextualizing one: truths are true in different contexts based on, or driven by, our purposive practices. It is only within such contexts and practices that any "truthmaking" takes place – or is even possible.[40]

In the end, I believe, we should at a meta-level defend a *pragmatically pluralistic view about truth itself*:[41] there are many truths about truth, including realism and the related correspondence theory of truth, to be defended *within* pragmatism. These truths about truth are themselves context-embedded; for instance, we may need a realist correspondence-theoretical account of truth within a political discourse opposing populism (and O'Brien), but we may, and in my view do, need a pragmatist account within a more purely academic discourse on truth.[42] A kind of *pragmatic realism* is certainly worth striving for: in the "post-factual" era of powerful populists, we should not *too much* emphasize the pragmatic "plasticity" of truth but, rather, the objectivity and realism inherent even in the Jamesian pragmatic conception of truth.[43] The "truth" about these issues is itself

---

[39] Pragmatism, of course, embraces thoroughgoing *fallibilism*: all our truth-claims are fallible, and any such claims may need to be corrected as our experience and inquiry unfold. On fallibilism in relation to scientific realism, see Niiniluoto 1999; see also, for example, Haack 1998, 2019.

[40] For my attempt to accommodate the concept of truthmaking (usually employed only by metaphysical realists) within a pragmatist metaphysics, see Pihlström 2009, chapter 2.

[41] For alethic pluralism (though in a form not based on pragmatism), see, for example, Lynch 2009. Incidentally, Wittgenstein (1980b, 75) once suggested that we should not choose between the classical "theories" of truth, as all of them contain valuable insights into truth, and none of them is the whole truth about truth.

[42] In principle, Rorty's neopragmatism may offer us valuable resources for switching between different context or "vocabularies" and for developing a self-critically ironic attitude to them, even the most "final" ones. Therefore, my assessment of Rorty here is not at all purely negative, though I do think we should be concerned with its potential dangers. Rorty himself was laudably active in promoting pragmatism in the former communist East-European countries that opened up to Western ideas of freedom and democracy in the late 1980s and the 1990s. The fact that the current situation in Europe does not look equally promising regarding, say, the development Deweyan ideas of democracy is of course one of the background factors that needs to be taken seriously by pragmatists now critically inquiring into the nature of truth in the contingent political and historical circumstances we find ourselves in.

[43] Critics of pragmatism also need to be constantly reminded that James (1975 [1907], 1978 [1909]) himself repeatedly emphasized that he is denying neither the "standing reality" external to us nor the idea of truth as a relation of "agreement" between our ideas and that reality; rather, James's investigations of truth are attempts to tell us what these notions can be taken to pragmatically mean – that is, what they are "known as" in terms of human experience. Another matter that needs

a pragmatic, contextual matter. This, I would like to suggest, is how the pragmatic conception of truth operates at the meta-level. Far from encouraging us to slide down to irresponsible relativism or populism, Jamesian pragmatism urges us to take responsibility for our practice-laden employments of the concept of truth within our everyday, scientific, ethical, political, and religious lives (and any other sectors of human life for that matter). This irreducibly ethical nature of truth, integrated with the explicitly normative notion of truthfulness, is something that arguably only a sufficiently deeply pragmatic account of truth can fully accommodate. Moreover, pluralism does not entail that *all* discourses that we may take as potentially truth-apt in the end are truth-apt. As I will suggest in Chapter 6, there are reasons – pragmatic reasons – to remain uncertain and undecided about the truth-aptness of religious discourses, for example, but this is, again, to respect the notion of truth instead of downgrading it.

It might be asked whether truth itself is "really" pragmatically "plastic" in the sense that any truths about truth depend on our pragmatic contexts or whether this contextuality or plasticity is, so to speak, merely epistemic in the sense that it only concerns our conceptions of truth (and their justifiability) instead of the nature of truth itself. Rather than backing out of this game, the pragmatist should, in my view, push pragmatism further, arguing that it is the nature of truth itself (not merely our conception of that nature) that contextually depends on our practices of living with truth and accounting for what we take to be its "nature" within our epistemic and ethical inquiries. We need more, not less, pragmatism; creating our concept of truth, we are also responsible for creating realistic (correspondence-theoretical) contexts for its employment.

As soon as we have climbed onto a meta-level viewing our practices of truth at a critical distance, there are many kinds of further reflexive questions that may be posed: can we really say, for instance, that philosophical theories (about truth, or about anything else), such as pragmatism, are themselves true or false, and in what sense exactly (e.g., in a pragmatist sense)?[44] Is it sufficient for a pragmatist to maintain that pragmatism itself

---

further elucidation is the fact that the contexts we operate within are constantly in flux; they cannot be just naively taken as self-standing fixed realities. Our ways of using the concept of truth themselves constantly shape the contexts within which we may employ different discourses on truth. This is a crucial element of the kind of pragmatic reflexivity emphasized above. On pragmatist (ontological) contextuality and reflexivity, see also Pihlström 2009, 2016, 2020a.

[44] This, in any case, is hardly a problem just for the pragmatist. The correspondence-theoretician might also have to hold, equally reflexively, that the correspondence theory of truth corresponds to reality (or is made true by the objective facts about what truth is, or something along these lines). Again, note, however, that I am not (unlike some other pragmatism scholars) claiming that the

is pragmatically true? This is related to the question how far a form of *pragmatic naturalism* can be carried in metaphilosophical reflections. According to philosophical naturalists, even realism may be an empirical theory about science and truth.[45] Whatever kind of naturalism is available to the pragmatist, it should at least be self-consciously *non-reductive*, and thus the pragmatic naturalist must constantly face the challenge that it may be problematic to use the concept of truth in the same sense when applied to philosophical theories as it is used when applied to, say, scientific theories. I must leave this issue open here.[46]

In any event, something like *critical philosophy* is vitally needed to stop the slide along the slippery slope from James via Rorty to Orwell's O'Brien (cf. also Skowroński and Pihlström 2019; see further Chapter 3). Critical philosophy (in my sense here) is both pragmatist and Kantian in its willingness to take seriously the reflexive questions that haunt us whenever we employ the notion of truth or other concepts we are normatively committed to in the very activities of using or presupposing any concepts whatsoever. In quasi-Kantian terms, I would like to phrase the main result of this chapter as follows: just like Kant saw empirical realism as possible only on the assumption of transcendental idealism, a reasonable form of realism in our contemporary society (and academia) not only needs to embrace a qualified (correspondence) account of objective truth but must at the meta-level be grounded in *transcendental pragmatism* that makes such realism and objectivity possible. It is a historical irony of pragmatism that already the founder of the tradition, Peirce (1877), appreciated the profound link between our very ability of fixing belief and the concept of truth. Even though we need not, as pragmatists today, stick to the Peircean version of pragmatism – and certainly this book does not argue for a Peircean approach but, rather, a (broadly) Jamesian one – we must never fail in the manner of Rorty, or Trump, to find that link important.

---

correspondence theory presupposes the naïve idea of "one-to-one" correspondence. When considering the relation between pragmatism and the correspondence theory, we should examine the most careful formulations of the latter (e.g., Niiniluoto 1999).

[45] In philosophy of science, such a naturalized scientific realism is taken to *explain* the success of science, just as "first-order" scientific theories would explain any empirical data.

[46] For my earlier engagements with naturalism in relation to pragmatism, see especially Pihlström 2003. For a highly relevant recent collection of essays on pragmatism and naturalism especially with regard to the philosophy of religion, largely inspired by Wayne Proudfoot's seminal contributions to these topics, see Bagger 2018. For an intriguing Jamesian examination of what it means to maintain that a philosophical theory is "true," see Gunnarsson 2020 (I will return to Gunnarsson's version of Jamesian pragmatism in Chapter 4).

Obviously, while I hope to have provided reasons for a moderate step toward realism that I think the pragmatist needs to take when considering the notion of truth along the lines proposed here, the more general realism issue at the core of pragmatism will not be settled in this chapter, or this book. A number of questions related to this overall theme will remain open. Let me, by way of closing this chapter, briefly comment on just one of them. Critically engaging with attempts to integrate realism with pragmatism in a (quasi-)Kantian context (including some of my own earlier proposals in this framework), Ilkka Niiniluoto (2019, 32–33) maintains that there is a tension between the pragmatist view that metaphysical theses about the "world in itself" are "fruitless," as we do not possess the metaphysical realist's imagined "God's-Eye View," on the one hand, and the claim that we should not draw any metaphysical distinction between the Kantian noumenal and phenomenal "worlds," as the two are "identical," on the other hand. This is, he argues, because our knowledge of the phenomenal world – the world empirically knowable by human beings through our epistemic practices, particularly science – would also yield knowledge of the metaphysical noumenal world if the two "worlds" are indeed one and the same.

While interpreting Kant as a "two worlds" thinker here, Niiniluoto is sensitive to the possibility of a "one world" reading, too.[47] I am not convinced, however, that the basic identity of the "two worlds" (from the perspective of the "one world" interpretation) causes the kinds of difficulties he suggests, because the identity claim should not (I would prefer to say) be understood as an ontological statement from a standpoint that would be prior to a *transcendental* analysis of the necessary conditions for the possibility of cognizing an objective reality in the first place – an analysis which includes, if this chapter is on the right track, also an ethical dimension. The "identity" here is something that a pragmatically conducted transcendental inquiry (rather than any ontological inquiry that would be methodologically and/or metaphysically prior to it) yields, instead of being available to us independently of

---

[47] I have suggested earlier that the pragmatist Kantian ought to defend the one-world reading of Kant's transcendental idealism, regarding the relations between things in themselves and appearances (see Carr 1999; Allison 2004; as well as Pihlström 1996, 2003). An important background for this discussion in the context of the realism debate of the past few decades is of course Putnam's (1981, 1990) struggle with "internal realism" in contrast to "metaphysical realism" – something that Putnam later significantly reconsidered (e.g., 2016). See Chapter 3 for some brief remarks on the relation between (Jamesian) pragmatism and Kantian transcendental idealism.

the transcendental standpoint. It is *not* an identity claim that we can make from a "God's-Eye View" that we might imagine to be somehow external to both of those "worlds".[48] When viewing our commitment to the concept of truth *from within* our practices of employing this concept, that is, in a context thoroughly structured by that commitment itself, we cannot take a step back and "measure" our realism against how things stand in the real world independently of our practices of pursuing truth about it. Our pragmatist investigation of truth is then *ipso facto* transcendental. I will try to clarify this thought in the later chapters more explicitly defending a "Kantian" account of (Jamesian) pragmatism.

I am tempted to view the pragmatic commitment to realism as a kind of necessary commitment to a *Grenzbegriff* we cannot avoid postulating as soon as we start inquiring (pragmatically and/or transcendentally) into what the objectively existing reality is "for us," or what is true about it. In sum, pragmatic realism in the sense in which I am prepared to be committed to it will have to be formulated in an unashamed Kantian way, as a kind of transcendental thesis, or combining transcendental pragmatism with empirical realism. The active interplay of pragmatism and transcendental philosophy will come up throughout the chapters to follow, while detailed systematic engagements with this issue are beyond the scope of the present investigation.

This chapter has, I hope, set the tone for the inquiries to follow. We will need to elaborate, guided by Jamesian pragmatism, much further on individual (especially religious) diversity and pluralism in truth-seeking (Chapter 2), sincerity and transcendental inquiry in the Kantian context of critical philosophy (Chapter 3), individual existential choices of life (Chapter 4), the very structure of our shared normative frameworks making any individual choices possible for us, already alluded to here

---

[48] Moreover, *pace* Niiniluoto, I do think we should remain committed – as this chapter hopefully to a certain degree demonstrates – to a minimally realistic assumption of pragmatic realism when inquiring into the relation between pragmatism and realism (cf. Niiniluoto 2019, 36), though undoubtedly I haven't always been careful enough to emphasize this. Even so, I warmly welcome Niiniluoto's argument that there is considerable unclarity and ambiguity in leading neopragmatists' like Putnam's, Nicholas Rescher's, and (of course) Rorty's views (as well as, presumably, my own) regarding the status of the existence of the realist's mind-independent world. (On Rescher's version of pragmatism and realism, see also Pihlström 2017.) From the point of view of the Kantian pragmatism I favor, one problem in Putnam's and many other neopragmatists' views is precisely their unwillingness to understand their own positions in transcendental terms. While Putnam's views on realism progressed toward an increasingly realistic position in his late years, he unfortunately seems to have moved farther away from any Kantian understanding of pragmatism – as laudable as his defense of irreducible normativity (Putnam 2016) in my view is.

(Chapter 5), and the heavy ethical burden of making sincere commitments when it comes to religious and other existential matters, in particular (Chapter 6). We will thus next turn to a deeper reflection on our individual, especially religious, pursuit of truth, thereby enriching our picture of Jamesian pragmatic pluralism.

CHAPTER 2

Religious Truth and Pluralism from a Pragmatist Point of View

Chapter 1 can be read as having reminded the reader, especially the pragmatist reader, that we ought to be very careful in dealing with the concept of truth. Starting from James's account of truth as "a species of the good" it is all too easy to arrive at Rortyan neopragmatism, which replaces the pursuit of truth with the pursuit of freedom, and then fall down along a slippery slope to the kind of fragmentation of truth – or even of the very possibility of sincerely pursuing the truth – familiar from contemporary populist politics as well as, more extremely, Orwell's dystopic fiction. Arguing that we need, pragmatically speaking, objective, realistic truth even in the absence of any overarching metaphysical realism, Chapter 1 arrived at a tentative defense of a pragmatically pluralist conception of truth, which also accommodates a moderate pragmatic form of realism within (transcendental) pragmatism. This is where the present chapter starts off: we ought to consider not just the concept of truth itself but the ways in which a pluralistic account of truth can be plausibly and responsibly maintained especially in a situation in which we need to acknowledge, for example, the political, ethical, and religious challenges of a multicultural society.

Religious pluralism and *religious diversity*[1] thus provide us with an ethically extremely important and politically problematic area of discourse where a pragmatic conception of truth desperately needs to be applied. I will in this chapter continue to employ Jamesian resources in my attempt to articulate a responsible pluralism we should maintain when it comes to religious diversity, and more generally the diversity of the existential commitments that individuals may sincerely make and hold. In short, we need a pragmatic approach to philosophical questions concerning the *conditions* of the sincere pursuit of truth in existential and religious matters.

---

[1] For recent collections of essays on these topics, see Grube and Van Herck 2017; Jonkers and Wiertz 2019.

While this chapter is partly expository, sketching a Jamesian and an Arendtian response to pluralism and diversity, my key aim is, precisely, to bring these different philosophical voices together in a way that is, as far as I know, only rarely encountered in the literature. A combination of Arendtian and Jamesian insights is needed in a self-critical reflection on how exactly the pragmatist should understand the sincerity of diverse individual pursuits of truth. This discussion will also prepare the ground for the investigation of pragmatist-cum-Kantian philosophical anthropology and the conditions of normativity in the next chapters.

2.1 Natality and Diversity

In the first chapter of *The Human Condition* (1958), Hannah Arendt introduced one of her key concepts, *natality*, famously arguing that plurality and diversity are conditions of all human activity – of the *vita activa*. We are similar by being all different from each other. Our being born as unique individuals indicates a capacity of beginning something new. This is why natality, our having been born, is for her the most central category of political thought (Arendt 1958, chapter 1). With human beings, the very idea of *initiation* – of bringing about something unprecedented – was brought to the world (Arendt 1958, chapter 24). The "newcomer" can "begin something anew," that is, act (Arendt 1958, 9); moreover, as unique individuals, we are singularly capable of acting in a *diversity* of ways and of thus creating unpredictable novelties to the world we inhabit together.[2] As Richard Bernstein (2018, 88) summarizes Arendt's point, *plurality* here means that "each of us has a distinctive perspective on the world".

According to Arendt's (1976 [1951], 457) equally famous analysis of totalitarianism, it is precisely human individuality, "anything indeed that distinguishes one man [*sic*] from another," that is "intolerable" from the totalitarian standpoint, because as long as human beings have not been rendered "superfluous" as individuals, there will be no total domination over them (see further Arendt 1976, chapter 12). Totalitarianism thus denies, and seeks to destroy, the kind of individuality manifested in the concept of natality. When people are confined (or, rather, stored like cattle, or even like inanimate objects) in concentration camps, they will no longer be able to initiate novelties, to begin anything new – nor, therefore, will

---

[2] On the history of the concept of novelty, see Kivistö 2018 (cf. also later for some remarks on novelty in Jamesian pragmatism).

they be able to continue to be human in a full ethical and political sense of the word.

Arendt writes: "Total domination, which strives to organize the infinite plurality and differentiation of human beings as if all of humanity were just one individual, is possible only if each and every person can be reduced to a never-changing identity of reactions, so that each of these bundles of reactions can be exchanged at random for any other." (Arendt 2003, 119.) It is from this pursuit of total domination, the "experiment of eliminating [. . .] spontaneity itself as an expression of human behavior and of transforming the human personality into a mere thing, into something that even animals are not," that the concentration camps emerge (Arendt 2003, 119). Moreover, it is not merely individuality and spontaneity as such but even individual death as one's own death – something that identifies one as a unique person – that a totalitarian regime like Nazism eliminates, thereby murdering the "moral person in man":

> The concentration camps, by making death itself anonymous (making it impossible to find out whether a prisoner is dead or alive) robbed death of its meaning as the end of a fulfilled life. In a sense they took away the individual's own death, proving that henceforth nothing belonged to him and he belonged to no one. His death merely set a seal on the fact that he had never really existed. (Arendt 2003, 133.)[3]

Totalitarianism hence abolishes our human individuality, and by destroying individuality it destroys "spontaneity, man's power to begin something new out of his own resources, something that cannot be explained on the basis of reactions to environment and events" (Arendt 2003, 135). At the same time, "spontaneity as such, with its incalculability, is the greatest of all obstacles to total domination over man" (Arendt 2003, 137).[4]

It may sound exaggerating to begin a chapter investigating the pragmatist resources for dealing with religious pluralism and diversity from these remarks by Arendt (who was certainly no pragmatist), summarizing her analysis of totalitarianism and its attempt to destroy human diversity. However, Arendt herself noted (perhaps exaggerating herself) that "[p]olitical, social, and economic events everywhere are in a silent conspiracy with totalitarian instruments devised for making men superfluous" (Arendt 2003, 140). It seems to me that *religious exclusivism*

---

[3] The elimination of death has been widely discussed in Holocaust literature. For a classical description, see Levi 1988; for a recent analysis in the context of the nonrepresentable in the Holocaust, see Patterson 2018.

[4] For a lucid discussion of this Arendtian analysis, see Bernstein 2018, 31–34.

should be included in this analysis. Indeed, it is, arguably, one of the conspirators and should be firmly resisted by anyone appreciating the kind of permissivist spirit of "inner tolerance" that James's pragmatism, in particular, emphasizes (cf. Axtell 2019, 233–234). We will, accordingly, in this chapter enrich our engagement with Jamesian pragmatism, particularly its conception of ethically, existentially, and politically relevant practice-embedded pursuit of truth, already begun in Chapter 1. In particular, this chapter moves the focus of the book from the general discussion of pragmatism and truth (and the threat of "post-truth") to a pragmatist attempt to articulate what it means for us to make existential (including religious) commitments in our lives – and what it means to remain engaged with the pursuit of truth when making such commitments.

I am not going to *argue* against religious exclusivism. Rather, its rejection is one of my *premises* in this discussion. In my view, responsible thinkers in philosophy and theology today ought to abandon religious exclusivism – in both its propositional and soteriological forms (i.e., regarding doctrinal truth and salvation) – as firmly as they would be opposed to, say, racism or totalitarianism.[5] I will examine *how* it should be resisted, and I will find my resources for this examination in Jamesian pragmatism, supplemented with Arendtian concerns with individuality, natality, and spontaneity. However, I will also point out that pragmatists crucially need to deal with the problem of truth in their articulation of inclusivism. One of the most promising ways of doing so is by interpreting and further developing James's pragmatic conception of truth as an interplay between "old stock" and "new opinion" in terms of "holistic pragmatism," as formulated by Morton White. I will only be able to very briefly comment on this idea toward the end of the chapter, but holistic pragmatism will be further explored and utilized in the overall argument of the book in Chapters 4 and 5, in particular. To a certain degree, then, this chapter provides a preliminary discussion whose full moral can only be drawn as the argument unfolds in the later chapters.

---

[5] Note also that I am in this book neither endorsing nor rejecting any religious views. To the extent that I am discussing philosophy of religion, I will stay at a critical meta-level (see especially Chapter 6). Furthermore, I think (as is usual in the Nordic countries) that theological research and education should be understood as independent academic pursuits of truth by no means answerable to any religious authority or dogma. Indeed, such research and education deepening our understanding of the complexity of the world, especially of religious traditions and their history, should increase our ethical and political abilities to live in a multicultural society expecting us to develop philosophies and theologies of inclusion instead of exclusion. This is one example of the fact-value entanglement open to pragmatist analysis (cf. Chapter 4): academic truth-seeking is not purely factual or intellectual but directly relevant to our lives amidst our various ethical and political challenges.

2.2   Pragmatist Individualism and Religious Diversity

The form of individualism James defended as a key element of his pragmatism is readily comparable to Arendt's notion of natality. For James as much as for Arendt, each human person is a distinct individual with a unique life-history as well as life-goals or projects, yet at the same time constitutively entangled with other selves. This is nowhere else as obvious as it is in James's explorations of the varieties of religious experience – to the extent that his individualism in *The Varieties of Religious Experience* (1958 [1902]) has often, and with some justification, been considered too extreme, ignoring the communal aspects of religious life (see, e.g., Taylor 2002).

A radical and profound form of individualism is undeniably at work in the way James defines, in Lecture II of the *Varieties*, what he ("arbitrarily", as he says) means by "religion": "*the feelings, acts, and experiences of individual men* [sic] *in their solitude, so far as they apprehend themselves to stand in relation to whatever they may consider the divine*" (James 1958 [1902], 42; original italics). However, this individualism does not encourage us to remain confined in our own uniqueness but on the contrary to open our eyes as wide as we can in encountering a diversity of others in *their* unique individuality. This is of course what James himself seeks to do in exploring the varieties of *others'* religious experiences in his *magnum opus*. Even if our primary interest is not in the detailed descriptions of those experiences James offers us, we should at the meta-level pay serious attention to his focusing on otherness in such a perceptive manner.

Moreover, opening his famous 1899 lecture, James notes: "Now the blindness in human beings, of which this discourse will treat, is the blindness with which we all are afflicted in regard to the feelings of creatures and people different from ourselves." (James 1962 [1899], 113)[6] In this lecture, James shares with us his personal experience of the difficulties involved in genuinely encountering otherness, which I am here quoting at considerable length in order to illustrate the phenomenological richness of his description of our relation to other human beings (cf. also Pihlström 2019b, 2020a):

> Some years ago, while journeying in the mountains of North Carolina, I passed by a large number of 'coves,' as they call them there, or heads of

---

[6] In addition to the authoritative version published in the critical Harvard edition, I have used James 1962 [1899], as well as the online version easily available here: www.uky.edu/~eushe2/Pajares/jcertain .html. On religious experience in a wider respect, integrating Jamesian as well as, for example, Schleiermacherian analyses, see Proudfoot 1985.

small valleys between the hills, which had been newly cleared and planted. The impression on my mind was one of unmitigated squalor. The settler had in every case cut down the more manageable trees, and left their charred stumps standing. The larger trees he had girdled and killed, in order that their foliage should not cast a shade. He had then built a log cabin, plastering its chinks with clay, and had set up a tall zigzag rail fence around the scene of his havoc, to keep the pigs and cattle out. Finally, he had irregularly planted the intervals between the stumps and trees with Indian corn, which grew among the chips; and there he dwelt with his wife and babes – an axe, a gun, a few utensils, and some pigs and chickens feeding in the woods, being the sum total of his possessions.

The forest had been destroyed; and what had 'improved' it out of existence was hideous, a sort of ulcer, without a single element of artificial grace to make up for the loss of Nature's beauty. Ugly, indeed, seemed the life of the squatter, scudding, as the sailors say, under bare poles, beginning again away back where our first ancestors started, and by hardly a single item the better off for all the achievements of the intervening generations.

Talk about going back to nature! I said to myself, oppressed by the dreariness, as I drove by. Talk of a country life for one's old age and for one's children! Never thus, with nothing but the bare ground and one's bare hands to fight the battle! Never, without the best spoils of culture woven in! The beauties and commodities gained by the centuries are sacred. They are our heritage and birthright. No modern person ought to be willing to live a day in such a state of rudimentariness and denudation. (James 1962 [1899], 114–115)

However, gradually recovering from this aesthetic and ethical (as well as, in some sense, existential) shock ignited by his observations, James continues:

Then I said to the mountaineer who was driving me, "What sort of people are they who have to make these new clearings?" "All of us," he replied. "Why, we ain't happy here, unless we are getting one of these coves under cultivation." I instantly felt that *I had been losing the whole inward significance of the situation.* Because to me the clearings spoke of naught but denudation, I thought that to those whose sturdy arms and obedient axes had made them they could tell no other story. But, when *they* looked on the hideous stumps, what they thought of was personal victory. The chips, the girdled trees, and the vile split rails spoke of honest sweat, persistent toil and final reward. The cabin was a warrant of safety for self and wife and babes. In short, the clearing, which to me was a mere ugly picture on the retina, was to them a symbol redolent with moral memories and sang a very pæan of duty, struggle, and success.

I had been as blind to the peculiar ideality of their conditions as they certainly would also have been to the ideality of mine, had they had a peep at my strange indoor academic ways of life at Cambridge.

Wherever a process of life communicates an eagerness to him who lives it, there the life becomes genuinely significant. Sometimes the eagerness is more knit up with the motor activities, sometimes with the perceptions, sometimes with the imagination, sometimes with reflective thought. But, wherever it is found, there is the zest, the tingle, the excitement of reality; and there is 'importance' in the only real and positive sense in which importance ever anywhere can be. (James 1962 [1899], 115; first and last emphasis added)

James then concludes by answering his own question in a memorable passage affirming the (at least potential) inner meaningfulness of a rich variety of different forms of life:

And now what is the result of all these considerations and quotations? It is negative in one sense, but positive in another. It absolutely forbids us to be forward in pronouncing on the meaninglessness of forms of existence other than our own; and it commands us to tolerate, respect, and indulge those whom we see harmlessly interested and happy in their own ways, however unintelligible these may be to us. Hands off: neither the whole of truth nor the whole of good is revealed to any single observer, although each observer gains a partial superiority of insight from the peculiar position in which he stands. Even prisons and sick-rooms have their special revelations. It is enough to ask of each of us that he should be faithful to his own opportunities and make the most of his own blessings, without presuming to regulate the rest of the vast field. (James 1962 [1899], 129)

In the context of this example, we should observe how fundamentally important pluralism, tolerance, and the recognition of otherness are for James. These are all intimately related to individual uniqueness, manifested in both enjoyment and suffering, and in the truly diverse ways in which life can seem meaningful – or meaningless – to different people in different situations. We are, James tells us, "absolutely" forbidden to judge others' lives to be meaningless just because they may seem meaningless to us. Yet, conversely, we might say that it is also wrong to attribute any such meaningfulness to them that is foreign from the others' own perspectives. This is precisely what goes wrong in, for example, "theodicist" claims that in the end suffering plays some functional role or serves some purpose hidden to the sufferer (see Kivistö and Pihlström 2016). Note that in forbidding us to pronounce "on the meaninglessness of forms of existence *other than our own*" James retains our right to judge our own existence as meaningless. There is, thus, a crucial asymmetry between positive and negative judgments about meaning.

Furthermore, James, on my reading, in the quoted passages employs not only the *pragmatic method* (cf. James 1975 [1907], Lecture II) but also something like the *phenomenological method* by showing us at first hand how easy it is to dismiss others' experiential perspectives on reality (cf. Pihlström 2019b). Simultaneously, he demonstrates how such blindness (or, analogously, deafness to what he elsewhere called the "cries of the wounded")[7] is detrimental to the ethically challenging attitude to the world generally that his pragmatism requires. This also emphasizes a close link between the epistemic project of knowing reality – of pursuing the truth – and the ethico-existential one of acknowledging others as individuals with their own distinctive (again both epistemic and ethico-existential) points of view.[8]

Religious (as well as, more generally, existential) individualism and pluralism in a Jamesian style can accordingly be seen as in their own way articulating something like the Arendtian appreciation of natality. This may seem rather obvious, but even so only few scholars have actually compared Arendt's views to James's.[9] One of the few who have seriously investigated both James and Arendt is Richard Bernstein, but even Bernstein makes no mention of Arendt in his major pragmatism book, *The Pragmatic Turn* (2010). He does examine, however, the ethical character of James's pluralism (see also, e.g., Pihlström 2013) – in a manner not very different from his insightful reflections on Arendt, truth, and critical thinking. Having cited James's criticism of "a certain kind of blindness in human beings," that is, our inability to perceive the inner significance of others' points of view, and of human diversity in its richness, Bernstein writes:

> [James] does *not* mean that when we make a serious effort to understand other points of view we will simply accept them or suspend our critical judgment. James's pluralism is not flabby or sentimental. It calls for a critical engagement with other points of view and with other visions. It is an engaged pluralism. Contrary to the picture of relativism that speaks of

---

[7] See the essay, "The Moral Philosopher and the Moral Life," in James 1979 [1897]; for excellent commentaries, see Marchetti 2015; Putnam and Putnam 2017.

[8] Several essays in Goodson 2018 discuss James's metaphors of "blindness" and the "cries of the wounded."

[9] For example, there is no mention of Arendt in Pawelski's (2007) otherwise useful book despite its focus on James's "dynamic individualism". Nor do the contributors to Goodson 2018 bring Arendt into any comparison with James's ethical views.

incommensurable frameworks and paradigms, James's pluralism demands that we reach out to the points of contact where we can critically engage with each other. (Bernstein 2010, 62)

Bernstein concludes, rightly in my view, that recent discussions of multiculturalism and identity politics still have a lot to learn from James's pragmatic pluralism, which also criticizes the idea that group identities are fixed and immutable by emphasizing the historical change, development, and mutation of identities (Bernstein 2010, 69). James, Bernstein reminds us, "was never sentimental about blindly celebrating differences" – that, indeed, would be a kind of blindness, too – but was "as concerned with searching for commonalities that can bind us together" (Bernstein 2010, 69).[10] The rejection of exclusivism must also be based on this willingness to learn critically from others' viewpoints. Endorsing diversity and celebrating individual or cultural differences must never be conflated with the uncritical acceptance of all points of view as equally true or valuable. The entire pragmatist tradition is, arguably, centered around the philosophical project of steering a critical middle course between the appreciation of individual differences and the rigorous pursuit of objective truth independent of perspectives. While perhaps emerging from individuals' pursuit of truth, truth itself even in the full-fledged pragmatist sense remains (humanly speaking) objective – or so I believe we should try to argue even when developing Jamesian individualist pragmatism (cf. Chapter 1). Pluralism should never be reduced to radical relativism according to which there can be no critical comparison of different points of view; on the contrary, pluralism should *motivate* such critical engagement with otherness. The problem of relativism is not easily eliminated, but taking it seriously – being constantly aware of the threat that one's healthy pluralism might slide into unhealthy relativism – already to a certain degree (albeit *only* to a certain degree) protects that pragmatic pluralist from the most irresponsible forms of relativism that hardly perceive their own problematic status.

Both Arendt and James were strongly opposed to any (e.g., Hegelian, totalizing, metaphysically realist) grand narratives that tend to subordinate the individual's unique perspective to some overall super-perspective, and thus also against what may be called theodicist grand narratives claiming evil and suffering to be somehow necessary from a "God's-Eye View".[11] As Bernstein (Bernstein 2010, 118) explains, Arendt rejected "both reckless

---

[10] For an illuminating discussion of Bernstein's reading of James's pluralism, see Green 2014.
[11] On James as an antitheodicist ethical thinker, see Kivistö and Pihlström 2016, chapter 5; on theodicies and metaphysical realism, see Pihlström 2020a, chapter 4. See also Chapter 6.

optimism and reckless despair," that is, all appeals to historical necessity, precisely because we can, due to our natality, our "capacity to initiate," always "begin something new". This comes very close to the *meliorism* defended by James (e.g., 1975 [1907], Lecture VIII), which is equally firmly grounded in the distinctive kind of individualism his pragmatism emphasizes. This individualism, however, must never be uncritical; hence, there is all the more reason to view Jamesian pragmatism through Arendtian spectacles of deep political concern.

2.3 Pragmatism and Truth

Arendt also offered us an insightful account of the significance of the concept of truth. As we saw in Chapter 1, she examines in "Truth and Politics" (originally published in 1967) the relation between truthfulness and political action, defending "disinterested pursuit of truth" (Arendt 2003, 573) and critically examining deliberate lying as a political force. Now, is disinterestedness, we already asked and must ask again, available in Jamesian pragmatism?[12] Or does individualism encourage political manipulation and disrespect for truth? In this chapter, the specific question is why the concept of truth remains important for the religious pluralism and diversity discussion in the first place, and why exactly we should aim at a pragmatist account of this concept. Let me now try to illuminate these questions.[13]

It is a commonplace to observe that there are diverse religious belief systems as well as diverse theological interpretations of them. Regarding the concept of truth, the obvious question to ask is whether, assuming that the relevant religious and/or theological discourses are "truth-apt" (i.e., the concept of truth can be usefully applied to them), at most only one or more than one position could be true within them. At the simplest level, the question thus is whether more than one religion can be true (assuming that religions can be meaningfully interpreted as sets of truth-claims).[14] If (at

---

[12] In a more comprehensive study, it would be possible to examine the issues of diversity and pluralism in pragmatist philosophy of religion more broadly by also taking into consideration Peirce's and Dewey's views. See also, for example, Pihlström 2013. For a comprehensive and original study of Peirce's philosophy of religion, see Atkins 2016.

[13] I am here relying on some formulations drawn from my contributions to Jonkers and Wiertz 2019, a recent volume on the religious pluralism debate. (See Pihlström 2019c, 2020a.)

[14] It is, of course, controversial whether religions *can* be interpreted as sets of truth-claims. If religions were mere rituals and practices without truth-aptness, then we would not have the problem addressed here at all, at least not as a problem relating to truth. I will return to the general question concerning the truth-aptness of religious discourse in Chapter 6.

most) only one religion can be true, then, insofar as there are many religious belief systems, all the others except the true one must be false (speaking, again, of religions simply as sets of beliefs, or as propositional statements believed to be true). Alternatively, all of them may be false. This is, roughly, the view known as *exclusivism*. The truth of any particular religion would exclude any other being true. At the level of individual beliefs or doctrines, the truth of any such belief would exclude the truth of all that are logically incompatible with it.

It might seem obvious, from a traditional theological (e.g., Christian) point of view, that exclusivism must be correct, and many religious thinkers and groups even today maintain exclusivists views, believing that they only are among the selected few to be saved by their true beliefs.[15] Leading philosophers of religion like Alvin Plantinga and William Lane Craig famously hold exclusivist positions (not to be studied here in any detail).[16] As mentioned earlier, I am not arguing against exclusivism here but rather trying to articulate a way of steering clear from it within a generally pragmatist approach; for me, the rejection of religious exclusivism is so fundamental that it is difficult to imagine an argument that would settle the matter, other than our general obligation of sincerely recognizing other human beings' perspectives on reality – that is, something like the avoidance of the kind of "blindness" that we just saw James criticize. One might say that rejecting religious exclusivism comes close to being an element of the "final vocabularies" (in a Rortyan sense) that my version of pragmatism is committed to – but in a Rortyan spirit (cf. Chapter 1), we should remain "ironic" about even such commitments by recognizing their historical contingency. It is in *this* contingent culture and society today that we, unlike many of our historical predecessors, can seriously reject exclusivism.

That we can and should do so ought itself to be taken seriously indeed: in my view, we should regard religious exclusivism as problematic as, say, racism – not only ethically but also more purely intellectually, regarding our duty to be self-reflectively and sincerely critical of our own belief systems and pursuit of truth. What the religious exclusivists in our culture lack is, precisely, sincerity. Perhaps, if one already happens to be a theist,

---

[15] I won't here dwell on the differences between propositional and soteriological exclusivism, though the distinction is important. Generally, we might say that it is the truth of the relevant religious belief system that is taken to play a crucial salvific role by (and for) those subscribing to the system. Cf. Grube and Van Herck 2017; Jonkers and Wiertz 2019.

[16] See, for example, Plantinga 2000. For an excellent substantial criticism of exclusivism based on an insightful investigation of "religious luck" from a broadly pragmatist perspective, see Axtell 2019.

then one may, *per* Plantinga's in a sense ingenious argument, find one's theism warranted (see Plantinga 2000). But at the meta-level the problem is that we should never just "happen to" endorse a belief of such fundamental importance and significance as Christian theism (or its denial). The prevalence of the paradigm of "Christian philosophy" in the philosophy of religion is as detrimental to the seriousness of the field as nationalism is for politics. Exclusivist self-righteousness has no room in pragmatist philosophy of religion.

Indeed, religious *inclusivism*, the denial of exclusivism, suggests that more than one religion can be true – in some not only epistemically but also, possibly, soteriologically or at least existentially relevant sense of the word. In our multicultural days taking various kinds of diversities very seriously, it might be regarded as an ethical duty for us to at least try to make sense of religious inclusivism of this kind, and this requires that we draw attention to the way the concept of truth functions in this area. In short, exclusivist arguments may seem to lead to discrimination or at worst violence,[17] whereas inclusivism might at least in principle support the peaceful coexistence of different religious outlooks, which is a vital challenge for us in the world today. In short, the ethical and political needs of religious toleration and mutual recognition of religious groups may – at least ethically and politically if not epistemologically and metaphysically – require that we aim at inclusivism, seeking to genuinely acknowledge (and not merely tolerate) others' religious outlooks, even when we cannot ourselves join in accepting them.[18] In brief, there are very strong ethical reasons to prefer inclusivism to exclusivism.

However, if we construe truth in the traditional metaphysically realistic correspondence sense, we easily end up in religious exclusivism. Thus, one way of keeping critical distance to the morally and politically arrogant exclusivism of philosophers like Plantinga and Craig is by construing truth pragmatically. But how exactly should this be done? In setting out to

---

[17] Racism leads to violence in this world, which, say, conservative Christian exclusivism typically does not do. But the exclusivist may firmly believe that the others (non-believers) will spend their *eternity* in damnation, and it is a mystery to me how anyone, at least any educated person, today can maintain a belief of that kind. If a theological view entails such an exclusivist belief, this should be considered a *reductio ad absurdum* of that view.

[18] On the central importance of the concept of recognition in religion, see Saarinen 2016; Proudfoot 2019; as well as Kahlos et al. 2019. Intuitively, recognition in this context means something stronger than mere tolerance (though something weaker than full-blown endorsement or acceptance), because we may, and do, also tolerate various religious, political and other outlooks in which we do not find much, or any, positive value. On the debate between inclusivism and exclusivism generally, see Griffiths 2001.

pursue this task, we are maneuvering on an Arendtian territory; we have to both appreciate the individual spontaneity highlighted by the concept of natality and continue to commit ourselves to the critical pursuit of truth – in science, politics, and religion alike.[19]

The obvious problem we need to deal with is that developing an inclusivist account of religious diversity, truly accommodating the attitudes of tolerance and recognition, might require us to sacrifice our traditional notion of objective, mind-independent truth, at least in the domain of religion but possibly more generally in "existential" matters. Different (mutually conflicting) religions can hardly be true in a full-blown objective sense of corresponding to the way the world is, if there is, realistically speaking, only one way the world (absolutely, mind-independently) is.[20] Therefore, it seems that a straightforwardly realistic conception of religious or theological discourse as truth-apt in a realistic sense entails exclusivism. Only if religious belief-systems can be genuinely false can any of them be claimed to be (objectively, realistically) true – or so the exclusivist would argue.

Now, it may be suggested that a pragmatist conception of truth inherited from James might offer some ways forward here by reconciling a (moderate) religious inclusivism according to which religious truth is not exclusively "one" with a (moderately, relatively, pragmatically) objective conception of truth enabling us to make sense of the idea that religious beliefs and theological doctrines purport to represent reality instead of being merely language-internal or completely perspectival constructions with no anchoring to any extra-human standard of truth. It might even be suggested that *only* a pragmatist account of realism and truth may enable us to construct such a reconciliatory meta-level position in the debate over religious plurality and diversity. This pragmatist move requires, however, that we understand the notion of truth itself not merely propositionally but also "existentially" as involving ethical truthfulness, as suggested in Chapter 1. Thus understood, our pragmatic conception of truth should

---

[19] In this context, a more general criticism of conservative religious exclusivism would emphasize that such a position does not encourage engaging in truly critical inquiry at all but, rather, in some kind of apologetics in which (in contrast to genuine inquiry) the "truth" is already known prior to the investigation. This more general critique could also be pragmatically formulated but must be set aside here. Conservative fundamentalists are not among my philosophical dialogue partners anyway; they are not in the (Rortyan) "audience" I am addressing by this book.

[20] This book, of course, cannot deal with the problem of realism in the philosophy of religion in any comprehensive way (though everything I say is, I hope, relevant to developing a reasonable form of pragmatic realism in this field). See, for example, Pihlström 2013, 2020a for a pragmatist approach to this issue.

also be well equipped to be employed in the Arendtian sense accounting for the political relevance of truth.

One might argue that we can be full-blown realists about reality and truth while being inclusivists about religious *epistemology*, denying that realism entails exclusivism in the ontological (and semantic) area if not in the epistemic one. A plausible option for religious and theological realists would then be to stick to realism in ontology (and semantics, regarding truth) while admitting that there could be more than one epistemically justified sets of beliefs. This is a possible position for those who have no problem in drawing a sharp distinction between ontology and epistemology.[21] For philosophers (of religion) following, say, Kant, Wittgenstein, or the pragmatists, however, such sharp distinctions are themselves problematic. In this sense, the above-sketched worry that realism about truth entails exclusivism is internal to a broadly speaking post-Kantian approach to the philosophy of religion (which I find plausible for independent reasons; cf. Chapter 3). Not only Kantians but also pragmatists, among others, deeply integrate ontology and epistemology (see, e.g., Pihlström 2013, 2020a), and therefore the exclusivist conclusions one may end up with at the ontological level of truth may be problematic at the epistemological level as well – as well as the ethical (and, theologically speaking, soteriological) level.

It needs to be re-emphasized that, far from leading to radical relativism or political opportunism, James's pragmatism functions as a (quasi-Arendtian) link between the crucial relevance of the concept of truth and the emphasis on individual plurality and spontaneity (see again Chapter 1). It is through Jamesian pragmatism that we can bring the notion of truth itself to bear on our analysis of plurality and unique individuality. Pragmatic pluralism insists that individual perspectives and commitments to truth-seeking *matter*. This is clear in James: truth is always truth-for-someone-in-particular, an individual pursuing truth both generally and in their existential or religious lives. Therefore, pragmatism is perhaps uniquely equipped to deal with the relation between religious pluralism or diversity (inclusivistically understood) and the problem of truth. As we saw in Chapter 1, truth(fulness) in the Jamesian sense is richer and broader than mere propositional truth. It is a *normative* property of our thought and inquiry in a wide sense, not just a semantic property of statements; moreover, its normativity is both epistemic and ethical. Jamesian

---

[21] For interesting perspectives on these issues, see again the essays in Grube and Van Herck 2017 and in Jonkers and Wiertz 2019, especially Dirk-Martin Grube's pragmatist contributions.

pragmatic truth *incorporates* truthfulness, as truth belongs to the ethical field of inter-human relations of mutual dependence and acknowledgment. It also incorporates an acknowledgment of the possibility of an inner truth (or truthfulness) of others' experiences, especially experiences of suffering. It is therefore an account of truth pragmatically serving our need to live in a situation of religious diversity, given the above-discussed ethical duty to avoid exclusivism.

Jamesian pragmatic truth is also inextricably entangled with our individual existential concerns in religious matters and beyond (cf. Chapter 4); therefore, it is indistinguishable from James's general individualism. A Jamesian approach to religious diversity starts at the individual level. Individuals' responses to their existential life-challenges having a religious dimension vary considerably, and any existentially or religiously relevant conception of truth must in some sense appreciate this temperamental variation – without succumbing to the temptations of uncritical subjectivism or relativism, though. If we for ethical reasons do wish to take seriously the Jamesian approach to individual diversity, we must pay attention to what he says about the "plasticity" of truth and about truth being a "species of good". One cannot genuinely pursue truth in the Jamesian sense unless one also acknowledges, or at least truthfully seeks to acknowledge, others' perspectives on reality – and, hence, Arendtian natality, the uniqueness of such individual perspectives, and their potentiality of opening up genuine novelties. Therefore, something like Jamesian pragmatic truth is precisely what accounting for religious inclusivism requires (to the extent that we find truth relevant in the inclusivism and diversity debate at all).[22] It must, however, incorporate both epistemic and ethical responsibility in truth-seeking: both objective inquiry and personal existential pursuits of truth – truth about the world as one uniquely responds to it given one's irreducible natality, and thus also truth about who one truly is.[23]

We may note in passing that, although I have here cited him mainly as a commentator of both Arendt and pragmatism, indeed one of the very few commentators bringing those two together, Richard Bernstein's own philosophical project is highly relevant to this way of understanding pragmatism, though a more comprehensive discussion would be beyond the scope of this inquiry. For example, in a relatively recent collection of essays on his work, aptly subtitled *Thinking the Plural*, both the editors

---

[22] Chapter 6 will offer another twist to this discussion by considering pragmatic agnosticism about truth-aptness itself.

[23] In Chapter 4, this notion will be further illuminated by a Jamesian analysis of the concept of individual vocation.

(Craig and Morgan 2017, xxv) and Bernstein himself (2017, 215) in his illuminating "Epilogue" characterize his *engaged fallibilistic pluralism* (canonically formulated in his 1988 Presidential Address to the Eastern Division of the American Philosophical Association) by contrasting it with a number of degenerated and narrower pluralisms, such as "fragmenting," "flabby," "polemical," and "defensive" pluralisms. There is, then, a "pluralism of pluralisms" (Bernstein 2017, 215) – according to Bernstein as well as to James (cf. Pihlström 2013) – that needs to be further examined and critically addressed. In addition to pluralism, a distinctively Bernsteinian philosophical move is the refusal to philosophize in terms of any dichotomies either between theory and practice or between the historical and the present (Craig and Morgan 2017, xxviii). This, as we may also learn from James and Arendt, is precisely the proper pragmatic attitude we need in philosophy today. My attempt to bring the Jamesian notion of truth in dialogue with the controversies over inclusivism and exclusivism can thus be characterized as an implicit defense of Bernstein's engaged fallibilistic pluralism.[24]

Furthermore, with regard to Bernstein's own reflection on what he means by engaged fallibilistic pluralism, there is a methodological lesson we should seriously consider. "To be *engaged,*" Bernstein tells us, "demands actively seeking to understand what initially strikes us as strange and different," and this is a *critical* project balancing a dialogical attempt at understanding with maintaining a critical distance (Bernstein 2017, 217–218). Fallibilism, in turn, rejects the dream of indubitability and the craving for absolutes while of course not rejecting the need to provide (fallible) reasons for one's claims (Bernstein 2017, 218–220; see also Bernstein 2005). Pluralism, finally, takes seriously James's rejection of "vicious intellectualism" and emphasizes the variety of perspectives from which the world can be viewed – not only theoretically but ethically and politically as well – while reminding us that we are not "prisoners" of our current point of view but can always "enlarge our perspective" (Bernstein 2017, 221–222). Moreover, Bernstein's reminder about the *fragility* of engaged fallibilistic

---

[24] It might be useful to cash out what Bernstein means by engaged fallibilistic pluralism by again employing the concept of recognition. The willingness to "listen to others without denying or suppressing the otherness of the other" (as Bernstein put it in 1988, quoted in Craig and Morgan 2017, xxv) is, arguably, precisely what philosophers working in the Hegelian-inspired tradition of systematic recognition theory based on Axel Honneth's and others' ideas are trying to articulate (see Chapter 5). On the other hand, Craig's and Morgan's volume does provide a balanced account of how Bernstein's pluralism and pragmatism are indebted not only to Hegel but to Kant as well. Perhaps the standard opposition between Kant and Hegel is also among those philosophical divisions that pragmatic pluralism may help us transcend.

pluralism is as important as that pluralism itself: we need to struggle to realize this form of pluralism in our individual and social lives (Bernstein 2017, 226).[25]

It is precisely at this point that Jamesian pluralism, as argued in this chapter, joins hands with Arendt's key concept of natality: we are all distinctive individuals with the capability of beginning something new. "Human plurality," Bernstein writes, "is based upon the unique distinctiveness of *every* individual. Plurality is the *sine qua non* of action and speech because speech and action can take place only *in between* human beings in the public spaces that they create" (Bernstein 2017, 223). This "in between" to a great extent defines our pursuit of truth and truthfulness. If we take this seriously, we may, I think, already have taken crucial steps toward appreciating the idea that one cannot really be sincere about one's own commitment to pursuing the truth unless one sincerely seeks to understand, and critically engage with, others' similar commitments and pursuits. This, of course, does not mean simply endorsing them; Bernstein is also very clear, both in his reading of James and in formulating his own pluralism, about the fact that engaged pluralism by no means entails any simplistic relativism. The kind of philosophical engagement open to the pragmatist, in particular, is inevitably *critical* engagement. Acknowledging plurality, diversity, and individuality should never downgrade the importance of taking a critical distance toward others', as well as one's own, existential pursuits; this, indeed, is an element of the kind of individual sincerity the Jamesian pragmatist cherishes.

I will next try to cash out – recalling Bernstein's phrase – "critical engagement" with others' perspectives (and one's own) by interpreting James's ideas in terms of what Morton White (e.g., 2002) labeled holistic pragmatism. It is (only) by appreciating the holistic character of our pragmatic world-engagement that we can both acknowledge the diversity of others' perspectives in a way necessary for ethically sensitive inclusivism and remain committed to the critical pursuit of truth, understood as a constant holistic incorporation of "new" ideas into our already existing stock of beliefs.

---

[25] A related concept that might, however, be useful for both Bernstein and his pragmatist interpreters is the Jamesian-Deweyan one of meliorism. If, indeed, "the past is never past" but the diverse horrors of history are permanently with us, how attractive is Bernstein's "sober optimism" (Craig and Morgan 2017, 197), after all? Why optimism, why not meliorism? For example, Megan Craig's reading of Bernstein's understanding of violence in its constant tendency to proliferation, articulated in dialogue with Arendt's emphasis on "thoughtlessness" (200–201), is sharp and thoughtful, but in my view there is no need to link "sober hope" (210) with optimism, especially in a pragmatist context derived from James.

2.4 Individuality and Novelty – and Truth Again

Whenever we set out to examine the Arendtian concept of natality or its Jamesian ramifications, it must be recognized, more generally, that *novelty* (a notion of fundamental importance for both Arendt and James) is a concept with an interesting history (Kivistö 2018); indeed, it is one of those everyday notions whose historicity and philosophical complexity we easily overlook, even in pragmatism scholarship. Pragmatists have also reflected on novelty in their own distinctive ways: Peirce and Dewey were concerned with novelty in metaphysics, science, and experimental inquiry, while James, unsurprisingly, has a broader account of novelty to offer, particularly due to the "will to believe" idea (see Chapter 4) as well as his account of truth and more general pragmatic holism.

It seems to me that there are two main *topoi* of novelty in James. The first is related to an idea central to the pragmatic account of truth itself, that is, the process of adding new experience to old fact (James 1975 [1907], Lecture VI), paving the way for the later pragmatic holisms of W. V. Quine and Morton White.[26] The basic point here is simply that "old" systems of belief or worldviews are constantly challenged and critically tested in terms of "new" empirical results, data, or experience. As we add novelties to the already existing body of accepted beliefs, our pragmatic "truths" grow. In this dynamic sense, truth, in one of James's memorable phrases, "happens" to our ideas. As already explained earlier, it is not a static property that individual beliefs or propositions just have or fail to have in isolation from other beliefs and our practices of fixing beliefs, but a more holistic property we attribute to our world-engagements and inquiries through which we also encounter various others with their own perspectival sets of "truths".

Secondly, and more generally, novelty in sensations is, according to James, rationalized by concepts (or conceptions); there is a constant critical interplay between the sensible and conceptual elements of our mental lives, as of course Kant had already maintained more than a century before James (cf., e.g., James 1977 [1911]). This view arguably amounts to "holistic pragmatism" in a broader sense: our world-engagement, also in religious and theological matters, is a holistic process incorporating both sensible (empirical) and conceptual (rational, normative) elements, and new sensible evidence needs to be

---

[26] Regarding James as a holistic pragmatist, see White's articulations (spanning several decades) of holistic pragmatism with both historical references and systematic elaborations in White 1956, 1981, 2002, 2005. One of the few prominent pragmatism scholars today who even seriously acknowledge White's role in the tradition is Misak (see her 2013, 209–211).

adjusted to the already existing conceptualizations we employ within our normatively structured and constantly rationally revisable habits of action (see also Chapter 5). Moreover, we must not overlook the ethical, political, or even metaphysical dimensions of novelty – and this is, again, precisely why I think James can be interestingly linked up with Arendt's notion of natality. There is, in a word, a kind of plurality inherent in novelty for James: novelties matter to us in a diversity of ways. They may also, at a meta-level, come to matter to us in *novel* ways.

We cannot here dwell on White's holistic pragmatism in any great detail (see also Chapter 4, as well as, e.g., Pihlström 2011b), but we should take a look at how he reads James. *The Varieties*, in White's words, examines "corroborative religious feelings harmonized with evidence of the normal senses"; hence, according to James, the "saint" may validly infer "God exists" from, for example, the feeling of an "objective presence" or an "unseen reality" (White 2002, 14–15). Intellect, will, taste, and passion all holistically operate together in the formation of our beliefs – and should, according to James, do so (White 2002, 19). There are, White notes, unfortunate remnants of "rationalism" in James, and therefore his pragmatism does not go all the way toward full-blown holism. In particular, mathematical truths and sensible truths, James seems to think, are to be tested in different ways (White 2002, 21). However, *Pragmatism* espouses a more holistic pragmatism, because according to James we are implicitly evaluating a "stock of opinions" whenever apparently testing only a single belief (White 2002, 21). This is how James formulates the matter in *Pragmatism*:

> The individual has a stock of old opinions already, but he meets a new experience that puts them to a strain. Somebody contradicts them; or in a reflective moment he discovers that they contradict each other; or he hears of facts with which they are incompatible; or desires arise in him which they cease to satisfy. The result is an inward trouble to which his mind till then had been a stranger, and from which he seeks to escape by modifying his previous mass of opinions. He saves as much of it as he can, for in this matter of belief we are all extreme conservatives. So he tries to change first this opinion, and then that (for they resist change very variously), until at last some new idea comes up which he can graft upon the ancient stock with a minimum of disturbance of the latter, some idea that mediates between the stock and the new experience and runs them into one another most felicitously and expediently.
>
> This new idea is then adopted as the true one. It preserves the older stock of truths with a minimum of modification, stretching them just enough to make them admit the novelty, but conceiving that in ways as familiar as the case leaves possible. An outree explanation, violating all

our preconceptions, would never pass for a true account of a novelty. We should scratch round industriously till we found something less excentric. The most violent revolutions in an individual's beliefs leave most of his old order standing. Time and space, cause and effect, nature and history, and one's own biography remain untouched. New truth is always a go-between, a smoother-over of transitions. It marries old opinion to new fact so as ever to show a minimum of jolt, a maximum of continuity. We hold a theory true just in proportion to its success in solving this 'problem of maxima and minima.' But success in solving this problem is eminently a matter of approximation. We say this theory solves it on the whole more satisfactorily than that theory; but that means more satisfactorily to ourselves, and individuals will emphasize their points of satisfaction differently. To a certain degree, therefore, everything here is plastic. (James 1975 [1907], 34–35; also quoted in part in White 2002, 21–22)

This passage is important for our quasi-Arendtian reading of James, because it articulates James's views on both individuality (individual satisfaction) and novelty, thus in a way paralleling Arendt's notions of natality and spontaneity. White elaborates on the passage as follows:

His point is rather that a whole thinker subjects a heterogeneous stock of opinions to a test in which logical consistency, and conformity to both experience *and* desire, is to be taken into account – in other words, that a whole thinker balances considerations of intellect, will, taste, and passion in an effort to deal with the challenge that has put the old stock to a strain. And although James recognizes the need to preserve that stock with a minimum of modification, he regards even the oldest truths in the old stock – those of logic and mathematics – as modifiable in the face of a challenge from the experience. (White 2002, 22)

James's key idea is, White explains, primarily normative: we *ought to* "marry old opinion and novel experience" (White 2005, 248). Accordingly, White maintains that James's pragmatic conception of truth should be revised as a doctrine about *how we ought to apply the word "true"* (to be distinguished from any definition of "true"): "we ought to apply the word 'true' to a new conjunction or stock of statements which will better accommodate the novel experience than the original conjunction or stock did. Such an expansion would make it clearer that a holistic or corporatistic epistemology does not culminate in a *definition* of truth [. . .]." (White 2005, 248) When James says our new theory "must mediate between all previous truths and certain new experiences", this "must" is a "normative 'must' that may be replaced by the phrase 'ought to'" (White 2005, 251).

James's "organicism" or "corporatism" amounts, then, to holistic pragmatism in White's sense – or, conversely, such holism is "Jamesian in spirit" (White 2005, 250). James is, White tells us, right to maintain that "our view of what ought to be may sometimes legitimately determine our view of what is the case" (White 2005, 249) – and this, of course, is a leading idea of James "will to believe," to be discussed in Chapter 4. Moreover, it is in this sense and for this reason that I have suggested that James's account of truth involves and incorporates individual existential truthfulness as a normative ethical ideal.

According to White, James is a precursor of pragmatic holism and holistic epistemology, also leading the way toward holistic pragmatism applied to ethics, which is White's own specific contribution to holism, crucially expanding Quinean holism focused on scientific testing of hypotheses (cf. Pihlström 2011b). He also encourages us to reject sharp dichotomies between mathematics, science, morality, and religion. (White 2002, 22–23) Still, some dualisms remain in all the classical pragmatists, White points out; none of them took holistic pragmatism all the way to where White himself proposes to take it, to the view that "*all* statements that are commonly said to express knowledge may be justified by the techniques commonly associated with empirical science" (White 2002, 53).[27] While we may perceive an indirect influence of James on Quine's "Two Dogmas" (White 2002, 155), and hence on White's own holistic views, it is a problem for James, in particular, that he stops short in his pragmatic holism by exempting *theological* statements from the totality of empirically testable conceptualizations of reality, treating them differently due to his mysticism (White 2002, 53).[28] Furthermore, James (following Hume) occasionally distinguishes too sharply between truths about "matters of fact" and those about "relations among ideas" (White 2002, 59).

Perhaps, then, James did not quite embrace holism – or the holistic account of our habit of accommodating novelties into our old stock of truth and experience – exactly in White's sense, precisely because he would have found it problematic to reduce all testing of hypotheses (however broadly conceived) to empirical science, even if "science" includes ethics along the lines suggested by White. It might be proposed that one of the main points of James's pragmatism is that we should avoid *that* kind of

---

[27] Indeed, while sympathizing with White's holism, I am not taking it quite that far, either, as I am (especially in Chapter 3) proposing to integrate pragmatism with a transcendental methodology. White's holism is thus too straightforwardly empirical for my Kantian pragmatism.

[28] Cf. here Gale 1999 on James's "divided self" – a division between the "Promethean pragmatist" and the religious mystic. For my own views on this distinction, see Pihlström 2008a.

reductive or even scientistic (imperialist?) holism and develop a different kind of holism recognizing the irreducible diversity of legitimate ways of evaluating our beliefs and hypotheses in the overall context of an individual (existential) subject's life. White, however, does acknowledge the *reflexivity* at work in James's holism regarding the need to (re)consider and adjust the epistemic status of the principles we both employ and simultaneously test, such as the conservation of energy in physics, which is in this regard analogous to holistic pragmatism itself. (Cf. also White 2005, 253.)

James's normative epistemology of science and morals hence also reflexively contains, as White acknowledges, an epistemology of epistemology. But even more importantly, James's pragmatist epistemology of inquiry as truth-seeking always also includes an ethical and existential dimension.[29] This makes it directly applicable to the epistemology of religious pluralism and diversity – an epistemology that can never be detached from ethics. Here we cannot end up with any conclusive interpretation of James's pragmatism in terms of White's holistic approach, or Arendtian natality, but the complex interplay of pluralism, inclusivism, and holism ought to be appreciated. In a word, they should all be brought into a *holistic reflective equilibrium* at the meta-level. This also indicates how centrally such an equilibrium functions as a method of holistic pragmatist inquiry (see again White 2002).

2.5 Acknowledgment and Translation

The pragmatist conception of pluralism, especially religious and existential pluralism, remains thin and shallow unless serious attention is somewhat more concretely drawn to the ways in which we ought to acknowledge others' perspectives on existential, political, and/or religious (or any other serious) matters. It might be suggested that such acknowledgment is impossible unless we can in some sense "translate" others' very different ideas to voices or vocabularies closer to our own. In a metaphorical sense, novelties can be brought into our holistic system of empirical, ethical, and existential beliefs by processes of translation from others' different belief systems and world-engagements. Let me therefore offer another twist in the exploration of Jamesian and (quasi-)Arendtian approaches to individuality, diversity, and pluralism by taking a look at a recent proposal by Naoko Saito to view the very project of philosophizing in close relation to

---

[29] Chapter 4 will offer some further analysis of James's pragmatic holism in relation to the "will to believe" account of religious faith.

the concepts of acknowledgment and *translation*. This excursus will, I hope, deepen our examination of pluralism and diversity by showing the richness of the resources of not only pragmatism but the American philosophical tradition more broadly for dealing with these issues.

In her book, *American Philosophy in Translation*, Saito does not restrict "American philosophy" to any geographical location. As a Japanese scholar, she is not only writing about philosophers based in America but *is* an "American philosopher" *engaging* in this tradition, giving her own voice to it. American philosophy, she maintains, receives its deepest articulation when "in translation". This is an original and bold suggestion itself derived from the American tradition, especially from Emerson's claims about "truth" being "translated".[30] Saito proposes a philosophical project of translation – not literally, but by making a rich set of "American" ideas available to a global community of thinkers troubled by various problems of our times, including "anxieties of inclusion" in political life, dystopic worries about "risk society," and the negative political emotions (e.g., fear, shame, guilt)[31] endangering genuine participation – arguing that we may deal with such issues by utilizing ("translated") American philosophy. It is in terms of such diverse problems of individual and social life ("problems of men," in Dewey's terms), with references to, for example, Ulrich Beck and Martha Nussbaum, that she explains our need to develop the American tradition (Saito 2019, chapter 1). In this sense, her discussion is, at a meta-level, pragmatist: philosophy must be put to practical use in order to ameliorate our lives.

The American philosopher *par excellence* for Saito is, however, no one among the great pragmatists but Stanley Cavell. Her work is to a large extent an articulation and rewriting of a Cavellian way of developing American philosophy. It is not as critical of pragmatism as Cavell, but it certainly avoids reducing American philosophy to pragmatism. Seeking to make a *metaphilosophical* point, Saito is trying to tell us how we should pursue philosophy today in the societies we live in, with the American tradition at our disposal – waiting to be translated to our specific philosophical (as well as political and educational) purposes. The reason I find this relevant to the discussion here is that the very idea of translating

---

[30] For a collection of essays on the idea of philosophy as translation, especially in relation to Stanley Cavell's work (figuring very strongly in Saito's more recent book as well), see Standish and Saito 2017.

[31] On the significance of fear as a political emotion, see Nussbaum 2018 (cf. Chapter 5); for the relevance of guilt to pragmatist engagements in ethics, see Pihlström 2011a.

philosophical "voices" to each other manifests a genuine concern with pluralism and diversity in a multicultural society.

Addressing our "politico-psychological crisis of democracy," Saito emphasizes the *antifoundationalism* available in American philosophy.[32] This philosophy "asks us to think in uncertainties, without relying on the illusion of a fixed ground and without falling into anarchism or relativism" (Saito 2019, 11). As a generalization concerning American philosophy – even in a narrow sense including primarily pragmatism and transcendentalism – this might sound implausible, because there are, for instance, pragmatists (Rorty being an obvious case in point) who can be classified as relativists.[33] "American philosophy" here seems to mean Saito's own specific understanding of a Cavellian appropriation of Emersonian-Thoreauvian transcendentalism synthesized with – translated into – Deweyan pragmatism, or vice versa (Saito 2019, 76). Translation for her is "a mode of thinking through which to enhance the possibilities, and to elucidate the shifting identities, of American philosophy" (Saito 2019, 11). Importantly, translation is not just a process of rendering thoughts in another language or context (linguistic, national, cultural, philosophical); it is a mode of *thinking*. This metaphilosophical moral is, I believe, one of the most significant messages Saito wishes to deliver. It is, moreover, in this sense of "translation" that American philosophy "is in itself in the process of translation" (Saito 2019, 11) – presumably all the time. It will never be completed but must always be begun, and translated, anew.[34] Translation, moreover, enables an on-going "internal criticism" of our philosophical tradition (Saito 2019, 13). Yet another metaphilosophical point Saito emphasizes is the Cavellian "truth of skepticism" (Saito 2019, 13): our primary relation to the world is, in Cavell's (1979) memorable phrase, "not one of knowing" but, rather, of "acknowledging" (see also Saito 2019, 103).[35] Acknowledging other voices by translating them – always inadequately and incompletely – to our own could be regarded as an articulation (or a translation?) of the Jamesian idea of avoiding "blindness" to others' experiences, and of the Bernsteinian one of engaged pluralism briefly discussed earlier.

---

[32] It should go without saying that my account of pragmatism and of the pragmatist approach to topics like truth, sincerity, and pluralism in this book is also intended as resolutely antifoundationalist. In Chapter 3, I will explain how this is nevertheless compatible with a qualified Kantian understanding of pragmatism.

[33] However, as we saw in Chapter 1, Rorty's position is complex, by no means directly reducible to any simple relativism.

[34] Arendtian natality could hence also be seen as an implicit idea in Saito's discussion.

[35] Compare this to the discussion of agnosticism in Chapter 6.

On these metaphilosophical grounds, Saito argues, we should be able to find resources in American philosophy to "think beyond," for example, the vocabulary of "mutual recognition" and the prevalence of "problem solving" associated with Dewey's pragmatism (Saito 2019, 12). The antifoundation-alist articulation of Emersonian "an-archic" perfectionism as understood by Cavell also enables us to transcend "the tragic" and to find "new hope" (Saito 2019, 12). Instead of recognition *à la* Axel Honneth and other contemporary theorists, the Cavellian philosopher advances a "politics of acknowledgment" (Saito 2019, 14, 103, 125–127).[36]

Given Saito's willingness to think "beyond the tragic," her book also seeks a kind of empowerment that (she believes) is available in American philosophy. While pragmatism must acknowledge the "tragic sense of life" (Saito 2019, chapter 3; see Hook 1974), there is no reason to remain stuck in the tragic human condition, as this can, she argues, be trans-formed precisely by taking seriously the skepticism and perfectionism Cavell urges us to develop.[37] It is by both acknowledging the "tragic sense of life" and thinking beyond the tragic that pragmatism is also able to transcend naively instrumentalist conceptions of "useful knowledge" and problem-solving (Saito 2019, 41, and chapter 3 *passim*). However, Dewey, one of Saito's pragmatist heroes, has traditionally been criticized for his lack of attention to the tragic. While Sidney Hook (1974) – himself a Deweyan pragmatist – did acknowledge the inescapable tragedy result-ing from the conflicts of moral ideals (Saito 2019, 42), Dewey scholars have debated over the resources of Deweyan pragmatism to do so. Saito criticizes readings that simply find Dewey guilty of naïve progressivism, but she also seems to believe that Deweyan pragmatism needs to be reconstructed in terms of (Cavell's) Emersonian perfectionism in order to genuinely account for the tragic dimension, and to overcome it (Saito 2019, 46–53).

---

[36] Cf. Koskinen 2017, 2019; Kahlos et al. 2019; Saarinen 2016. On recognition and acknowledgment in a pragmatist context of responding to experiences of suffering, see Kivistö and Pihlström 2016, as well as Pihlström 2020a. See also, again, Chapter 5. When defending the politics of acknowledgment as a project "acknowledg[ing] the obscure dimensions of human life and the unredeemable debt we owe to others, our endlessly asymmetrical relation to others with its infinite sense of responsibility" (Saito 2019, 130), Saito might more explicitly recognize Emmanuel Levinas as an ethical thinker coming very close to this idea (though for Levinas the relevant asymmetry between the other and myself would, indeed, be ethical rather than political). I argue in Pihlström 2019b and 2020a that Levinas comes close to Jamesian pragmatism precisely in his emphasis on the irreducible other (see also Pihlström 2009).

[37] It may be noted that the phrase, "the tragic sense of life," was used much earlier by Miguel de Unamuno, a Spanish writer and philosopher whose book with that title (Unamuno 1913) also cites James.

At this point, pragmatists more inclined toward James might ask, "why Dewey?" Why, that is, should the "American philosopher" seek resources for acknowledging tragedy, yet moving on with a "new hope," from Dewey's views instead of James's? Among the pragmatists, James, in my view, is *the* philosopher of the tragic, and his pragmatist (and "antitheodicist") analysis of the human predicament does not necessarily need assistance from Cavell. Furthermore, an obvious follow-up question then is, "why perfectionism, why not meliorism?".[38] It is difficult for me, I admit, to fully grasp Saito's intended meaning of "perfectionism". This may be clearer for those better versed in Cavell (and Emerson), but for anyone coming to Saito's version of American philosophy from a slightly different perspective, for example, a Jamesian one, the very idea of perfectionism may seem problematic. Sure, we can and should indefinitely ameliorate our practices, but there is no way for us to "perfect" them. Saito maintains that perfectionism employs "the teleological idea of perfection without final perfectibility" (Saito 2019, 66), but I can barely see why the idea of making things better needs to operate in terms of any teleology. The Emersonian perfectionist views the negative political emotions of shame and guilt as "driving forces for perfecting democracy" (Saito 2019, 119), but perfection is to be understood as involving imperfection (Saito 2019, 121–122); Saito's (and Cavell's) an-archic perfectionism "seeks always a better state and yet does not rely on any transcendental (or, i.e., foundational) ground that would supposedly provide stability" (Saito 2019, 122). If so, I fail to see how this differs from Jamesian meliorism. I would suggest replacing the term "perfection" by "amelioration".[39] Nor do I agree that "transcendental" can

---

[38] Similarly, in briefly commenting on Bernstein earlier, I felt it necessary to ask, "why optimism, why not meliorism?".

[39] In this regard, my comment is analogous to the suggestion earlier to replace Bernstein's "sober optimism" by "meliorism". Incidentally, Saito seems to find my own work on evil and suffering to remain stuck with something like the tragic sense of life. However, I must mildly protest against the claim that my "worldview," "grounded in the idea of evil," "tilts pragmatism toward foundations – a foundationalism of the tragic and of evil" (Saito 2019, 58). This is something Saito interestingly contrasts with Cavell's "contesting of tears" and Paul Standish's "rebuking of hopelessness," and even with Emerson's "awareness of the futility of grieving," refusing to absolutize despair and the tragic (Saito 2019, 58). I am happy to agree with this resistance to any absolutism or foundationalism. The antitheodicism I have defended – rejecting attempts to render evil and suffering meaningful or harmonious in terms of any theistic or secular theodicy – is not intended to lead to nihilism or cynicism but precisely (as Saito thinks Emerson does) to shift moral responsibility "onto one's self" (Saito 2019, 59), especially regarding our responses to others' suffering. Far from being absolute or fundamental, evil and suffering should be seen as contingent and avoidable – not necessary. The Jamesian meliorist is as fully committed to a campaign against them as the Emersonian-Cavellian perfectionist. Perhaps it would, thus, be possible to "translate" Saito's perfectionist American philosophy to the more Jamesian pragmatist version I am trying to articulate in this book.

be equated with "foundational"; what my account of Jamesian pragmatism actually proposes is (in Saito's terms) a "translation" of transcendental inquiry from foundationalism into pragmatist antifoundationalism.

Just like perfectionism does not presuppose any final perfectibility, Saito argues, philosophy as translation appreciates the "untranslatable" and is thus, again, opposed to any absolute foundations (Saito 2019, 88). It is on the basis of this antifoundationalism that we can also perceive how morality "pervades life" (Saito 2019, 90) – though again I would add that this is a conclusion the Jamesian pragmatist meliorist may draw quite as naturally as the Cavellian perfectionist. The themes of skepticism, the untranslatable, and transcending the tragic, when finally brought together by Saito, can in my preferred terms be regarded as constituting a holistic totality in her attempt to put American philosophy into work in self-critical reflection and empowerment of our practices. This attempt is, despite Saito's apparent lack of interest in James (in comparison to Cavell and Dewey), clearly analogous to what I am trying to do in this book.[40]

Saito repeatedly refers to Deweyan pragmatism as "criticism" – as, indeed, "criticism of criticisms" or "higher-level criticism" (e.g., Saito 2019, 28). This invites a comparison of pragmatism to the tradition of critical philosophy inaugurated by Kant (to be further pursued in Chapter 3). However, Saito, like many American philosophers, seems reluctant to interpret pragmatism, or even transcendentalism, as Kantian transcendental philosophy. Her remarks on reality "always being translated," on our needing "the background of the unsayable, the ungraspable" in order to see (or say) anything, and on a sense of the "obscure" preconditioning pragmatism (Saito 2019, 35) might, however, suggest precisely this comparison. Could philosophy as translation actually involve a transcendental grounding of the sayable in the unsayable?

What I think should be added to what Saito offers us is an explication of the notion of criticism in terms of critical philosophy in the Kantian sense – and thus also a discussion of the concept of the transcendental in relation to the Kantian vocabulary in addition

---

[40] In this regard, one of her most interesting discussions is the comparison (Saito 2019, 106–111) of Cavell's views to Hilary Putnam's (who was indebted to Cavell in many ways). The main disagreement between these two Harvard giants concerns skepticism. Putnam was always critical of skepticism as a philosophical challenge, and even Cavell's unusual understanding of ("the truth of") skepticism never won his sympathies, though he seems to have admired Cavell's notion of acknowledgment. Saito unsurprisingly sides with Cavell, but I suppose a Jamesian-inspired pragmatist might, again, take the Putnamian side in this debate. However, even when rejecting skepticism there is no need to disagree with Cavell and Saito on the need to maintain a "sense of anxiety and groundlessness" (Saito 2019, 111).

to transcendentalism.[41] In addition, it would be interesting to see how Saito (or Cavell, for that matter) might respond to the claim that there is no *practical* difference between what she calls perfectionism and what other (especially Jamesian) pragmatists have called meliorism. At least it is difficult for me to locate such a difference. Be that as it may, one of my main reasons for citing Saito's work at some length here has been to draw attention to the entanglement of the ethical and the epistemic, in itself a highly Jamesian (if also a Cavellian) theme: in Cavellian terms, there is, for us, no possibility of reducing our skeptical predicament and the responsibility for acknowledging others to any (mere) epistemic task of knowing the world better. Our acknowledging others' viewpoints also carries with it an inherent pluralism. We constantly need to translate our responses to otherness to other possible, and novel, responses – and so it goes. Without this practice of translation (in a broad sense), in its diverse constellations and contextualized engagements with otherness, there is no critical acknowledgment or appreciation of pluralism and diversity at all. The pragmatic need to embrace something like Saito's philosophy of translation itself is therefore both epistemic and ethical, even though I have argued that the project Saito offers us is better cashed out in terms of Jamesian meliorism than with (in my view) her unfortunately titled "perfectionism".

2.6 Silence

We have in this chapter seen how James develops a pragmatist view of individuality – of natality in Arendt's sense – and how this view can be holistically employed in accounting for the ethical needs of inclusivism in the multicultural world we live in. We might thus say that James ought to be taken seriously in this discussion for (quasi-)Arendtian reasons, and this can be done by elaborating on his ideas in terms of White's holistic pragmatism. The struggle with truth – epistemologically, ethically, politically, existentially, and religiously – is an essential dimension of any serious appropriation of Jamesian pragmatism in this context. We have also proposed a way of enriching this discussion of pragmatism in terms of Saito's elaboration of Cavellian acknowledgment and "philosophy as translation".[42]

---

[41] Saito occasionally speaks about "transcendental knowledge" (Saito 2019, 15, 146), but that does not sound like the kind of knowledge that we, according to Kant, have about, say, the forms of intuition and the categories of the understanding.

[42] A more detailed analysis of Saito's work would also have to deal with her (and Paul Standish's) appropriation of the idea of *truth* being "translated" (see again Standish and Saito 2017).

Let me close this chapter by noting that an inclusivist account of religious (or more generally existential or valuational) diversity should appreciate not only the irreducible plurality of religious (and other) outlooks and pronouncements (e.g., religious or theological doctrines), and the processes of translation among them, but also the different ways in which religious experiences may be *silently* – and therefore untranslatably – had and undergone. It is vitally important for us to acknowledge not merely the philosophical, existential, and religious "voices" we can hear and (in some sense) "translate" but also the voiceless, the silent. Silence itself, though *per definitionem* unable to voice its differentiations, is also plural: there can be a diversity of silences, including religious silences. For example, Job's God's devastating silence (before the speech from the whirlwind) is very different from religious mystics' silence (on mysticism, see again James 1958 [1902]), which is, in turn, different from the divine silence discussed by atheists arguing from divine hiddenness to the non-existence of God (a debate not to be analyzed here). These silences, and many others, can also constitute elements of religious and more generally existential diversity as we know it.[43] They may also need to be in some sense "translated" to each other – insofar as it is even in any remote sense possible to translate an untranslatable silence.

One of our ethical tasks in the world today is to resist the intolerance of religious exclusivism as stubbornly as we must resist the intolerance of political totalitarianism. This must be done in such a way that the firm rejection of the arrogance of claiming to possess the one and only truth, or to be able to voice the one and only correct doctrine, does not make us slide down the slippery slope of relativism into the disappearance of truth altogether (cf. again Chapter 1). It is for this task that we need – pragmatically need – pragmatism, in the broad sense including, among other things, Bernstein's engaged pluralism, White's holism, as well as Saito's Cavellian-inspired philosophy of translation, and with some stretch even Arendt's philosophy of natality and spontaneity. Bringing all these "voices" together under a broadly Jamesian umbrella has been the distinctive concern of this chapter, hopefully supplementing the pragmatist picture of truth and individual sincerity we already started to canvass in Chapter 1.

---

[43]   On the history of silence, see Corbin 2018 [2016]. See also the discussion of the appropriate responses to the Holocaust in, for example, Adams 2016 and Patterson 2018. Many of the essays on realism and truth in Holocaust representation available in Adams's collection are also highly relevant to our concerns in this chapter. (See also Chapter 6.)

CHAPTER 3

Around or through Kant?
Kantian Transcendental Pessimism and Jamesian Empirical Meliorism

After having focused on the notion of truth in the framework of a Jamesian pragmatist understanding of pluralism and diversity, it may seem surprising to turn to Kant. Isn't Kant's transcendental philosophy antithetical to all such pluralisms and contextualisms? Obviously I do not think so. On the contrary, the kind of pragmatism I am advancing in this book is fundamentally indebted to Kantian critical philosophy.

While James himself famously, or notoriously, claimed philosophy to have progressed not "*through*" but "*round*" Kant from British empiricism to "the point where now we stand" (i.e., presumably, his own pragmatism), respecting the "English spirit" as intellectually, practically, and morally "saner", "sounder", and "truer" than Kant's (James 1978 [1898], 138–139), a number of scholars have compellingly shown how profoundly Kantian many of James's own ideas were – and how deeply Kantian the pragmatism he co-established thus more generally is.[1] The details concerning the complex relationship between Kant and James remain controversial for interpreters of both philosophers and for historians of pragmatism, but at an abstract meta-level it is relatively easy to identify important analogies between the two thinkers, despite James's (at times arguably exaggerated) hostility toward Kantian transcendental[2] apriorism and the heavy "German" style of philosophizing generally, which he seems to have considered a clear manifestation of a kind of "intellectualism" foreign to practical human life and its real concerns.

---

[1] See, for example, Bird 1986; Carlson 1997; Pihlström 1998, 2003, 2008a, 2009, 2010a, 2013; as well as several contributions to Skowroński and Pihlström 2019.

[2] Obviously, the term "transcendental" must be understood in its strictly Kantian meaning throughout this discussion. Even many pragmatists – including James and Dewey – have notoriously confused the transcendental with the transcendent. In brief, whereas a transcendental investigation inquires into the necessary conditions for the possibility of something that we take for granted within our practices (e.g., linguistic meaning or cognitive experience), transcendent speculation goes beyond the limits set by such conditions. For a pragmatist who in a general naturalistic spirit avoids any commitment to the transcendent, it is perfectly fine to engage in transcendental argumentation concerning such conditions and limits.

These analogies are significant when we continue our examination of the resources of Jamesian pragmatism for dealing with the challenges of diversity, pluralism, and individual sincerity in our existential and ethical pursuits.

This chapter will substantiate the remarks on the Kantian (transcendental) features of Jamesian pragmatism made so far only in passing in the previous chapters. After a general discussion of the role of transcendental arguments and transcendental reflection in pragmatism, I will explain why I think that the most important similarity between the two key figures of this chapter, Kant and James can be found in their philosophical anthropologies, that is, in their transcendental-cum-pragmatic accounts of the human condition. This interpretation of "transcendental pragmatism" will be highly significant for my investigation of the pragmatist pursuit of existential and religious truths in the later chapters.

3.1   Transcendental Pragmatism

Let me, in an introductory fashion, first explain at a general level why, unlike many other readers of Kant and James, I do not think that pragmatism and Kantian-inspired transcendental reflection are incompatible – and why, in fact, I rather believe them to be mutually supporting and enriching – and then indicate some of Kant's and James's most significant points of agreement, before moving on to a detailed examination of their pessimism and meliorism (respectively). My reader may legitimately wonder why I need to go through the rather complicated route of integrating pragmatism with transcendental philosophy and arguing for my broadly Jamesian account of the pursuit of truth and sincerity in this context – rather than, for instance, in a more straightforwardly pragmatist context of Peircean truth-seeking or Deweyan democracy. This chapter offers, I hope, a partial answer to this very large question.

As tentatively suggested in the introduction, there is a sense in which pragmatism may be viewed as a naturalized and historicized version of *transcendental idealism* – with our shared social practices in a sense taking the place of the transcendental subject in world-constitution – and it is clear that a Kantian reconstrual makes more sense of the pragmatist idea that we "constitute" the (empirical) world than any merely factual or causal rendering of such constitutive activity. Thus, we have to go through Kant because only by "retranscendentalizing" the Jamesian pragmatist claims about our constituting truth and reality within and through our purposive practices of inquiry, conceptualization, and general world-engagement do those claims become plausible at all. But this is not the only reason why we need to add a transcendental twist to the otherwise philosophically more straightforward path of pragmatist argumentation. Another key reason is that I am in this book asking *transcendental questions* about the necessary conditions for the possibility of certain "given" elements of our human world, such as normativity (see Chapter 5) as well as the pursuit of truth in general, and in order to be able to sincerely do so, even the pragmatist should consider such issues from a transcendental point of view.[3] They cannot be satisfactorily answered within a pure naturalistic conception of our lives and practices in a natural world.

But what exactly should we mean by the "transcendental" here? In order to make a case for the compatibility of pragmatism and transcendental philosophy, something more must be said about this very concept (cf., e.g., Pihlström 2003, 2004). It is, I believe, plausible to view this integration of two apparently rather different philosophical outlooks as a manifestation of what has been labeled the "repositioning of the idea of the transcendental" (Malpas 2003, 3) – a phenomenon we may find in late twentieth- and early twenty-first-century philosophical literature, both analytic and "Continental". Just as many other thinkers that do not clearly belong to the "transcendental tradition" (cf. Carr 1999) may receive transcendental reinterpretations, it is possible to read pragmatists like James to belonging to at least the margins of this tradition.[4]

One important twist of the transcendental tradition, albeit one not particularly closely related to pragmatism, is the debate over *transcendental arguments* that was initiated in analytic philosophy by P. F. Strawson and Barry Stroud in the 1950–1960s. Both in its early formulations and later incarnations in analytic epistemology, this discussion focuses on the question of how to refute skepticism about the external world. Transcendental arguments, modeled on Kant's original arguments, seek to establish necessary conditions for the possibility of given actualities of experience. In a strong form they would show, for example, that a skeptical view questioning the reality of the external world would be unable to make sense of our being able to find ourselves self-conscious subjects. Some contemporary philosophers maintain that such anti-skepticism is too bold and that

---

[3] In addition, Kant is a necessary background figure for a Jamesian antitheodicist approach to the problem of evil and suffering. This theme can only very briefly be visited in this chapter; see also Chapter 6, as well as, for more details, Kivistö and Pihlström 2016, chapter 5.

[4] Instead of defining the "transcendental tradition" in any explicit manner, we may understand it as a heterogeneous tradition beginning with Kant and Kantian philosophy and encompassing thinkers as diverse as, among many others, Wittgenstein, Husserl, Davidson, and Putnam. See again Malpas 2003; for recent discussions of Wittgenstein as examining the transcendental question concerning the limits of language and the conditions of meaning, see the essays in Appelqvist 2020.

successful transcendental arguments must thus be weaker, and hence more modest or less ambitious, than transcendental arguments have traditionally been thought to be. This is the legacy of Stroud's (1968) seminal critique of Strawson's way of employing transcendental arguments. Stroud argued that preserving realism requires admitting that no ontological, non-psychological conclusions about the world can be derived from psychological premises about how we "must" think about the world.[5]

It might be suggested that transcendental pragmatism could be developed by making transcendental argumentation "modest" in this sense, giving up any claims to apodictic certainty. While certainty is indeed a false ideal for the fallibilist pragmatist, I do *not* think that the pragmatist "repositioning" of transcendental arguments should adopt this line of thought, suggesting that these arguments would have to be ontologically speaking less ambitious than previously imagined. But I do believe that we have to give up *essentialist* conceptions of the true nature of transcendental arguments, and more generally, of transcendental philosophy, because it is always possible to come up with novel reconstruals of such arguments in different contexts. The question thus concerns the appropriate ambitions we should have in transcendental investigation, rather than any simple opposition between "more" and "less" ambitious transcendental arguments. The pragmatist ought to take a thoroughly pragmatic view here: transcendental arguments can be used, more or less ambitiously, for various philosophical purposes in different frameworks of inquiry, and as in any pragmatist inquiry, it is important to be aware of the relevant purposes defining the use of the relevant kinds of argument. This is the first important thing to note about what we may consider the "pragmatization" of transcendental arguments and transcendental philosophy. Instead of essentialism and ahistoricism, we need a pragmatically sensitive local and pluralistic understanding of transcendental philosophy. This also entails that it is by no means necessary to view transcendental arguments exclusively in the epistemological context of anti-skeptical argumentation. Transcendental arguments also play an important role in ethics and the philosophy of religion, for instance.[6]

---

[5] For this debate, see several essays in Stern 1999. The modern classics of the discussion are Strawson 1993 [1959] and Stroud 1968 (also available in Stroud 2000, a volume with several other relevant writings). See also Strawson's later (1985) reconsideration of his position; cf. Stern 2000; Glock 2003. For more recent discussions on the relation between transcendental arguments and philosophical naturalism, see Smith and Sullivan 2011.

[6] For a comprehensive discussion of transcendental arguments in ethics and metaethics, see Brune et al. 2017.

When browsing the literature on transcendental arguments, one often gets the impression that merely the argumentative form would somehow be crucial in identifying this type of argument. However, the standard form of a transcendental argument is something like this: (1) (Necessarily) if A is possible, then C; (2) A is actual, hence possible; (3) therefore, C.[7] This scheme roughly covers historically famous cases of transcendental arguments. For example, we find Kant arguing in the First Critique as follows: we have cognitive experiences of external objects; necessarily, in order for such experience to be possible, our cognitive faculty must organize those experiences and their objects spatio-temporally and in terms of the categories of the understanding (e.g., causality); therefore, we do organize the world we experience spatio-temporally and categorially. Similarly, Wittgenstein argues in the *Investigations* that linguistic meaning is possible only if meaning is public and that, hence, there can be no private language.[8]

As such, this simple model of transcendental arguments hardly differs from an ordinary *modus ponens* inference. The distinctive character of the necessity attached to transcendental conditions identified in transcendental arguments may be debated, though. For example, in Kant's arguments about the transcendental conditions of possible experience, the relevant conditions are claimed to be necessary presuppositions of something whose possibility is taken as given (viz., cognitive experience of objects external to our minds); the fact that there is any such experience is itself contingent, and hence the relevant kind of necessity is, as we may say, "presuppositional".

My point here is that mere argumentative structure does not provide us with the essence of transcendental arguments – and therefore certainly does not prevent the pragmatist from utilizing such arguments for specific purposes. I am tempted to view transcendental philosophy as a Wittgensteinian family-resemblance notion: no single criterion can be used to differentiate this type of philosophy from other types of philosophy (see again Pihlström 2003, 2004). Even so, it is meaningful to speak about the "transcendental tradition" (cf. Carr 1999), denoting the loose, family-resemblance-like tradition beginning with Kant to which I am also willing to include, with all necessary qualifications and reservations, pragmatists like James – against their own self-image. It is within such a broad tradition that we may also find questions such as the ones addressed in this book arising, that is, questions

---

[7] Here A stands for some actual feature of our experience or practices, while C stands for its condition.
[8] The interpretation of Wittgenstein as a transcendental philosopher is controversial, though; see the essays in Appelqvist 2020.

concerning the conditions of our being able to commit ourselves to the pursuit of truth, to normative judgment, and to personal existential convictions, among other things.

The Strawson-Stroud debate, with its various more recent manifestations (see, e.g., Stern 1999, 2000), might lead us to think that the problem of skepticism is essential to transcendental arguments. That is, one might understand such arguments as inherently anti-skeptical. In this book, I am not investigating skepticism, and generally we may consider the pragmatist tradition itself thoroughly anti-skeptical in the sense that the pragmatist typically refuses to play the skeptic's game. It is not *this* problem that I think the pragmatist should respond to by means of transcendental arguments. Hence, there is also no need to resort to a "less ambitious" form of those arguments in the sense of admitting that no full-blown answer to the skeptical scenarios can be provided.

Whereas many analytic epistemologists dealing with the problem of skepticism in the context of transcendental argumentation seek to develop a form of transcendental argument not committed to anything like transcendental idealism, to the extent that they even speak of an "idealist objection" to transcendental arguments,[9] my pragmatist-cum-Kantian reconstruction of transcendental philosophy takes more seriously the central (albeit not ahistorically essential) role played by such idealism in the transcendental tradition (and, indeed, in a reinterpreted form in the pragmatist tradition, too). I do not find transcendental idealism a dangerous metaphysical ghost to be exorcized from a sane transcendental philosophy; nor, however, do I find it a "merely methodological" view that can be embraced without making any metaphysical commitments.[10] A pragmatist transcendental philosophy may very well develop the idea

---

[9] In a sense, this objection goes back to Stroud's (1968) seminal argument against Strawson, according to which one would have to presuppose a version of idealism (or verificationism) in order to be able to argue from something that we must think to something that obtains, or must obtain, in the world outside our thought. Just like Kant, the (Jamesian) pragmatist refuses to draw any principled dichotomy between the structure of our thought and the structure of the world in the first place; it is a key point in their transcendental investigation to emphasize the intimate relationship between those structures.

[10] While the former seems to characterize the epistemological use of transcendental arguments to combat skepticism, the latter seems to be manifested in the work of some influential historical scholars of transcendental philosophy (e.g., Allison 2004; Carr 1999). In my earlier work on pragmatist metaphysics (e.g., Pihlström 2009, 2015), I try to avoid both, emphasizing that we may use the transcendental method precisely for metaphysical purposes insofar as we understand metaphysics itself in a pragmatist fashion avoiding metaphysical realism (or what Kant called "transcendental realism"). This interpretation of the nature and methodology of metaphysics goes beyond the present undertaking, though (apart from a few concluding remarks toward the end of the book).

that the (empirical, experienceable) world is at the transcendental level constituted by human subjectivity, albeit not a solipsistic transcendental ego but human subjectivity as engaging in normatively structured practices of conceptualization and inquiry. This may even be regarded as a naturalized and historicized account of transcendental idealism, although very few pragmatists wish to call it that. In any event, there is no need for the "modesty" that some anti-skeptical transcendental arguments seek because we need not operate within an anti-skeptical project that would have to avoid idealism at all costs in the first place.

A further important point about transcendental argumentation to be appreciated by the pragmatist is the inconclusive and in a sense inevitably *circular* nature of such argumentation. While transcendental arguments have traditionally since Kant been taken to yield apodictically certain *a priori* knowledge, this assumption must be relaxed in the pragmatist reappropriation of the transcendental tradition. While more "Continentally" oriented philosophers finding transcendental structures of reflection in, say, Heidegger may speak about the situatedness and "facticity" of our subjectivity (or "being-in-the-world"),[11] the pragmatist may draw attention to our having to investigate the necessary conditions for the possibility of the given actualities of our experience always from within the contingent practices through which we encounter the world we live in. Such contingency is always there no matter how ambitiously transcendental our philosophical analysis seeks to be. Moreover, the pragmatist tradition itself has enormously useful resources for investigating the historically relativized and contextualized status of the *a priori* (see especially Lewis 1923; cf. Pihlström 2003). Rather than diminishing the importance of the transcendental approach, the contingency of our practices and their normative structures (cf. Chapter 5) on the contrary re-emphasizes the need to investigate, "from within", how exactly – that is, in terms of which philosophical presuppositions – we are committed to viewing the world from within those practices. This is a crucial element of our pragmatist pursuit of truth in this practice-embedded sense.

This understanding of transcendental philosophy – indeed, an account of transcendental reflection in a much broader sense than technical transcendental argumentation – should be seen as highly central to an analysis of our commitment to the pursuit of truth and individual sincerity amidst a diversity of both individual and social habits and practices. In short,

---

[11] Malpas's (2003) volume contains many relevant contributions to this discussion. For Malpas's own analysis of the circularity of transcendental reasoning, see Malpas 1997.

a transcendental strategy of this type manifests the *reflexivity* present in any serious pragmatist examination of our practices and commitments. Just as Kant had to use the very same human reason he was "critiquing" in his critical philosophy for engaging in that critical pursuit itself, the pragmatist must examine our human practices of pursuing the truth and making sincere individual commitments in ethical, existential, and religious matters from within those same practices themselves.[12]

Having, I hope, achieved a preliminary understanding (available to the pragmatist) of the variability, indefiniteness, and negotiability of the concept of the transcendental – in a word, having secured a kind of contextualizing pluralism (cf. Chapter 1) pertaining to this concept – and having also very briefly characterized the circularity and inconclusivity of transcendental argumentation (regarding skepticism, for instance) as well as the role played by rearticulations of transcendental idealism and transcendental subjectivity in the "transcendental tradition", we may now move on to a slightly more substantial comparison between Kant and James and note some of their obvious similarities, before entering the key topics of this chapter in more detail.

First, in theoretical philosophy, especially epistemology and metaphysics, James shares what we might call Kant's *constructivism*, that is, transcendental idealism, at least in spirit though certainly not in every detail of letter: the empirical world experienceable and knowable by human beings does not come to us as "ready-made" or "given", equipped with "its own" pre-categorized metaphysical structure, but is continuously shaped and structured by our cognitive capacities – not, to be sure, by a fixed and unchanging set of twelve categories of the understanding (according to James) but by our on-going and constantly critically revised *practices* of inquiry. That is, we cannot (and should not imagine that we can) know "things as they are in themselves" (*Dinge an sich selbst*) but only things that have been to a considerable degree structured by us, albeit obviously not created by us *ex nihilo*.[13] Some of the best Jamesian pronouncements of this

---

[12] This idea will receive further elaboration in Chapters 4–6, with pragmatist explorations of individual religious commitments, the always already presupposed normativity of our practices, and our very ability to engage in religious discourses. One may think of the comparison between James and Kant in (the rest of) this chapter as preparatory for those analyses.

[13] Regarding the denial of any human creation of the world *ex nihilo*, it is clear that both Kant and James are in some basic pre-philosophical sense realists: both maintain that there is something out there that we did not make up. It is better to speak about our "structuring" reality into a human shape than about our "constructing" reality, as the latter phrase has too radically constructivist connotations. As noted in Chapter 1, James also endorses the correspondence account of truth in its obvious, uncontroversial sense.

general (quasi-Kantian) constructivism are Lectures II and VII of *Pragmatism* (James 1975 [1907]), dealing with the pragmatic method and the metaphysical dependence of "things" on our purposes and interests, respectively.[14] In brief, a transcendentally reinterpreted Jamesian pragmatism insists that our practices – our habitual ways of acting and being in the world – play a constitutive, hence transcendental, role not only in making cognition and meaning possible but even in making the existence of objects ("for us") possible.[15]

Secondly, in practical philosophy (ethics) and the philosophy of religion, James, while of course firmly rejecting Kantian strict rationalist deontology in favor of a more experimental, non-apriorist, and non-foundationalist ethical approach,[16] can be interpreted as having come up with a way of postulating God's reality (and possibly human immortality) in a way strikingly resembling Kant's (1983 [1788]) "postulates of practical reason". There is no way we could metaphysically or theoretically speaking *know* anything about God (or any other transcendent metaphysical and theological matters, including things in themselves), but our ethical orientation to life may nevertheless necessitate a theistic postulation, because otherwise we could not be coherently committed to what the moral law requires us to commit ourselves to, that is, what Kant calls the highest good (*summum bonum*), the eventual harmony of moral virtue and happiness. For Kant as much as James, it may therefore be *ethically necessary* to have faith in God[17] – though it must also be kept in mind that James's God is

---

[14] Elsewhere, I have tried to interpret these key formulations of pragmatism and/or pragmatic constructivism as attempts to argue that our metaphysical "structuring" of the world is always also ethical, that is, that there is no way in which ethical considerations could be eliminated from our metaphysical theorizing. See, for example, Pihlström 2009, 2013.

[15] Again, let me note that the Jamesian pragmatist should, in my view, interpret this in a substantially metaphysical sense, not as a merely epistemic or merely methodological understanding of constructivism (transcendental idealism), albeit within a conception of metaphysics that gives up the metaphysically realist assumption of a "ready-made" world. This "metaphysical" sense does not entail, however, that the pragmatic world-constitution would be, say, causal; it is, indeed, a transcendental constitution of the practices (contexts, frameworks) within which worldly objects are possible for us.

[16] For James's single most important essay on ethics, see "The Moral Philosopher and the Moral Life" (1891) in James 1979 [1897]; Marchetti (2015) provides one of the most insightful readings of this Jamesian text (see also Marchetti 2019).

[17] It seems to me that James would have no difficulty in agreeing with the Kantian idea that "practical necessity can bequeath necessary, practical reality" to concepts that remain problematic from the point of view of theoretical reason, such as "the practical reality of autonomy" as well as the existence of God and the immortality of the soul (Vanden Auweele 2019, 54–55). See, for example, James 1958 [1902], Lecture III. This issue concerning our commitment to the practical reality of the object of religious faith will also be relevant to the considerations of the final substantial section of this chapter.

a finite God, not the single over-arching absolute divinity of traditional theism. Even though this ethical necessity is usually not cashed out in terms of any explicit transcendental argument, in the loose (family-resemblance-like) characterization of transcendental argumentation available to the Jamesian pragmatist, we may also view this Jamesian commitment to the practical reality of the divinity as transcendentally grounded – because grounded in the way we (may) have to orient our lives in order to be able to make sense of the possibility of our ethical commitments.[18]

In terms of Kant's three great questions – "What can I know?", "What ought I to do?", "What am I entitled to hope?", presented toward the end of the first *Critique* (Kant 1990 [1781/1787], A805/B833; see also, e.g., James 1977 [1911], chapter 2) – James is therefore a semi-Kantian thinker at least with respect to knowledge (we can only know a world that is to a great extent a result of our own constitutive and structuring activities, albeit a more pluralistic and malleable one than Kant had maintained) and hope (we can legitimately hope that there is God, or that there are at least some kind of superhuman forces concerned with the "salvation" of the world, and that we might have an immortal life, though again there is much more plurality in the ways in which these beliefs are construed from the Jamesian pragmatic point of view in comparison to Kant's). Moreover, even though the ethical question concerning what we ought to do is the one where the two philosophers are perhaps most obviously divided, the meta-level idea that religion and theology should be based on ethics rather than vice versa is something they deeply share. There is a sense in which ethics, for both Kant and James, comes first and orients our entire philosophical investigation, no matter what we are philosophically inquiring into, and therefore their profound agreement in ethics cannot be located in the *content* of ethical theory.[19] In particular, metaphysics (including the metaphysics of theism, or religious metaphysics generally) must be grounded in ethics, rather than the other way round (cf. Pihlström 2009, 2013).

Furthermore, James's ethics, despite his tendency (as a pragmatist) to assume some form of consequentialism according to which the outcome of our actions is what ethically matters, is "Kantian" in the sense that we must, as analyzed in Chapters 1 and 2, be fundamentally committed to

---

[18] See the discussion of James's "will to believe" in Chapter 4. The will to believe type of argumentation and transcendental argumentation are, surprisingly, similar at least in the sense of focusing on what we must do and think in order to be able to account for something that is possible for us.

[19] Of course, in a sense James rejects the very idea of ethical theory (cf. again Marchetti 2015); this is a clear difference between the two philosophers, as Kant formulated one of the most important theories in the history of ethics.

taking seriously other individuals' perspectives, against a "certain kind of blindness" to the inner worth of others and a deafness to the "cries of the wounded" that we constantly hear around us.[20] In fact, I will in the following suggest that this yields a key *metaethical*[21] similarity between Kant and James.

It may be proposed that whereas Kant's philosophy is generally known as transcendental idealism, James's version of pragmatism – despite his rejection of the a priori transcendental method and some of the scornful remarks he makes about the use of the transcendentalist vocabulary – can be labeled *transcendental pragmatism* (see Pihlström 2003, 2009; cf. also Chapter 1). This is above all because our human practices, driven by our natural needs, interests, and purposes, provide us with a quasi-transcendental framework within which knowledge, the objects of know-ledge and representation, as well as moral deliberation are so much as possible. James as much as Kant is investigating the necessary conditions for the possibility of things we take for granted; he just (unlike Kant) locates such conditions of meaning, cognition, experience, and objecthood in our constantly changing, historically transforming, and always reinter-pretable practices rather than any permanent ahistorical structures of the human cognitive capacity. Another reason why this practice-oriented view is not very far from Kant's general position is that according to Kant practical reason is ultimately "prior to" theoretical philosophy: even in its theoretical use, human reason is guided by the practical (moral) interest. James could not agree more profoundly about this idea.

I will next argue for James's fundamental Kantianism by moving around these more familiar comparative discussions, however. It seems to me that several earlier contributions to the interpretation of Kant and James (among them possibly some of my own earlier works) have already taken some steps toward demonstrating how clearly Kantian James's pragmatic constructivism and especially his ethically grounded conception of religion are, insofar as a pluralistic "softening" of the original Kantian transcendental framework is regarded as a serious option (which, clearly, many Kantians would not do). I will, instead, move right through the theme that in my view unites Kant and

---

[20] As noted in Chapter 2, these phrases come from "On a Certain Blindness in Human Beings" (in James 1962 [1899]) and "The Moral Philosopher and the Moral Life" (1891, in James 1979 [1897]), respectively.

[21] By using this word I am not indicating that either Kant or James would have made a clear distinction between metaethics and (normative) ethics as contemporary ethical theorists tend to do. Rather, the fact that a kind of meta-level reflection on what ethics is – what constitutes a genuinely moral point of view – runs through these philosophers' ethical writings; moreover, an ethical reflection runs through their *entire* writing.

James at the most fundamental level – that is, *philosophical anthropology*.[22] After all, Kant maintained that his three questions can be summarized as the single question, "What is man?", and it is precisely this question that James, as a kind of "transcendental humanist", is also trying to answer (cf. also Carlson 1997). I will suggest that these two philosophers' many remarkable similarities are basically a corollary of their shared conception of humanity, which can, perhaps contrary to some expectations, be regarded as *pessimistic* in an important sense.[23] After having devoted the bulk of this chapter to a comparison of Kant's and James's (ethical and religious) pessimisms and meliorisms, I will add some final remarks on their shared commitment to critical philosophy, already invoked in Chapters 1 and 2.

3.2   Jamesian Meliorism

Our reception of both Kant and James has, I believe, suffered from overly optimistic readings that may make them seem less sophisticated thinkers than they really were.[24] Kant is often portrayed as a rationalist Enlightenment optimist who despite his faith in reason brings God back into his transcendental system through a backdoor, while James may be seen as a "positive thinker" inspiring (famously) not only the philosophy of life employed at Alcoholics Anonymous but positivity- and happiness-focused self-help more generally, including the theology of wealth and flourishing.[25] This is in my view seriously wrong and needs correction.

I have tried to argue on earlier occasions that James's pragmatic method should actually be characterized as a "negative" method in the sense that it primarily focuses on the potential *ethically problematic* effects of our concepts and conceptions that are to be pragmatically examined (see Pihlström 2013, 2014a). I now wish to draw attention to some new scholarly

---

[22] This is also something I have tried to analyze earlier in a way relevant to this comparison: see Pihlström 1998; cf. also my more recent explorations of pragmatic yet transcendental philosophical anthropology in Pihlström 2016.

[23] I have previously (Pihlström 2008a) suggested that for James "empirical meliorism" is based on "transcendental pessimism", but at that stage I did not realize how crucial a certain kind of pessimism is for Kant himself.

[24] More generally, I suggested in Chapter 2 that otherwise highly insightful pragmatist philosophers may be led to slightly problematic directions by subscribing to optimism (Bernstein) or "perfectionism" (Saito).

[25] Note, by the way, that the analogy to recovery from alcoholism is not irrelevant even in relation to Kant, who compares our tendency to be tied up with evil to alcoholism; see Kant 1983 [1793/1794], 6:28n; cf. Vanden Auweele 2019, 21. Regarding James's influence on positive thinking with a conservative Christian twist, Norman Vincent Peale's inspiration by James has sometimes been mentioned (I am grateful to Ken Stikkers for this information).

work on Kant emphasizing *his* negative and pessimistic conception of the human being. For my comparison of James and Kant, I will particularly use Dennis Vanden Auweele's very interesting study, *Pessimism in Kant's Ethics and Rational Religion* (2019), because his interpretation is rather unique in its emphasis on Kant's pessimism.[26] Not only Kant's conception of the limits of human reason (on the side of theoretical philosophy) but also, and more importantly, his rejection of theodicies and his account of radical evil (on the practical philosophy side) are key elements of what may be regarded as his pessimism – a humanistic version of pessimism that deserves to be taken seriously also in a Jamesian pragmatist context.

This is a form of pessimism that need not, however, destroy our ability to be good – either epistemically or ethically. Rather, it is a way of taking seriously our true human predicament in its epistemic, ethical, and existential fragility. I believe this is something that unites Kant and James at a fundamental level of philosophical sincerity, and therefore Kantian pessimism needs attention in this context.

Pessimism here needs to be understood as a *transcendental* ground for the very possibility of our being and doing good – of our striving for a better world, again both epistemically and ethically – to the extent that we can claim a kind of transcendental pessimism and empirical meliorism to be firmly integrated in James (cf., e.g., Pihlström 2008a). It is, if you will, a condition identifiable by a transcendental argument investigating what needs to be presupposed for us to be able to commit ourselves to ameliorating our lives; in order for such an argument to be available to us, the above-sketched integration of pragmatist and transcendental approaches is needed. Kant's pessimistic account of the human being thus plays a crucial role in my pragmatist development of transcendental philosophy. At a meta-level, this interplay of pessimism and meliorism should make us rethink the philosophical anthropology shaping both Kantian critical philosophy and Jamesian pragmatism. We must, Kant and James seem to agree, start from a reflexively critical analysis of our human situation, seeking to understand our finite and fragile condition as sharply and honestly as possible; only against that background of criticism can we pragmatically try to construct a better human world (epistemically and ethically). For Kant, such a critical analysis shows that we are unable to know anything about things as they are in themselves (including theological issues such as the existence of God and

---

[26] I find Vanden Auweele's reading to be fundamentally in agreement with my own earlier work on Kantian antitheodicy (Kivistö and Pihlström 2016), though the actual theodicy discussion remains relatively brief in his book. See also Madore 2011 (and cf. later in the text).

human immortality) and that we are not by our nature good but desperately need the moral law set by our autonomous reason in its practical use. For James, an analogous critical analysis starts from the impossibility of theodicies that would allegedly render suffering justified from a transcendent or absolute point of view not tainted by the diversity of human concerns, and from the framing of the very pragmatic method by the problem of evil, the recognition that there are real losses and real sorrows in human life, no matter how positively meaningful and flourishing our life could at best be (cf. Kivistö and Pihlström 2016, chapter 5). Just as Kant's *Religionsschrift* (1983 [1793/1794]) begins with the well-known analysis of "radical evil" as a natural human inclination, James's *Pragmatism* (1975 [1907]) begins and ends with a discussion of the problem of evil and the rejection of theodicies.

It seems to me that James indeed does not go "around Kant" but right through him when it comes to a certain kind of pessimism about the human condition. This might sound like an implausible reading of a philosopher who wrote essays such as "The Energies of Men" and "Is Life Worth Living?" (both in James 1979 [1897]); however, the key idea is not that meliorism would be wrong but that it is based on a deeper pessimism. Moreover, the specific word is not essential – we definitely do not have to talk about "pessimism" at all – but the general commitment to something like anti-optimism and the rejection of any naïve "positive thinking" are what matters. Indeed, a kind of quasi-Jamesian moral "heroism" is precisely what is needed for the Kantian moral subject to overcome – even partially – the natural inclination to prioritize evil maxims instead of moral ones. Vanden Auweele (2019) rightly emphasizes that from a Kantian point of view human nature has no inherent inclination to goodness but needs reason (the moral law) as its guidance. James may be slightly more optimistic about this specific matter, but he also argues that we need to be educated out of our instinctive blindness and deafness.[27] For James, such education takes place through the employment of the pragmatic method taking seriously the potential practical results of our ideas, a method framed by an antitheodicist understanding of the problem of evil: neither Hegelian nor Leibnizian attempts to render unnecessary suffering meaningful in a transcendent sense are, for James, humanly acceptable, as they disregard the concrete experience of the victims of evil and suffering (cf. James 1975 [1907], Lecture I). To take such evil and suffering seriously is to pursue truth about the human condition, avoiding the fake news of false optimism.

---

[27] See again the extensive quotes from James's "Blindness" essay in Chapter 2.

We should thus follow James (James 1975 [1907], Lecture VIII) in viewing pragmatism as proposing a form of meliorism reducible neither to naively optimistic views according to which the good will ultimately inevitably prevail nor to dark and cynical pessimism according to which everything will finally go down the road of destruction.[28] Pragmatism generally mediates between a number of implausible philosophical extremes (including strong realism and idealism as well as the tough-minded and tender-minded "temperaments"),[29] and similarly Kant's transcendental philosophy mediates between (again) realism and idealism as well as, among other things, rationalism and empiricism and dogmatism and skepticism. The mediating role played by meliorism is a key dimension of the more general pragmatist-cum-Kantian picture of the human being. This is how James characterizes pragmatism's commitment to meliorism:

> Now it would contradict the very spirit of life to say that our minds must be indifferent and neutral in questions like that of the world's salvation. Anyone who pretends to be neutral writes himself down here as a fool and a sham. [. . .] Nevertheless there are unhappy men who think the salvation of the world impossible. Theirs is the doctrine known as pessimism.
>
> Optimism in turn would be the doctrine that thinks the world's salvation inevitable.
>
> Midway between the two there stands what may be called the doctrine of meliorism [. . .]. Meliorism treats salvation as neither inevitable nor impossible. It treats it as a possibility, which becomes more and more of a probability the more numerous the actual conditions of salvation become.
>
> It is clear that pragmatism must incline towards meliorism. (James 1975 [1907], 137)

Earlier in the same volume, James contrasts meliorism with determinism, because the latter – no matter whether it is a mechanistic materialist form of determinism or an absolute idealist one – claims that "necessity and impossibility between them rule the destinies of the world", while the former "holds up improvement as at least possible" (James 1975 [1907], 61).[30] Pragmatism figures as a pluralistic philosophy of promise and hope, refusing to ever take "salvation" for granted (like dogmatic religious outlooks optimistically tend to

---

[28] Excellent relatively recent discussions of James's meliorism can be found in commentaries such as Marchetti 2015 and Campbell 2017; see also several relevant essays in Goodson 2018.

[29] On philosophical temperaments, see James 1975 [1907], Lecture I. I have discussed this mediating role of pragmatism on a number of earlier occasions, for example, Pihlström 2008a, 2013.

[30] Cf. Gunnarsson's (2020) comprehensive analysis of James's rejection of determinism, to be discussed in Chapter 4. Gunnarsson, in my view problematically, speaks of James's optimism rather than meliorism.

do), nor claiming it to be impossible (as materialist and determinist views hopelessly pessimistically do, with their bleak picture of an ultimately inhuman universe), but the fact that such a promise is needed in the first place follows from our highly insecure, vulnerable, and both epistemically and ethically incomplete human condition.

In particular, sincerely understanding this incompleteness is essential in our ethical relations to other human beings around us. More specifically, James's above-cited examination of "a certain blindness in human beings" (cf. Chapter 2), as an inclination or tendency to overlook the significance of otherness and other human beings' distinctive points of view that might make *their* lives meaningful in ways we cannot easily understand, is analogous (or even James's own version of) Kant's treatment of "radical evil", which is also characterized as an inclination (*Hang*), that is, the tendency rooted in us to choose maxims contrary to the moral law – an inclination to evil (*Hang zum Böse*). These notions reflect the two philosophers' fundamental agreement about transcendental pessimism. According to both, we need to be educated out of these inclinations. This happens, in Kant, primarily by the practical use of reason (which ultimately leads to religion; cf. later), and in James by an engagement in holistic practices more generally (i.e., not merely reason-use as such), religious practices included. Both are versions of the idea that human beings need to be *encultured* in order for them to be able to be moral – to adopt a "strenuous mood", as James memorably put it. Pessimism and meliorism work together here, as it is only on the grounds of pessimism that the melioristic project of making the world – especially human beings – better makes sense. This ultimately amounts to a holistic pragmatic philosophical anthropology (cf. also Chapter 4).

Without appreciating a basic vulnerability in the lives we share with other human beings, no "cries of the wounded"[31] can be heard, and no pragmatic method can get off the ground. Therefore, James's physiological metaphors of human finitude should be taken seriously as fundamental to his pragmatism: he finds both *deafness* (to what he calls the cries of the wounded) and *blindness* (to others' experiences in general) significant to his analysis of our responses – or, better, failing responses – to vulnerability and suffering. In an opening comment to the 1899 "blindness" lecture, he notes (also quoted in Chapter 2): "Now the blindness in human beings, of which this discourse will treat, is the blindness with which we all are

---

[31] On this key Jamesian notion, see, for further discussion, Putnam and Putnam 2017, as well as Kivistö and Pihlström 2016, chapter 5.

afflicted in regard to the feelings of creatures and people different from ourselves." (James 1962 [1899], 113) Similarly, the human being, according to Kant (1983 [1793/1794], 6:32), "is by nature evil", and this fact about our condition manifests itself in our disregard for moral duty when it conflicts with our natural pursuit of happiness.

It must be noted, however, that there are also important divergences between Kant's and James's distinctive accounts of our inclinations to evil. For Kant, radical evil is not merely the empirical tendency to prioritize one's own happiness, well-being, or personal needs and interests in contrast to the moral law (though this is something we have a tendency to do); it is, more strongly, our *free choice* of maxims that prioritize happiness to moral law, that is, our tendency to freely choose to follow maxims that conflict with the categorical imperative. Our autonomous reason is self-divided here. It is crucially important for Kant that we are *responsible* for these choices and prioritizations and that *we* are therefore, indeed, "radically" evil ("at the root", recalling the Latin etymology of *radix*); the unhappy choice arises from ourselves. Ultimately, our tendency to freely choose to be evil in this sense is as inexplicable and incomprehensible as our acting (when morally good) out of pure respect for the moral law as moral subjects (see Kant 1983 [1793/1794], Book I; Bernstein 2002, chapter 1).[32]

3.3 Kantian Pessimism

It is, arguably, precisely due to the "radical" character of evil (in the etymological sense of *radix*) that human beings are unable to achieve by their own efforts what Kant in the second *Critique* (1983a [1788]) called the highest good (*summum bonum*); in this pursuit commanded by the moral law itself (and thus by our practical reason), we seem to need, in addition to our autonomous reason, something like divine grace, and we need to be able to *legitimately hope* that we might deserve such grace on the basis of our moral commitment. James (1979 [1909]) revisits an essentially similar idea when advancing pragmatism as a pluralistic philosophy of hope, insisting that we need to do our best in the effort of the "moral salvation" of the world while at the same time trusting that other (superhuman) agents will do their best, too.[33]

---

[32] Furthermore, in Pihlström 2014a, chapter 1, I suggest that we should understand Kant's notion of radical evil in terms of Peirce's metaphysics of "real generals", such as habits and dispositions; the extent to which this realistic Peircean account is compatible with James's somewhat more nominalistic pragmatism (cf. Pihlström 2009) is another matter and cannot be discussed here.

[33] In the *Religionsschrift*, Kant also mentions "supernatural cooperation" (1983c [1793/1794], 6:44).

We should, however, take a slightly closer look at the way in which pessimism figures in Kant's practical philosophy and philosophy of religion, in particular. Here I will help myself to Vanden Auweele's insightful reading. He defines "Kantian pessimism" as a view emphasizing "*the lack of any capacity for human nature to be or navigate toward moral goodness*", entailing that "*human nature requires a radical revolution through means exceeding that nature*" (Vanden Auweele 2019, xvi; original emphasis; see also 65), and he strikingly suggests that pessimism is not merely a part of Kant's philosophy but is present "in the whole of his philosophy" (Vanden Auweele 2019, xviii). In some more detail, he summarizes Kantian pessimism as the conjunction of three theses. First, human nature (or natural processes generally) "do by themselves not facilitate moral goodness"; indeed, there is "something profoundly amiss with human nature". Secondly, therefore, our development toward goodness "must include a radical change"; in terms of the *radix* etymology, again, human nature needs to be "altered from the ground up", not merely trained or reformed. Thirdly, Kant espouses a skeptical view about our actually being able to reach the highest good (Vanden Auweele 2019, xviii). The human being simply does not have a "holy will" that would not experience a conflict between moral duty and natural inclination (Vanden Auweele 2019, 44–45, 51). This seems to be a similar kind of transcendental anthropological "fact" about us as, say, our not possessing the faculty of "intellectual intuition" that would know its objects directly without the mediating role of the senses (as analyzed in the Transcendental Aesthetic of the first *Critique*).[34] It is a fundamentally important element of our pursuit of truth about the human condition that we appreciate such "transcendental facts" that define our human world and its limits; it is a way of disregarding the truth to speculate about what human life could be like in the absence of such conditions. Therefore, naively optimistic views claiming that human beings are "intrinsically" or "essentially" good rather than evil are, strikingly, comparable to post-truth fragmentations of truth-seeking.

Note how close Kant's pessimism comes to Jamesian meliorism. As Vanden Auweele puts it, this pessimism "does not cancel out the possibility of a better future, but warns against the belief that natural processes by themselves navigate toward that end. Progress is hard and difficult, not inevitable." (Vanden Auweele 2019, xx) What is required is "moral

---

[34] Vanden Auweele (2019, 109) in my view aptly characterizes the propensity to evil as "an anthropological idea of a transcendental nature, meaning it applies universally to human beings but is contingent to their nature". Analogously, human finitude and mortality can be claimed to be "transcendental anthropological" features of human existence (Pihlström 2016).

education that cultivates and augments [our] rational interest in moral behavior" (Vanden Auweele 2019, 20). Accordingly, just as the Jamesian meliorist may still have confidence (however meager) in the possibility of a better outcome, or "moral salvation" of the world (for which the assistance of "higher powers" may be needed), the Kantian pessimist does not claim human beings to be "necessarily corrupted" but only "naturally corrupted" (Vanden Auweele 2019, 101; cf. 109, 116): the *Hang zum Böse* rooted in us does not make morality impossible for us but only very difficult. Otherwise the very pursuit of moral goodness (a pursuit we have a duty to engage in) would become an incoherent goal. Moral virtue must still be a human *possibility*; our nature cannot be so thoroughly (necessarily, unavoidably) corrupted by our propensity to evil that we could not even *aim* at being morally good – to even occasionally occupy what James called the "strenuous mood".[35] The possibility of moral goodness in this sense only concerns human beings, because neither angels (who would possess a "holy will") nor mere animals would be able to act virtuously due to a conflict between duty and inclination.[36]

Another potential comparison to James would also be highly natural here: perhaps our way to goodness is something that only opens through a radical conversion (see the relevant sections on conversion in James 1958 [1902], Lectures IX–X). At least in Kant's view, no minor adjustments are sufficient, but human nature needs to be "radically sculpted" to "overhaul" its natural behavior (Vanden Auweele 2019, 65); what is needed is a "dramatically changed second nature". While this kind of radical moral education is difficult, Kant is not a thoroughgoing or absolute pessimist in the sense that he would deny its possibility. James's position may also be seen as cautious if not skeptical regarding our ability to achieve the highest good – or "moral salvation", as James calls it – as it is not easy for us to overcome the blindness that comes naturally to us. Moreover, we may note that just as Kantian radical evil and Jamesian moral blindness are analogous notions, so are the ethico-religiously central concepts of the highest good and the moral salvation of the world.[37] While Kant urges us to be

---

[35] The second and third book (*Stücke*) of the *Religionsschrift* can, I think, be read as an extended argument concerning the way in which the good can nevertheless overcome our evil propensity – but not without religion. In James, too, the hope for moral salvation is inextricably tied up with his defense of the possibility or even pragmatic necessity of adopting a religious outlook.

[36] This possibility of goodness could also be analyzed in terms of Peircean metaphysics of "real generals", including real (also unactualized) possibilities (in terms of which, as I will suggest in Chapter 4, we may understand, for example, personal life-vocations).

[37] It might be suggested that the Jamesian idea of "moral salvation" comes close to Kant's hope that "the world must be moralized" (Vanden Auweele 2019, 126).

committed to moral duty despite its difficulty, James offers us an uncertain universe with ineliminable responsibility:

> It is then perfectly possible to accept sincerely a drastic kind of a universe from which the element of 'seriousness' is not to be expelled. Whoso does is, it seems to me, a genuine pragmatist. He is willing to live on a scheme of uncertified possibilities which he trusts; willing to pay with his own person, if need be, for the realization of the ideals which he frames. (James 1975 [1907], 142–143)

There is hardly a better description of personal sincerity in James's oeuvre. For James, this "trust" may also be directed, religiously, at "super-human forces" that may assist us in advancing the moral ideal of salvation (James 1975 [1907], 143). In the Kantian context, a "conversion" to moral seriousness despite the uncertainty of our condition is, however, primarily a rational and ethical one. Because our human nature does not possess the tools to reach moral goodness, we require "the intervention of reason that radically remodels nature" (Vanden Auweele 2019, 5). This ultimately leads to religion, but we cannot hope to just volitionally adopt a religious faith because of its beneficial effects in our moral pursuits; as Vanden Auweele notes (2019, 23), Kant rejects Pascal's Wager as firmly as James (1979 [1897], chapter 1) does.[38] Yet, we do need actively embraced faith in order to direct our behavior from what we merely naturally are to what ethical duty – in our "strenuous mood" – requires. Insofar as the key to Kant's pessimism is our inability to be naturally good (i.e., our inclination to evil instead of moral virtue), for James the fundamental problem seems to be that the very possibility of morality is endangered by the fact that we appear to be living in a material world devoid of any higher meaning and value, if the scientific account of the world is on the right track. For both, we need to overcome our mere nature and become fully human – and this is itself an irreducibly ethical quest.

While Vanden Auweele does not explicitly speak about transcendental pessimism (or meliorism, for that matter), his reading of Kant fits very well my attempt to reconcile transcendental pessimism with empirical meliorism. He notes that "the rationally justified hope for a future in which humanity is set right shines so powerfully that one is blinded to the darkness it is supposed to cover up" (Vanden Auweele 2019, 22). Rational hope does shine, but we can only notice it against the pessimistic

---

[38] Cf. Chapter 4. On the similarities between Kant's practical postulation of God and James's "will to believe" idea, see, however, Pihlström 1998, 2013.

darkness around it. Again, the same holds for James's melioristic conviction that things *can* be made better while success is never guaranteed.

There is no need to here dwell on the way in which Kant (1983 [1791]) in his "Theodicy Essay" firmly rejects all actual and possible (e.g., Leibnizian metaphysically optimist) theodicies allegedly rendering evil and suffering (or "counterpurposiveness", *Zweckwidrigkeit*) meaningful and (in some sense) purposeful.[39] It suffices to observe here that antitheodicism is an essential element of Kant's pessimism. There is no way in which we could by our limited rational resources justify, or even reconcile ourselves with, all the evil and suffering we find around us in the world we live in; moreover, it can be suggested that our moral duty to treat other human beings not merely as means but also as ends (according to the second formulation of the categorical imperative) would have to preclude the instrumentalizing tendencies of theodicies, that is, the temptation to see others' suffering as a means to some imagined higher end (cf. also Chapter 6).

No rationalist dogmatic faith in a harmonious divine plan rendering all counterpurposiveness ultimately purposeful can thus be humanly accepted, because it is in the end a form of the "blindness" James criticized, though not exactly in the same sense. It is a form of blindness (and deafness) due to its inability to appreciate the experience of utter meaninglessness in suffering. In this antitheodicism, Kant and James stand united.[40]

3.4 Ethics and Religion

As was already remarked earlier, the Jamesian pragmatic postulation of God's existence – based on a "will to believe" leap (cf. again Chapter 4) – resembles the Kantian rationally legitimate hope for God's existence as a "postulate of practical reason". This leap, or hope, is necessary for us (given the kind of beings we are, and given the pessimism sketched earlier), because otherwise we cannot be fully committed to the requirements of morality. It is, thus, for melioristic reasons that we need to take the "will to

---

[39] Vanden Auweele's (2019, 7–10) brief discussion of this issue is solid, though it fails to deal with Kant's very interesting reading of the Book of Job – a serious omission in my view (cf. Kivistö and Pihlström 2016, chapter 2). Kant's account of that ancient text arguably sets the tone for a number of more recent, and very different, antitheodicist projects, including James's.

[40] For more detailed reflections on this topic, see my previous engagements with the theodicy issue and antitheodicism, including Pihlström 2013, 2014a, 2020a; Kivistö and Pihlström 2016. See also Chapter 6.

believe" step toward practically postulating a Kantian divinity that (we may
hope) can ultimately guarantee justice as the harmony of virtue and
happiness, though, given our pessimistic condition, we can never know
for sure anything about such an outcome.

On the basis of the considerations of meliorism and pessimism, it is possible
to further deepen our comparison between Kant and James by noting how
closely similar their ways of subordinating religion to morality are. It is
through religion – to which our reason in its limited condition brings us –
that our blindness and our propensity to evil may be (partially, temporarily)
overcome and the moral pursuit strenuously advanced – to the extent that we
may (again) follow Vanden Auweele's (2019, 131, 173) suggestion according to
which Kant's philosophy of religion is "an integral part of practical philosophy
by making religion into a tool for cultivating moral resolve", and the functions
of religion are to be subordinated to the ethical one. They are, clearly, to be
subordinated to ethics according to James as well.

An obvious question that arises here is how *sincerely* a morally motivated
religious believer can adopt religious faith, knowing that it ultimately only
plays an instrumental role for advancing ethical rather than religious ends.
This is a question that comes up, in my view, as clearly in the Kantian
framework (see Vanden Auweele 2019, chapter 6) as in the Jamesian one
(see especially Pihlström 2008a, chapter 2, and 2013, chapter 1). It is,
indeed, a question we need to address in order to make any sense of the
idea of truth-seeking, or the pursuit of truth, in religious contexts. If
religion is only, or even primarily, intended to help us adopt the strenuous
mood and pursue moral ends that ought to motivate us independently of
religion, does it have any autonomous or even any genuine role to play in
our lives? If we were fully conscious of the primarily (or exclusively) ethical
function of religion, this would be "the end of religion"; a truly Kantian
form of Christianity would, rather, have to be embraced without our being
aware of its essentially serving our "moral courage" (Vanden Auweele 2019,
191). This is how Vanden Auweele formulates this worry:

> Religions can only achieve its [*sic*] function, that is, to cultivate moral
> resolve, if they are taken to be true, not if they are adopted because it is
> prudent to adopt a religion. One believes in Christianity because one thinks
> Christianity is true, not because one thinks Christianity would be prudent
> to believe in (this would make for a hypocritical believer). (Vanden Auweele
> 2019, 192)

In other words, the morally instrumental function of religion is problematic for the sincerity of religious faith. "Instrumental belief is not real

belief" (Vanden Auweele 2019, 193), and therefore our realizing the "practical usefulness" of religious belief would destroy that belief *qua* religious. As was already noted, Kant just like James later rejected Pascal's Wager, which (at least according to a received view) proposes to infer the rationality of religious faith from the predictably beneficial outcome of that faith (and from the fact that its probability, however small, is not zero).

This "sincerity objection", as we might call it, is arguably a worry that can be raised with full force only in the context of the kind of Kantian-cum-Jamesian pessimism-cum-meliorism that has been sketched earlier. We may be persuaded by Kantian and Jamesian arguments that religion is necessarily, at least in the sense of practical necessity, needed for us to be able to overcome our instinctive blindness and/or our natural inclination to prioritize evil maxims. It is only a short step from this insight to the conclusion that this is *all* religion is ever needed for. Could religious faith, then, even turn into a kind of *placebo* therapy that we know "works" (ethically, or perhaps just prudentially) but not because there is a "real" objective mechanism there but because such a motivating force tends to be effective for beings like us with our cognitive and ethical condition, including our limitations?[41] At least it would seem that for a *placebo* effect to be real we cannot know that the therapy involved really has no efficient power. Paradoxically, for our being able to effectively "use" religion as a "tool" for our moral resolve, we must *not* know, or perhaps not even be able to know, that it is "merely" such a tool. We must, in some sense, be able to be sincerely committed to religion without having climbed onto a reflective meta-level affirming the moral value of such commitment, in order for that religious commitment to serve its ethical function – yet this sincerity itself must arise from our ethical stance toward religion. Do we, then, in a certain sense have to *cancel* our pursuit of truth in order to arrive at a truly pragmatic truth in religion? There is no way out visible in this *impasse*; the demands of individual (existential) sincerity – of our pursuing the truth about our deepest commitments and their ethical value – are so heavy that they may threaten our being able to maintain such sincerity at all.

It is, it seems to me, essentially the same kind of sincerity that Kant emphasizes when he rejects theodicies in the Theodicy Essay and that he also praises in an eloquent footnote toward the end of the *Religionsschrift*. This is, indeed, what Kant finds the most striking feature in Job's character

---

[41] See also Pihlström 2008a for a Jamesian investigation of this issue. We will return to the Jamesian "will to believe" in Chapter 4.

in contrast to Job's "friends" (who seek to formulate theodicies, in contemporary parlance).[42] More precisely, Job's key virtues, according to
Kant, are his "sincerity of heart" (*Aufrichtigkeit des Herzens*) and "honesty
in openly admitting one's doubts" (*die Redlichkeit, seine Zweifel unverhoh-
len zu gestehen*), which establishes "the preeminence of the honest man over
the religious flatterer [*Schmeichler*] in the divine verdict" (Kant 1983 [1791],
8:267):

> Job speaks as he thinks, and with the courage with which he, as well as every
> human being in his position, can well afford; his friends, on the contrary,
> speak as if they were being secretly listened to by the mighty one, over whose
> cause they are passing judgment, and as if gaining his favor through their
> judgment were closer to their heart than the truth. Their malice in pretend-
> ing to assert things into which they yet must admit they have no insight, and
> in simulating a conviction which they in fact do not have, contrasts with
> Job's frankness [*Freimütigkeit*] [. . .]. (Kant 1983 [1791], 8:265–266)

At this point it might be suggested that the Kantian prospective believer
actually needs Jamesian meliorism to overcome the pessimism that now
extends to our ability to invoke religious considerations in any serious and
sincere sense in this context. Within the Kantian system itself, the sincerity
of religion may indeed be lost, as Vanden Auweele correctly worries. In
brief, it may be suggested that from a pragmatic point of view our sincere
faith may itself bring its own verification along with it – and this is
something that seems to be available to James but not (at least not fully)
to Kant. This would be an example of a case in which the employment of
the Jamesian "will to believe" strategy is pragmatically legitimate; after all,
one of the types of cases that James (1979 [1897]) considers in "The Will to
Believe" is precisely the case where strong belief is required for the belief
itself to be able to be (made) true (see Chapter 4). However, even here (at
least when we are examining the religious case) it seems that we do need to
make sure the faith that is to be voluntarily embraced *is* sincere to begin

---

[42] While I have in this chapter relied heavily on Vanden Auweele's in my view excellent account of
Kantian pessimism, which includes the rejection of theodicies (as manifestations of a kind of
misdirected theological optimism), Vanden Auweele curiously neglects Kant's very important
engagement with the Book of Job (which is the starting point for the entire antitheodicist inquiry
in Kivistö and Pihlström 2016). He (Vanden Auweele 2019, 193) does draw attention to Kant's praise
of sincerity in *Religionsschrift*, though. This is what Kant says: "*O Aufrichtigkeit!* du Asträa, die du
von der Erde zum Himmel entflohen bist, wie zieht man dich (die Grundlage des Gewissens, mithin
aller inneren Religion) von da zu uns wieder herab? [. . .] Aber *Aufrichtigkeit* (dass alles, was man
sagt, mit Wahrhaftigkeit gesagt sei) muss man von jedem Menschen fordern können, und, wenn
auch selbst dazu keine Anlage in unserer Natur wäre, deren Kultur nur vernachlässigt wird, so würde
die Menschenrasse in ihren eigenen Augen ein Gegenstand der tiefsten Verachtung sein müssen."
(Kant 1983 [1793/1974], 6:190n.)

with. It cannot be – any more in the Kantian than in the Jamesian situation – adopted *merely* for instrumental reasons or on purely practical and functional grounds due to results or benefits that would be external to it. Its moral worth needs to be something that sincere faith "internally" (inherently) carries with it, even if the contingent outcome were not to be realized, after all. Only by adopting *such* a pragmatic faith in God's reality can the potential pragmatic Kantian be both genuinely religious and genuinely ethical.

From the Jamesian pragmatist point of view, it may even be suggested that the "truth" of religion would pragmatically amount to its ethical functionality in our lives. That is to say, Vanden Auweele and many others who fail to approach the Kantian issue of sincerity from the Jamesian pragmatist standpoint rely on an essentially *non-pragmatic* dichotomy between the issues concerning the theoretical truth (vs. falsity) of religion, on the one hand, and the practical usefulness or functionality of religion, on the other hand. If we frame our examination of the relation between religion and ethics in a thoroughly pragmatist manner, this dichotomy must itself be overcome. Just as the concept of truth itself involves a dimension of ethical truthfulness (see Chapter 1), the pursuit of religious truth is indistinguishable from the moral pursuit. The ethical *transcendentally* constitutes the religious. By understanding both the Kantian and the Jamesian commitment to individual sincerity in this pragmatic-cum-transcendental sense, we can make better sense of both views, and of their integration. The practical – that is, ethical – functionality of religion is, then, constitutive of its pragmatic truth, or in other words, the theoretical "metaphysical" truth of a religious outlook *is* its pragmatic functionality in the (would-be) believer's system of belief, that is, ultimately in their (form of) life in a holistic sense.[43] Pragmatism, after all, is for James a "philosophy of hope", but this notion of hope must not be contrasted to Kant's but rather be understood as fully congruous with Kant's treatment of religion in terms of legitimate rational hope.

It will inevitably remain an open issue here whether Jamesian pragmatism can ultimately keep its promise of delivering a melioristic account of religion that does not rely on a dichotomy between ethical or pragmatic and purely theoretical truth but can, rather, resolve the question of sincerity that seems to arise in the Kantian context which proposes to account for

---

[43] At this point, a comparison between the Kantian-cum-Jamesian position formulated here and the Wittgensteinian tradition in the philosophy of religion naturally invites itself (cf. also Pihlström 2013). Note also that I am of course not taking any stand on whether there *are* religious truths; I am merely inquiring (at a transcendental level) into the conditions of there possibly being any.

religion in terms of practical reason. The main conclusion for us (for now) is that it is right here that Kant and James are deeply engaged with essentially the same problem, and while their transcendental and pragmatist methods of inquiry seem very different, they are actually fully congruous in their common attempt to understand the human condition – its shared practices and "transcendental facts". In my view, Kantian practical (moral) theism needs to be informed by Jamesian pragmatist considerations in order for the sincerity issue to be adequately dealt with. But in the context of the present inquiry this remains a mere hypothesis to be further critically tested by means of both historical and systematic investigation.[44] However, merely by formulating this hypothesis I hope to have been able to elaborate on the idea tentatively defended in Chapters 1 and 2, viz., that Jamesian pragmatism entangles the concepts of truth and truthfulness with each other.

It is, at any rate, an essential element of this Kantian-cum-Jamesian sincerity that naïve optimism is rejected across the board, both in ethics and in religion – and not merely as a contingent falsehood but at a pragmatic transcendental level as a view that fails to make sense of the human condition. Optimism does not just happen to be false; nor are theodicies just contingently mistaken. Their confusions lie much deeper. Therefore, the sincerity needed in the formulation of a properly Kantian (and Jamesian) religious faith is essentially the same sincerity that we need for the rejection of theodicies, along the lines of Kant's Theodicy Essay, and therefore the kind of pessimism briefly analyzed earlier is a key element of such sincerity. Only by taking others' meaningless and non-instrumentalizable suffering philosophically – ethically – seriously can we hope to formulate anything like an adequate account of morality and religion; overcoming theodicies is, indeed, part of overcoming the "blindness" James was sincerely worried about (cf. Chapter 6).

3.5 Sincerity and Self-Deception

The contrast between sincerity (truthfulness) and insincerity or self-deception might also give us a clue to appreciating the relation between Kant's Theodicy Essay and his account of "radical evil" in the *Religionsschrift*. Our dishonest tendency to deny our radical evil – the tendency to prioritize

---

[44] Some Kantian scholars might, for example, argue that from Kant's perspective there is a sense in which a religious attitude "comes first", after all, and the critical account of the moral grounds of religion only gives a voice to those who already have religious faith. I will, however, here stay within the more standard understanding of Kant's religion as subordinate to ethics.

maxims that set our own advantage prior to the moral law – is perceptively emphasized by another recent Kant commentator, Joël Madore (2011, e.g. 63), whose reading is in many ways close to, though not identical with, Vanden Auweele's. Madore suggests that some "supernatural cooperation" (comparable to James's similar concept) seems to be needed for us to overcome the "natural tendency to self-deception deep-seated within the most profound depths of human freedom", casting "a shadow on the moral call" and "darkening our sense of ethical responsibility" (Madore 2011, 86). In our "repeated practise of self-deception", Kant (as analyzed by Madore) reminds us, we need a kind of "rebirth" (Madore 2011, 119) – in a word, again, a Jamesian-like conversion. James comes, as we have seen, very close to this Kantian view that human beings are neither perfectly good nor hopelessly evil (Madore 2011, 113); this, indeed, seems to be a fundamentally melioristic conception of the human nature the two philosophers share. Conversion is always *possible*, no matter how unlikely it is for us. While Madore does not deal with James at all, his analysis of the Kantian oscillation between a kind of "defeatism" and an optimistic faith in humanity (cf. Madore 2011, 117) is readily comparable to Jamesian meliorism.[45]

The "sincerity objection" analyzed earlier is, however, crucial for the picture of Kant we find in Madore's account, too. Only a sincere faith may save us from moral despair, we are told (Madore 2011, 132), but it is precisely this sincerity that may be extremely difficult if not impossible for us to achieve, precisely because of the essentially pragmatic character of the religious commitment itself, when grounded (as it should) in ethics. At least it would seem that we cannot self-consciously practice pragmatic faith in order to be able to arrive at a moral conversion. One's religious commitment is, in brief, either insincere (and self-deceptive) or, if sincere *qua* religious, not fully ethical, and hence ultimately unjustified. This is a dilemma that the Kantian – or the Jamesian – religious moralist cannot leave behind for good but must constantly return to.

In the end, Madore tells us, Kant's critical philosophy, in its reflection on human nature, "ineluctably oscillates between the promise of freedom and the limits of reason", or (with reference to Dostoevsky's *The Brothers Karamazov*) between the compelling characters of Ivan and Alyosha (Madore 2011, 142). If our picture of Kant comes down to this, it seems to me, once again, that it is not at all implausible to view James's melioristic

---

[45] Madore (2011, e.g. 139) also joins those who emphasize Kant's opposition to theodicies: the "*scandal*" of evil is "a moment of utter powerlessness and despair no end, no purpose, could ever rationalize, no matter how *ennobling*".

(and antitheodicist) pragmatism as thoroughly Kantian in spirit. It is precisely this double-edged nature of the human moral pursuit that needs to be emphasized in the context of pragmatic meliorism as well. There is no royal road out of the dilemma of sincerity; it needs to be acknowledged as partly defining the human condition.[46] Thus, our engagement with the relation between Kant and James demonstrates how different and challenging sincerity is for us.

It must also be acknowledged, however, that James's pessimism may be weaker than Kant's, because moral education or enculturation *is* possible, according to James, *from within* "human nature". The uprooting needed is not as radical as in Kant's case. In addition, there are certainly differences between Kant's and James's conceptions of the nature of religious belief, or belief in general: there is no remnant of exactly the kind of voluntarism we find in the James of "The Will to Believe" in Kant (cf., however, Chapter 4). Nevertheless, these differences should never blind us to the fact that it is precisely in its emphasis on sincerity and the ethical necessity (if also practical impossibility) of avoiding the self-deceptive tendencies rooted deep in our human heart – and human reason – that James operates within a strikingly Kantian philosophical context.

3.6 Humanism and Critical Philosophy

It is impossible to defend the transcendentally pessimistic conception of humanity without a fundamental commitment to what Kant called critical philosophy – even though, as we have just learned, critical philosophy itself remains in a state of oscillation between freedom and evil. But precisely for this reason, the chief task of philosophical inquiry is always critical.[47] Critical philosophy needs to be applied to our understanding of the duty of sincerity itself, as well as to an analysis of the conditions for the possibility of sincerity. In this sense, the examinations of the Jamesian pragmatist account of truth (in Chapters 1 and 2) as well as the treatment of the will to believe (in Chapter 4) are, in a broad sense, transcendental engagements with how sincerity in the pursuit of truth is possible for beings like us.

Critical philosophy, broadly understood, integrates the Kantian pursuit of reason and the Jamesian pursuit of the holistic and pluralistic development of "the whole man in us". It is (only) through critical philosophy that

---

[46] The discussion of agnosticism in Chapter 6 may be read as a further elaboration of this idea.

[47] Note also that among the pragmatists, Dewey defined philosophy as "the critical method of developing methods of criticism"; see the closing comments in Dewey 1986 [1929], 354.

we can establish methods of conversion that might (but also might not) lead to moral goodness and progress. It is, moreover, (only) through critical philosophy that we become aware of the kind of pessimism we need to be committed to in order to sincerely understand our human condition, especially the Kantian inclination to evil and the Jamesian instinctive blindness. For the uncritical (naïve) gaze, these unwelcome features of our condition are not visible. In a more pragmatist terminology, we need a genuine – again sincere – commitment to never-ending *inquiry*, also in ethical and theological matters. In this way, the "philosophical anthropological" attempt to understand what we as human beings are like (including the issues of pessimism and meliorism) are deeply entangled with the fundamental questions concerning reality and truth, that is, the realism issue in all its pragmatic richness. Everything that has been said in this chapter about the ethical and religious aspects of pessimism and meliorism has thus been essentially related to the pursuit of truth about the human condition.

To engage in critical philosophy – or pragmatic inquiry – in pursuit of the kind of melioristic account based on the background of pessimism is, moreover, to be committed to a Kantian-cum-Jamesian *humanism*, in contrast to various currently popular transhumanist, posthumanist, or antihumanist ways of thinking.[48] However, in order to be able to maintain a sound version of humanism, the pragmatist needs to respond to Kantian-inspired issues recently raised by Henrik Rydenfelt (2019b) in a brilliant critique of pragmatist humanism. In seeking to point out an inconsistency, or at least a tension, right at the heart of the Jamesian brand of pragmatism I have defended, Rydenfelt claims that the pragmatist cannot have it both ways: a pragmatic account of meaning (derived from Peirce's original ideas, especially the Pragmatic Maxim) and the (quasi-Kantian) "pragmatic humanism" claiming that we in some sense pragmatically "construct" (or, as I have preferred to express it in this chapter and elsewhere, "structure") reality are hard to reconcile with each other. The reason for this is that the kind of pragmatic humanism Rydenfelt criticizes is indebted to Kantian transcendental idealism to the extent that it needs (its own version of) the notion of the *Ding an sich*.[49] Even the "one-world" interpretation of transcendental idealism (cf. Allison 2004 [1983]) is, according to Rydenfelt, vulnerable to the Peircean criticism according to which we cannot form

---

[48] The notion of pragmatist humanism will also be summarized in Chapters 5 and 6.
[49] For comparison, see my brief engagement with Niiniluoto's (2019) criticism of pragmatism toward the end of Chapter 1.

any meaningful conception of anything that is absolutely incognizable to us (while being possibly cognizable to a different kind of intelligence). Rydenfelt summarizes his criticism as a dilemma: "On the one hand, if we can conceive of cognition that (supposedly) transcends the limits of our human capacities, that cognition is at once turned into a possible human cognition. On the other hand, if something really were beyond all possible human cognition, we could not even have a conception of it." (Rydenfelt 2019b, 50)[50]

This is a serious challenge, because the Kantian approach to ethics and religion clearly reaches out to the noumenal realm even when no literal metaphysical postulation of "two worlds" is accepted. What is distinctive in Rydenfelt's elegant argument is the way he uses Peirce to locate a problem within the pragmatist tradition itself, insofar as that tradition is given a Kantian twist. One way out of this antinomy might be to take seriously the idea of the Kantian thing in itself as a *Grenzbegriff*, a mere limit to our cognition.[51] It would then still be from within our cognitive capacities, or more generally from within the human condition we are investigating – without strictly speaking postulating anything (any "thing") that would be incognizable, or cognizable only to a different kind of intelligence – that any limits to our cognition would, or could, be posited. The postulation of things in themselves in this *Grenzbegriff* sense might play a role in our account of pragmatic realism; however, in my attempts to develop a Kantian transcendental pragmatism (or "pragmatic humanism") in this chapter, and this book, no sufficient attention can be drawn to what Kant meant, or what we should mean, by things in themselves. The problem is serious and deserves further scrutiny.[52]

It is essential for our engagement of both the epistemic-cum-metaphysical and the ethical-cum-existential challenges of Kantian pragmatism that the

---

[50] This could be compared to earlier criticisms of transcendental idealism, including Strawson's account of the "bounds of sense" in the 1960s and Jaakko Hintikka's discussion of the "paradox of transcendental knowledge" in the 1980s. See, for example, Strawson 1966 and Hintikka 1996, as well as the brief discussion of transcendental arguments in the beginning of this chapter.

[51] See again my brief comments on Niiniluoto's views in Chapter 1.

[52] Another option, one that Rydenfelt himself seems to favor, would be a Peircean form of "anthropomorphism", which would regard human cognition as "naturally 'tuned' into the way the world is" (Rydenfelt 2019b, 53). However, I believe an appropriate form of pragmatic transcendental idealism accommodating empirical realism would somehow have to acknowledge, in the spirit of general fallibilism, that we might even be radically mistaken about the way the (empirical) world is. That, too, is part of our human predicament that needs to be transcendentally analyzed. For the (Jamesian rather than Peircean) pragmatist as well as the Kantian, it is important to carefully distinguish between humanism and anthropomorphism. If Peirce preferred the latter, then so much worse for his version of pragmatism, I'm afraid.

(pragmatically and transcendentally) inquiring subject that critically turns toward a reflection on their own capacities and limitations (from within a context or practice always already shaped by those capacities and limitations) is a *human being*. Even though classical transcendental philosophers like Kant and Husserl investigated the possibility of experience or consciousness in general, in principle pertaining to any rational or cognizing beings, for a pragmatist version of transcendental philosophy – for the pragmatist twist I am hoping to make in the transcendental tradition inaugurated by Kant – the emphasis on humanism is crucial.[53] Given the diversity of human needs, interests, and practices, a pragmatically humanist transcendental investigation may also be directed to specific discourses and forms of human life, such as religion – in addition to the more general or global philosophical questions concerning the possibility of experience as such. For the (Jamesian) pragmatist, Kantian-like transcendental inquiries are always inevitably directed at practice-embedded and historically contextualized issues that may receive different manifestations in different natural, social, and historical surroundings. A pragmatist transcendental reflection on what it is to live a human life amidst its ethical, existential, and (possibly) religious concerns should not sacrifice the "ambitiousness" of a truly transcendental investigation even when taking seriously the irreducible variability of our practices and the plurality of our ways of making sense of our existence. In this chapter, my aim has been to offer an ambitious, albeit pragmatic, account of the problem of ethical and religious sincerity at the heart of the pessimistic view of humanity we have seen Kant and James both maintain.

The question "What is man?" indeed integrates all the three Kantian questions. James, we may conclude, essentially shares Kant's humanistic conception of the human being; to be a pessimist, or a meliorist,[54] is to be a humanist transcendentally and existentially, and therefore seriously and often painfully concerned with the human condition at the level of the transcendental and existential questions concerning the very possibility of ameliorating our practices of life. Kantian pessimism is profoundly opposed to the kind of both epistemic and ethical optimism we have inherited all the way from Aristotle and ancient philosophy in general; despite its actively forward-looking character, pragmatism inherits this

---

[53] However, even this humanism does not provide an ahistorical *essence* of transcendental philosophy (recall that in the beginning of this chapter I started from an antiessentialist characterization of transcendental argumentation as a family-resemblance concept).

[54] On pragmatism and meliorism, see also, for example, Bergman 2019.

pessimism, recognizing that we live in an epistemically and ethically problematic world with finite human capacities requiring critique. Yet, Kantian critique, in turn, is itself fundamentally melioristic, as it seeks to ameliorate our human condition, again both epistemically and ethically. This humanistic conclusion will be further elaborated on in the chapters to follow.

CHAPTER 4

The Will to Believe and Holistic Pragmatism

This chapter has three main aims. Having in Chapters 1–3 reflected on Jamesian pragmatism, especially its conceptions of truth and truthfulness as well as its philosophical anthropology (in relation to Kantian critical philosophy), I now hope to introduce and defend a pragmatist account of the *fact-value entanglement* and *holistic pragmatism* as a pragmatist theory of inquiry, especially inquiry into values and normativity. I will thus reflect on the potential relevance of holistic pragmatism in the philosophy of value and normativity in general and ethics in particular, also yielding (I will suggest) a robustly pragmatist response to the thoroughgoing *Entzauberung* ("disenchantment") of the world taken to follow from the advancement of the sciences, a philosophical and cultural issue James was deeply concerned with throughout his career (without using this specific term, though).[1] More historically, this task will involve interpreting and evaluating James's famous, or notorious, *"will to believe" argument*, from the perspective of holistic pragmatism (while normativity more generally will be examined in Chapter 5).

In many ways this chapter will continue the investigation of what it means for us to sincerely pursue the truth in, for example, religious, valuational, and existential matters that crucially shape our lives as the distinctive individual lives they are. Concepts not yet centrally employed in the previous chapters, including dis- and re-enchantment, as well as freedom, vocation, and habituality, will also be taken up, and holistic pragmatism will be elaborated on somewhat more comprehensively than in the earlier chapters. While this chapter develops a complex line of thought employing a multifaceted conceptual machinery, I hope to be

---

[1] It would be impossible to provide any extensive treatment of the notion of *Entzauberung* (which goes back to Max Weber), or its history, here; I am just loosely using this concept, and I will more or less take it for granted and offer my thoughts as a contribution to an implicit dialogue with Hans Joas's (2017) impressive (also to some extent pragmatism-inspired: see especially his chapter 2) critical examination of its legacy.

able to show how the Jamesian will to believe and holistic pragmatism may enhance our understanding of ourselves as individuals living amidst our constantly critically renewable (epistemic and ethical) habits of normatively coping with the challenging world around us, with no neat separation between the factual and the valuational aspects of that world.

As already indicated in passing in the previous chapters, holistic pragmatism turns out to be a promising approach in various fields of philosophical inquiry. It is helpful in the philosophy of science, including the human and social sciences; in ethics, including applied ethics; in argumentation theory, especially the relations between factual and normative beliefs and belief-revision in argumentation; in the history of pragmatism; and in the philosophy of religion (among other fields). I will begin this chapter by briefly examining a neopragmatist argument for the fact-value entanglement due to Hilary Putnam. I will then show how this line of argument can be made more precise and systematic by employing White's holistic pragmatism. Next, I will turn to James's "will to believe" argument, interpreting it in the context of holism – and thus also seeking to show that there is a clear sense in which James himself was a holistic pragmatist in White's terms. Even though the kind of Kantian transcendental understanding of pragmatism defended in Chapter 3 will be largely bracketed in this chapter, this does not mean that it would be forgotten. On the contrary, when investigating the ways in which a Jamesian will to believe is possible, or even necessary, for us in certain practice-embedded situations of human life, we continue to ask transcendental questions about the ways in which we inevitably have to make certain philosophical and/or existential commitments in order to be able to engage in the kind of truth-seeking (or "*weltanschaulichen*") activities we actually do engage in.

The need to develop a pragmatist "re-enchantment" of the human world,[2] or at least a critical response to thoroughgoing scientistic disenchantment,

---

[2] Note also that my broadly Kantian pragmatism starts from the fundamentally Kantian idea that human beings are finite, limited, bounded by their fragile human condition, therefore needing rational critique. Regarding the prospects of a critical evaluation of *Entzauberung*, this also means that we must take seriously the fact that we are unable to know anything about the transcendent, and as moral agents we are "unholy" and in the need of moral law: human beings do not possess a "holy will" which would necessarily accord with the moral law; on the contrary, we are "radically evil" in the sense of being naturally inclined to prioritize self-serving maxims conflicting with the moral law. This sets limits to how much re-enchantment, or *Wiederverzauberung*, we can expect to achieve within a Kantian pragmatism. Another caveat is also in order: one may argue (as Matthias Jung did, commenting on a draft of this chapter) that no re-enchantment is needed in pragmatism at all, given that the world is always already meaningful and value-laden, never devoid of values and meanings (see the discussion below on the fact-value entanglement). I will, in any event, use the notions of disenchantment and re-enchantment rather intuitively, without drawing any detailed attention to

runs implicitly throughout this discussion and will become more explicit toward the end of the chapter when I raise some reflexive issues concerning holistic pragmatism. In terms of the Jamesian will to believe idea, I will also suggest how one's personal vocations and existential decisions could "re-enchant" the world one lives in. At the meta-level, one might even suggest that the will to believe can be applied to the fundamental choice between viewing the world under the aspect of *Entzauberung* and viewing it in terms of (partial) *Wiederverzauberung*. Examining this possible switch of perspective is highly significant for our pragmatist account of truth-seeking.

By recognizing the *existential openness* of such a choice, my James-inspired view may come close to Hans Joas's (2017) project of opening more dialogical space for religious believers and non-believers to engage in constructive dialogue.[3] However, my explorations will not be merely focused on religious or transcendent forms of *Verzauberung* (or re-enchantment); the issue is more general, extending to the fact-value entanglement as well as personal existential (including vocational) commitments to forms of significance within an individual life. My argument for the general relevance of the Jamesian will to believe may thus also be implicitly slightly critical of Joas's project, because in my view a kind of re-enchantment is possible also for non-believers.[4]

4.1 The Fact-Value Entanglement

Moral and more generally normative realism and antirealism have been endlessly debated in recent and contemporary philosophy. The basic question is whether (moral) values and norms are merely subjective, or whether there are objective (moral) values and norms. J. L. Mackie's (1977) famous *queerness argument*, claiming that objective and action-guiding moral values would be "queer" in comparison to any other entities we encounter in the thoroughly *entzauberte* natural world as described and explained by the advanced sciences, was countered, I believe rather successfully, by Putnam's (1981, 1990) *companions in the guilt argument*. Putnam reminds

their Weberian history or any systematic elaborations. James was certainly philosophically and existentially – deeply personally – worried about the fact that a purely scientific worldview might remove all values and meanings from our world.

[3] The examination of agnosticism in Chapter 6 will also bring this discussion one step further.

[4] Joas's (2017) investigation of the history of *Entzauberung* is of course much more sociological than my philosophical explorations, but he has also been influenced by James, albeit primarily James's (1958 [1902]) psychology of religious experience. See the introduction ("*Einleitung*") to Joas 2017; on Joas's reading of James's *Varieties*, in particular, see his chapter 2. I find Joas's treatment of Schleiermacher as a predecessor of James highly relevant and historically clarifying.

us that if moral values are queer, then our scientifically unavoidable commitments to, for example, rational acceptability, warrant, justification, and
other epistemic values are equally queer. He writes:

> Our life-world . . . does not factor neatly into "facts" and "values"; we live in
> a messy human world in which seeing reality with all its nuances . . . and
> making appropriate "value judgments" are simply not separable abilities. . . .
> It is all well and good to describe hypothetical cases in which two people
> "agree on the facts and disagree about values," but in the world in which
> I grew up such cases are unreal. When and where did a Nazi and an anti-
> Nazi, a communist and a social democrat, a fundamentalist and a liberal, or
> even a Republican and a Democrat, agree on the facts? Even when it comes
> to one specific policy question . . ., every argument I have ever heard has
> exemplified the entanglement of the ethical and the factual. There is a weird
> discrepancy between the way philosophers who subscribe to a sharp fact/
> value distinction *make* ethical arguments sound and the way ethical argu-
> ments *actually* sound. (Putnam 1990, 166–167)

The key ideas here include the unavoidable need to use "thick" moral
concepts, the recognition of our "messy" life-world and language-use (here
Putnam's pragmatist, especially Deweyan influences are clear), a version of
pragmatic pluralism or *conceptual relativity*, as well as the project of developing
"ethics without ontology" (Putnam 2004) – against "Ontology" in general.[5]
All of these ideas are central to Putnam's version of neopragmatism, culminating in a resolutely non-metaphysical defense of the fact-value entanglement.
In Putnam's view, any facts we may meaningfully even speak about already
involve some human values. Putnam elsewhere continues:

> If we *disinflate* the fact/value dichotomy, what we get is this: there is
> a distinction to be drawn (one that is useful in some contexts) between
> ethical judgments and other sorts of judgments. This is undoubtedly the
> case. . . . But *nothing metaphysical follows from the existence of a fact/value
> distinction in this (modest) sense.* (Putnam 2002, 19)

> The language of *coming to see* what [the ethical] standpoint requires of one is
> internal to that standpoint and not a piece of transcendental machinery[6]
> that is required to provide a foundation for it. . . . Ethical talk needs no
> metaphysical story to support it (or, in a postmodernist version of the
> metaphysical temptation, to "deconstruct" it); it only needs what ethical

---

[5] I discuss these issues in some detail in a number of earlier works: see, for example, Pihlström 2005,
2009, 2015, 2020a. On pluralism, see also Chapter 2. For Putnam's late views on realism, ontology,
and normativity, see Putnam 2016.

[6] This wording indicates that Putnam (in my view) is unfortunately insensitive to *transcendental*
pragmatism, though he has been heavily influenced by Kant, too.

talk – both in the narrower senses of "ethical," and in the wide sense of talk about the good life – has always needed: good will, intelligence, and respect for what can be seen as grounds and difficulties from within the ethical standpoint itself. (Putnam 2002, 94–95)

I have not quoted Putnam at length in order to provide any careful analysis of his views but merely to illustrate what a pragmatist account of the fact-value entanglement looks like.[7] I will, however, next seek to show how what White called holistic pragmatism can be employed in an analysis and elaboration of the Putnamian idea of the fact-value entanglement. (In the next chapter, I will further argue for the relevance of holistic pragmatism to our philosophical understanding of normativity as a general trait of the human form of life.)

4.2   Holistic Pragmatism

Holistic pragmatism, as developed by White, may be used to make Putnam's account of the fact-value entanglement and pragmatic realism about the normative more precise. There is, however, a sense in which both Putnam's position and White's holistic pragmatism are insufficiently metaphysical in order to serve as full-blown accounts of the human condition (as "philosophical anthropologies", that is). In order to be truly helpful in a pragmatist response to the disenchantment vs. re-enchantment issue, in particular, they need some more robust metaphysical elaboration. White's holistic pragmatism also enables us to appropriate James's pragmatism in novel ways, as I will show in due course.

Even though White's holistic reading of James was already cited and briefly commented on in Chapter 2, let me again briefly explain what holistic pragmatism amounts to. Unsurprisingly, it is a synthesis of pragmatism and holism. While pragmatism urges us to examine the meanings of our (intellectual, scientific, rational) concepts and/or conceptions and beliefs in terms of the potential practical effects of their objects,[8] *holism*

---

[7] For a more comprehensive discussion of his version of pragmatic moral realism, see Pihlström 2005. In addition to Putnam's well-known reflections on the fact-value entanglement, Rorty's equally holistic rejection of any such dichotomy between fact and value could also be discussed here. For example, in his 1997 essay on James's philosophy of religion, "Religious Faith, Intellectual Responsibility, and Romance" (in Rorty 2007), Rorty in a sense defends a relatively similar holism as White and Putnam do. However, having already made some critical remarks on Rorty's views on truth and freedom in Chapter 1 and having earlier criticized Rorty's philosophy of religion in more detail (see Pihlström 2013), I must here set aside any Rortyan twists of this matter – as interesting as they might be.

[8] As every scholar of pragmatism knows, this idea can be traced back to Peirce's "How to Make Our Ideas Clear" (1878), in which the Pragmatic Maxim was first formulated; James, Dewey, and others

specifies this idea by emphasizing "wholes" or "totalities", in contrast to isolated atomistic particulars, both in semantic accounts of the meanings of concepts and in epistemic discussions of the justification of beliefs. W. V. Quine's semantic and epistemological holism (as articulated in Quine's "Two Dogmas of Empiricism" in 1951) is presumably the most widely known version of pragmatic holism, according to which scientific theories face the "tribunal of experience" as corporate bodies. The unit of empirical testing and experimentation is an entire scientific theory, or even our scientific worldview as a whole, not a single belief (sentence, statement). The analytic/synthetic and the a priori/a posteriori distinctions cannot be made entirely precise, or maintained as strict dichotomies; according to Quine, there is no general definition of analyticity available for us to be able to do so. In particular, there is no way to divide the totality of scientific statements or beliefs into an analytic part and a synthetic part, and even logical truths are not immune to revision.[9]

Quine's holism was carried further in a series of works spanning several decades by White (1973 [1949], 1956, 1981, 2002, 2005), who argues that not only are *logical* (analytic) and *empirical* (synthetic) statements "in the same boat" and tested as a totality, but also *ethical*, and more generally *normative*, statements are elements of this holistic "web of belief" along with factual or descriptive statements and beliefs. This is crucial for understanding our human form of life, as guided and thoroughly structured by normative principles and commitments (see also Chapter 5).

Ethics, according to White (2002, xi), "may be viewed as empirical if one includes feelings of moral obligation as well as sensory experiences in the pool or flux into which the ethical believer worked a manageable structure". Hence, just like the analytic and the synthetic in Quine, the normative and the factual are parts of the same holistic "web" or network of beliefs. Descriptive statements and normative ethical principles form conjunctions that must be tested holistically, just as Quine argued that scientific and logico-mathematical beliefs should. There can be no scientific experimentation in ethics, of course,[10] but there *can* still be something like testing moral ideas and hypotheses in the "laboratory of life" (as

then provided broader applications of the principle (cf. also, e.g., Misak 2013; Pihlström 2015). For a recent general discussion of the pragmatist theory of belief, see Zimmerman 2018.

[9] We may skip this famous argument here. For an illuminating discussion of holistic pragmatism in Quine and White (and others), see Misak 2013, chapters 11–12.

[10] Unless one includes (unlike me) the kind of "experimentation" that researchers engaged in, for example, "trolley problems" are conducting in order to learn about people's moral intuitions, possible (arguably) relevant to questions concerning the ethics of artificial intelligence, for instance.

Putnam 1997 aptly put it in the context of the philosophy of religion). Logic, science, and ethics form a unified whole without epistemic dichotomies. As logical principles *may* be given up in the face of "recalcitrant experience" (cf. again Quine 1980 [1951]), descriptive or factual statements *may* be denied in order to preserve a normative principle we do not want to give up, or a principle we cannot give up because we are so strongly committed to it as an element of our lives and practices. Therefore, ethics is not inferior to science, or immune to empirical evaluation; feelings of obligation together with sensory observation link ethical sentences to the natural world. *Pace* Quine, ethics is thus "anchored in experience" (White 2002, 160). Both ethics and science are, for White, fallible and corrigible but equally cognitive enterprises.

The classical pragmatists, especially Dewey, maintained very similar views.[11] More generally, ethics, science, economy, law, as well as, possibly, religion are all normatively structured areas of human culture forming a holistic totality instead of distinct spheres with definite boundaries. Pragmatist philosophical anthropology, or the pragmatist understanding of the human condition, *is* therefore a pragmatically holistic *philosophy of culture* investigating the human being as a cultural being engaging in a number of mutually intertwined normatively governed practices.[12]

While I believe we may fruitfully employ holistic pragmatism in our articulation of (say) pragmatist semantics, epistemology, metaphysics, and ethics, some minor revisions to White's views are needed. White speaks about moral "feelings", but this should be extended to cover moral experience much more broadly. Feelings of obligation can be inspired by experiences of suffering or injustice, for example – others' or one's own.[13] There could also be (meta-level) feelings or experiences of our never being able to meet our moral obligations (e.g., for Levinasian reasons, invoking one's

---

[11] So did in his own way the less well-known Finnish philosopher Eino Kaila (2014 [1939]) in his theory of "practical testability", distinguished from the empirical testability of scientific theories (cf. Pihlström 2012b, 2019d).

[12] See again Chapter 5. While holism may in some sense be contrasted with individualism, in this context pragmatic holism and individualism are compatible, because an individual person may consider her/his own belief system along the lines of holistic pragmatism, seeking to harmonize its factual and normative commitments. Pragmatism typically views the human being as an individual-in-a-community, reducing neither one to the other. Thus, I see no inevitable conflict between the kind of Jamesian individualism formulated in Chapter 2, in particular, and the holism examined here – any more than an Arendtian account of one's unique natality needs to conflict with political engagement.

[13] This would then be a way of incorporating "thicker" moral concepts into the holistically pragmatist consideration of the fact-value entanglement. See Müller 2018 on a holistic pragmatist account of pacifism based on a closely related idea.

infinite responsibility to and for the other), even leading up to what we might call feelings of one's "transcendental guilt" (cf. Pihlström 2011, 2014). This would amount to a never-ending inescapable guilt for being unable to ever fully hear all the "cries of the wounded" (invoking, again, a term used by James 1979 [1897]) that need to be heard. Such moral experiences may be part of the interplay of normative and factual elements of our world-picture.[14]

As an example of holistic pragmatism at work, consider the following argument:

(1) One can be morally responsible for one's actions (or have moral duties) only if one acts freely (i.e., is a genuine agent).
(2) One can act freely only if one possesses a free will.
(3) Only individuals (can) have wills.
(4) Therefore, groups and collectives (e.g., business corporations) cannot have a will of their own.
(5) Therefore, groups (etc.) cannot act freely and are not genuine agents.
(6) Therefore, groups (etc.) cannot be morally responsible.
(7) Therefore, there is no such thing as moral or social responsibility, nor any moral duties, attributed to business corporations.

Now, according to holistic pragmatism, if we find the conclusion ethically unacceptable, we may revise or reject one of the factual premises. Thus, if we find it ethically impossible to maintain, for instance, that business corporations cannot be morally or socially responsible for their actions, we may revise our picture of what agency (including freedom, the will, etc.) *is*. The revised picture of agency must then of course also be made compatible with the rest of our beliefs. Moreover, we must provide further reasons for the ethical "impossibility" motivating this belief revision. What is essential is that we examine our entire set of factual and normative beliefs as a totality, as a field within which everything is related to everything else. (This view could thus also be labeled "relationalism".) There is, then, at least potentially, an endless process of *mutual holistic adjustment* of beliefs and evidence at work here – like in any empirical inquiry. Arguably, at least some version of doxastic voluntarism is presupposed by holistic pragmatism, as one needs to be able to *choose* which beliefs to revise or reject. This again motivates a comparison to James's "will to believe", but here I will not take any firm stand on what kind of voluntarism exactly needs to be assumed.

---

[14] For an insightful pragmatist analysis of transcendental guilt and meliorism, see Zackariasson 2019.

Arguably, we can extend holistic pragmatism from the epistemic justification of different kinds of beliefs or statements to whatever is the practical equivalent of such normative justification in the critical evaluation of cultural *practices* and *institutions*. While remaining distinguishable from each other, our value-laden, normative practices (e.g., science, economy, politics, religion, and art) are dynamically interrelated and must themselves be "tested" holistically – whatever it ultimately means to "test" them.

4.3 Jamesian "Will to Believe": A More Thorough Holism?

Let us move on to the more historical part of this chapter, and thus (finally) to a reconsideration of James's "will to believe" idea (henceforth WB), which is highly relevant here first of all as an attempt to bridge the fact/value gap (and thus also for a reconsideration of the prospects of "enchantment"), but more generally as a pragmatist approach to the issues of individual sincerity and pluralism we have encountered in the previous chapters. In what sense exactly (if any), I now want to ask, is James a holistic pragmatist, or a pragmatist holist? *Not* in the sense of any *totalizing* holism, of course – not, that is, in the sense of reducing everything into one total overall picture of the world. Nor in the sense of any straightforward metaphysical commitment to the existence of "wholes" independently of their individual parts. Clearly, James's holism, whatever it is, cannot be phrased in terms of any kind of monism. But presumably we can say that James is a holist in the sense of taking seriously the "whole man [person] in us", without any reductive preference for intellectual – or any other – perspectives at the cost of others?[15] Those different, related yet mutually irreducible perspectives can definitely be weighed along the lines of White's holistic pragmatism as elements of an interconnected totality, "the whole man" [*sic*].[16] *This* kind of holism is central to Jamesian philosophical anthropology, integrating pluralism, anti-reductionism, and pragmatism, and it will also turn out to be a key to a pragmatist "re-enchantment" of the normative human world.

---

[15] See also Joas's (2017, e.g. 27, 64–65) discussion of James's resistance to reductive "nothing but" explanations of religion. Joas examines James mainly as one of the founders of the study of religious experience, while offering interesting comparative remarks not only on James and Schleiermacher but also on Peirce and Josiah Royce. Where I might be in a mild disagreement with Joas is regarding his emphasis on James's sharp distinction between religion and morality (Joas 2017, 66–67). What he means is presumably the distinction between religious experience and religion as a system of moral rules; while this may characterize the *Varieties*, the WB idea is in my view designed to overcome the dichotomy between morality and religion in the (quasi-Kantian) sense that religious faith may be arrived at on moral grounds (cf. also Chapter 3).

[16] Cf. also White's (2002, 2005) explicit comments on James, already cited in Chapter 2.

James's (1979 [1897]) controversial WB argument seems, at least prima facie, to be in tension with the criteria of the scientific method that Peirce had formulated in his seminal paper, "The Fixation of Belief" (1992–1998 [1877]; also in Peirce 1931–1958, vol. 5). While James dedicated *The Will to Believe* to his friend Peirce, the latter found its method problematic or even harmful for the scientific thinker. If Peirce was right in this judgment, it is doubtful whether WB can be maintained as an element of any pragmatist pursuit of truth (cf. Chapter 1). At the minimum, the potential role played by WB in the pragmatist conception of our pursuit of truth needs to be critically investigated. We may approach this issue by considering whether WB is *virtuous* or embodies some kind of epistemic *vice*, and then return to holism.[17]

James famously – or notoriously – argued against W. K. Clifford's (1879) *evidentialist* principle according to which "it is wrong, always, everywhere, and for anyone, to believe anything upon insufficient evidence". He suggested that we may, when faced by a "genuine option" not to be settled by merely intellectual or evidential considerations, voluntarily adopt a belief at our own risk. He saw Clifford's evidentialism as exemplifying the epistemic vice of overly strict methodology of belief-fixation, often preventing us from believing truths. From the perspective of Peirce's pragmatist theory of inquiry, however, James's suggestion that our "passional nature" legitimately may (and does) play an active role in the fixation of beliefs may amount to excessive *credulity*. Does it, we might ask, even collapse to the "method of tenacity" in Peirce's terms (as distinguished from the scientific method)? Some less sophisticated critics of James's pragmatism, including Bertrand Russell, have claimed that the WB strategy licenses *wishful thinking* and thus conflicts with the norms of critical scientific inquiry. We may interpret these and other historically important attacks on James as (explicit or implicit) attributions of the epistemic vice of credulity to anyone following the WB method. The WB has by some

---

[17] Some historical predecessors of Jamesian doxastic voluntarism would include at least the following: the "*credo quia absurdum*" idea by Tertullian (3rd century CE); believing "in order to understand" (*credo ut intelligam*), as proposed by Anselm of Canterbury (as well as in his own ways already Augustine); the development of voluntarism in later medieval philosophy (Duns Scotus, William Ockham); Blaise Pascal's principle known as "Pascal's Wager", betting on the hypothesis that God exists, which James rejected as an artificial mechanical calculation "lacking the inner soul of faith's reality" (see James 1979 [1897], 16); as well as Soren Kierkegaard's existential philosophy of the "leap" and absurdity. Doxastic voluntarism as a systematic philosophical background issue can also be raised in this context (but cannot be settled here). In any case, there is no need to embrace any extreme doxastic voluntarism (and James explicitly rejects anything like that: we cannot just "will to believe" that the $2 in our pocket actually amounts to $100).

critics even been mocked as the "will to deceive" and the "will to make-believe".[18]

Such critical voices are to be heard and taken seriously. Peirce, for instance, wrote: "I thought your *Will to Believe* was a very exaggerated utterance, such as injures a serious man very much, but to say what you now do [in *A Pluralistic Universe*, 1909] is far more suicidal. ... [P]hilosophy is either a science or is balderdash." (Peirce's letter to James, March 9, 1909; quoted in Perry 1935, II, 438.) But he also noted: "That everything is to be tested by its practical results was the great text of my early papers; so, as far as I get your general aim in so much of the book [*The Will to Believe*] as I have looked at, I am quite with you in the main. ... [Yet,] it is not mere action as brute exercise of strength that is the purpose of all, but say generalization, such action as tends toward regularization ... " (Peirce's letter to James, March 13, 1897; Peirce 1931–1958, 8.250.)

Russell, in turn, claimed: "It is curious that, in spite of being an eminent psychologist, James allowed himself at this point a singular crudity. He spoke as if the only alternatives were complete belief or complete disbelief, ignoring all shades of doubt. ... We habitually act upon hypotheses, but not precisely as we act upon what we consider certainties; for when we act upon a hypothesis we keep our eyes open for fresh evidence." (Russell 1972 [1945], 815) This seems to be incorrect, however: James focuses on "complete belief or complete disbelief" *only* in the case of "genuine options," which are "momentous" in the sense that they cannot be avoided – because doubt would pragmatically amount to the same thing as disbelief. (We will get back to this shortly.) For example, remaining in a state of doubt regarding the question of whether to marry a certain person or not – waiting for new evidence for or against the success of the potential marriage – is *practically equivalent* to deciding *not* to marry that person.

At a more general level, James's and Peirce's disagreement, in particular, poses both philosophical and historical questions. How, for instance, does our evaluation of the WB as an epistemic vice (or as a virtue) influence the methodology of the philosophy of religion, especially the controversy between evidentialism and fideism?[19] How, furthermore, does the WB

---

[18] Among recent pragmatism scholars, Aikin and Talisse (2018) offer the harshest critique of WB as *immoral*. Klein (2018) in my view rightly shows that their critique fails to do justice to James's criteria for legitimate WB cases.

[19] While evidentialism requires that religious beliefs ought to be supported by religiously neutral evidence, or rational considerations more generally, in order to qualify as rationally acceptable, fideism distinguishes sharply between reason and faith, suggesting that religious faith needs no evidence. It seems to me that James's WB, as such, does not neatly fall into either one of these basic categories. Cf. Pihlström 2013 for further discussion.

method figure in the emergence of James's own pragmatism and his study of religious experience?[20] Moreover, if the WB strategy is evaluated as a vice (or as a virtue), is it primarily an *epistemic* vice or a *moral* vice (or virtue)? How exactly should the distinction between epistemic and moral vices (and, correspondingly, virtues) be drawn? It is right here that we may bring James into a dialogue with White and holistic pragmatism. These questions are fundamental to the understanding and critical evaluation of pragmatism as such, as they may challenge pragmatist reinterpretations of the boundary between the theoretical and the practical more generally.[21]

Let us now, guided by this list of questions (not all of which can be explicitly responded to here), briefly examine James's WB and its basic ideas. James's oft-quoted fundamental thesis is this: "*Our passional nature not only lawfully may, but must, decide an option between propositions, whenever it is a genuine option that cannot by its nature be decided on intellectual grounds; for to say, under such circumstances, 'Do not decide, but leave the question open,' is itself a passional decision – just like deciding yes or no – and is attended with the same risk of losing the truth.*" (James 1979 [1897], 20; original emphasis) A few pages earlier James tells us what makes an option "genuine" (James 1979 [1897], 14–15): it has to be (i) "live" in the sense that *both* of the rival hypotheses are "live" ones for the subject; (ii) "forced", that is, the decision cannot be avoided, as we cannot refuse to face the issue and there is no "third way"; as well as (iii) "momentous", that is, a unique, highly significant, non-trivial chance. Crucially, suspending judgment may be equally risky as believing, or refusing to believe (see, however, Chapter 6). An option is here defined as a choice between rival hypotheses – a choice in our lives.

James is a thoroughgoing fallibilist: objective evidence is never complete. Especially in religious, metaphysical, and other existential matters, there is no conclusive evidence or absolutely decisive intellectual considerations available in order for us to fully settle issues such as, for example, God's reality. Therefore, the individual believer – as an existential subject – has a personal right to embrace (for example) the religious hypothesis that

---

[20] The term "pragmatism" is not yet used in *The Will to Believe* in 1897, though arguably pragmatism as a philosophical orientation is already strongly present there (while Russell claims that WB is only a transitional doctrine on James's way toward pragmatism, which is, by his lights, even worse). I will raise the issue of pragmatism emerging out of James's earlier WB essays in my critical comments on Gunnarsson (2020) in this chapter below.

[21] We will return to this issue, too. In a more comprehensive investigation, one should also pursue a metaphilosophical assessment of the significance of the historical (still on-going) controversies around James's WB doctrine to the theory of inquiry both within pragmatism (including holistic pragmatism) and more broadly. Hookway's (2011) work is instrumental in bringing James's WB into comparison with virtue epistemology.

God exists (or is real) if, and only if, it is a genuine option for her/him and cannot be settled on purely intellectual or evidential grounds. Thus, "we have the right to believe at our own risk any hypothesis that is live enough to tempt our will" (James 1979 [1897], 32).

Is this a *right* or a *will* to believe? (James later said he should have spoken about a "right".) James's much-discussed examples include the mountain climber who needs to decide whether to make a dangerous but possibly life-saving leap, as well as marriage – both cases of personal risk where courage and determination are needed. Personal risk of error is contrasted to a real chance of success, of getting things right. WB, furthermore, is not restricted to religion; even atheism could (in principle) be defended by WB. James didn't try to convince the atheist that they should believe in God but to convince someone already inclined to believe that it is not wrong to do so (Jackman 1999). Typically, WB concerns the issue of whether the universe is at bottom "moral or immoral". In this sense, we might say that it is ultimately a WB decision to view the world either as "disenchanted" or as (partially, potentially) "re-enchanted"; no scientific evidence or purely intellectual consideration will ever finally determine such an issue for us. James seems to have maintained that science does not *force* us to an uncompromisingly *entzauberte* worldview; accordingly, WB can be employed to partially (critically, fallibly) re-enchant our world for us.

Different variants of what James takes to be justified WB must be distinguished. In some cases the belief may be necessary to *create its object*, or to create its own truth.[22] The mountaineer can succeed in their dangerous leap only by believing they can make it; the person considering marriage can succeed in their marriage only by believing in it and living the kind of life that belief requires. In other cases, the belief may be needed in order for us to be able to *obtain evidence for its possible truth*. This is problematic, though: in science, one *doesn't* have to believe that the hypotheses one sets out to test are

---

[22] This is probably the point where the WB discussion comes closest to James's pragmatist account of truth, discussed in Chapters 1–2. On the other hand, some scholars (e.g., Gunnarsson 2020) want to clearly distinguish between the WB essays and the later writings on truth. (I will get back to this issue below.) In any event, this is presumably one of those Jamesian views that might be taken to come close to the populist "post-truth" discourse: does Donald Trump, for example, really believe that if he shouts (or tweets) what he believes is the case, that belief will "create its object" and become true, at least in the extremely naïve "cash value" sense of convincing his loyal supporters? No matter how exactly the relation between the WB idea and the pragmatist conception of truth is interpreted in James, it is clear that James never goes that far. He never denies the importance of realistic facts "out there" but emphasizes the role of volitional commitment in our *sincere* doxastic attempts to come to terms with our situation amidst the facts we find ourselves surrounded by. WB, no matter how problematic it is as a method of inquiry, is an attempt to find the truth; Trump's tweeting is no such attempt at all but, instead, a mockery of our truth-seeking practices.

true. On the other hand, more generally this could still be the case: for Kuhnian reasons, we can only acquire evidence in the context of *some* beliefs or commitments already taken for granted (see Kuhn 1970 [1962]). But then again, those commitments are usually *not* made by WB methods but by becoming enculturated to a reigning scientific paradigm.[23] Finally, believing a certain hypothesis may lead to *favorable (e.g., moral) results* in the individual believer's life. This, for James, is the central consideration in the case of religion.[24] At this point, WB also touches upon (while not reducing to) James's conception of truth, which also (equally notoriously, according to critics like Russell) emphasizes the satisfactory consequences of true beliefs (cf. Chapter 1).

The main point to be made here is that James can be usefully read in the context of pragmatist holism, especially given his reference to "the whole man in us". Several commentators emphasize that WB does not just come into the picture if it turns out that the issue we are considering cannot be settled in terms of evidence and intellectual considerations; rather, the "whole man in us" is at work all the time, already *prior to* determining whether intellectual considerations are sufficient or not. Even so, we must distinguish between cases where we need to will to believe a hypothesis in order to "record" its truth and those where we need to will to believe it in order to "contribute" to its truth (cf. Campbell 2017, chapter 3). WB in this sense requires courage, an active will (not merely a right) to believe. (Cf., e.g., O'Connell 1984; Pappas 1994.) It also involves *sincerely*, and hence self-critically, developing one's "intellectual character".[25] To embrace the WB strategy is thus (partly) to develop a certain kind of intellectual or doxastic self or personality – inevitably holistic, pertaining to the whole person, and thus also fundamentally morally relevant. Therefore, WB, as interpreted in the context of holistic pragmatism, is ultimately a position within pragmatist philosophical anthropology.[26]

---

[23] The issue regarding the epistemic situation of the (prospective) theist considering WB and the scientist seeking new hypotheses is more complex, however; see Klein 2015 and 2019.

[24] It can even be compared to Kant's view (in the Second Critique) of God's existence as a "postulate of practical reason" (see Pihlström 2013, as well as Chapter 3), but in this chapter I cannot pursue this line of thought (discussed in detail in some of my earlier work on James). In an obvious sense, it is always eventually an empirical question whether beneficial results – or any results at all – will ensue in someone's life based on their adoption of a worldview or religious hypothesis on WB grounds. On the other hand, such results will never be known in advance; the WB strategy always looks to the future in uncertain circumstances.

[25] See also several essays in Rydenfelt and Pihlström 2013, especially Axtell's (2013) contribution.

[26] Koopman (2017) argues that James's WB should be placed in the context of his psychology of the will and thus of a naturalistic theory of "self-transformation", for example, habit-modification.

What James offers us is a truly *pragmatic view of rationality*: we should not divide our doxastic lives into purely intellectual or rational and "merely pragmatic" spheres; on the contrary, these are thoroughly intertwined, and our exercise of rational capacities of belief-fixation (including the acquisition of relevant evidence) is itself thoroughly pragmatic and practice-involving. This could be regarded as the key meta-level moral to be drawn from James's WB argumentation. This is also one reason why the WB argument should in my view be placed in the context of James's overall pragmatism, even though the term "pragmatism" does not yet occur in the 1897 text.[27] This is also why James is *not* a simple fideist in the philosophy of religion. Rationality is not excluded but thoroughly pragmatized. On the other hand, James might also be interpreted as claiming that in the end there *is* evidence for (a certain kind of) religious hypothesis, based on religious experience (cf. James 1958 [1902]; see, e.g., Putnam and Putnam 2017). In any event, WB considerations are, we might say, "internal" to the subject's ("the whole man's") reflections on *who* s/he ultimately is, or who s/he wishes to become – instead of being external considerations of the possibly beneficial effects of believing, such as the well-being that religious faith might bring to the believer.

This account takes a step toward resolving the problem of sincerity that was identified in the Kantian-cum-Jamesian context elaborated on in Chapter 3. WB needs to take place internally within the genuine religious considerations of an individual pursuing the truth (in a way relevant to their existential concerns, including the truth about who they are "deep down"), rather than just externally as a search for the factual, contingent benefits of faith. Only thus applied does WB have any chances to come even close to the ethically demanding view of religion we saw Kant maintain and James approximate.

There are, recall, different strands of holism in James. There is (as we saw in Chapter 2) the "wedding" of new fact or experience into old opinion, or into an old stock of beliefs, comparable to the holisms we find in Quine and White. Our responses to such novelties need to be ethically – pragmatically – evaluated by our ability to hear what James called the "cries of the wounded"; therefore, there is no gap between the factual and the normative (as later more explicitly argued by White). But then there is also the holism of the "whole man in us" – a meta-level pragmatic holism. WB could in an extreme metaethical case even amount to *choosing* (deciding) whether it makes sense to listen to the "cries of the

---

Dianda (2018) also proposes to read the WB argument in the context of James's *Principles* (1981 [1890]) and *Varieties* (1958 [1902]).

[27] WB could even be used to argue for pragmatism itself – and we will return to such reflexive matters toward the end of this chapter.

wounded", that is, to acquire moral evidence at all, or to keep on adjusting new experience into the old stock of factual-cum-normative beliefs. One might wonder whether morality is an illusion or something to be taken seriously;[28] however, one might then use WB to actually decide in one's life that morality *does* matter, after all. Again, this could be seen as a pragmatist resistance, by means of WB, to any reductive scientistically *entzauberte* world-conception claiming moral values to be fundamentally illusory or (in Mackie's terms attacked by Putnam) "queer". It would be a WB-based way of adopting and maintaining a fundamentally sincere attitude to how one pursues truth in one's life.

As explained in the previous chapters, it seems to me that there are two main dimensions of novelty in James. The first is related to his account of truth: again, this is a matter of adding new experience to old fact (James 1975 [1907], Lecture VI), leading up to the holisms of Quine and White. "Old" systems of belief or worldviews are constantly challenged and thus also in a sense critically tested in terms of new empirical results, data, or experience. Secondly, and more generally, novelty in sensations is, according to James, rationalized by concepts; there is a constant interplay between the sensible and conceptual elements of our mental lives (cf. James 1977 [1911]). This is holistic pragmatism in a more general sense. Furthermore, the Jamesian articulation of novelty might in fact be yet another pragmatist way of re-engaging the *Entzauberung* theme (cf. again Joas 2017). In a thoroughly *entzauberte* world there are no genuine novelties to be expected, while in a (moderately) "re-enchanted" world we may trust our practice-embedded human perspectives to yield new experiences and conceptual articulations of reality.[29] This may not, and certainly need not, be a religious or transcendent sense of *(Wieder-) Verzauberung*, but it does add a Jamesian twist to the *Entzauberung* discussion.

In comparison with the only kind of novelty available to a more radically secularized neopragmatist like Rorty, the Jamesian possibility of transcendence may even function as a quasi-transcendental condition enabling some of us to view our lives in terms of "re-enchanting" religious vocabularies, too; just like in Kant (cf. Chapter 3), there is in James at least a hint toward the view that our moral obligation to pursue the moral law could not really

[28] It is a well-known biographical fact that James's early mental breakdown around 1870 was primarily based on his worry that the scientific worldview might render moral responsibility illusory. Arguably, one might need WB to recover from such a sense of moral nihilism, and famously James stated in 1870 that his "first act of free will shall be to believe in free will". (Cf. Gunnarsson 2020.) I will briefly return to freedom toward the end of this chapter.

[29] Moreover, we must not overlook the ethical, political, and metaphysical dimensions of novelty – here James's ideas can be interestingly compared with, for example, Arendt's notion of natality, as suggested in Chapter 2.

be made sense of without such a reaching out to the transcendent. If this is a plausible way of understanding James, then WB is not that far away from Kantian transcendental argumentation, after all.

4.4 Virtues, Vices, and Habits

As we have already observed, the classical pragmatists were certainly not in agreement about these issues. Peirce maintained in "The Fixation of Belief" that, when employing the scientific method, we let our beliefs about reality to be fixed by "Real things" that are independent of us (i.e., independent of our – or any number of individuals' – wishes, thoughts, etc., though not necessarily therefore independent of "thought in general"). This distinguishes the scientific method from the methods of tenacity and authority, as well as the aprioristic "method of what is agreeable to reason". Does the WB method allow us to (tenaciously?) fix beliefs based on our wishes, prejudices, or personal existential commitments, rather than "Real things"? If so, is it an epistemic vice, after all (assuming that Peirce, in "Fixation", tells us what it means to be a virtuous believer)? Does it justify credulity and wishful thinking in opposition to critical, evidence-based belief-fixation based on the scientific method? Does it take us into a wrong direction in our pursuits of truth? And if WB is, or exemplifies, a vice – or a virtue – which specific vice(s), or virtue(s), does it manifest?

If WB manifests credulity, or wishful thinking, then it is presumably (primarily) an epistemic vice. Courage and cowardice in religious, existential, and other existential or *weltanschaulichen* matters may here be opposed to each other. If, on the other hand, WB exemplifies courage in, for example, adopting a religious or existential hypothesis without sufficient evidence at one's personal risk, then it is perhaps a virtue, after all – unless it stretches the boundaries of courage too far and becomes epistemically hazardous. A pragmatically holistic evaluation of virtues and vices in the context of an entire human life is here needed.[30]

---

[30] Peter Hare (2015, 143) once suggested that virtue epistemology could enrich or "thicken" holistic pragmatism; see also Hookway 2011. We might pause here to reflect a bit on the relation between the WB and Pascal's Wager. The latter, one might argue, does not manifest courage, after all; rather, it is a strategy that prefers to be on the safe side. It could turn out that God exists, however improbable this is; therefore, it is *safer* to bet on the hypothesis that God does exist, as there could be an infinite loss to be suffered otherwise. For James, in contrast, it would in a sense be "safer" to just rely on contemporary science and to reject theism. It is more courageous to embrace the "religious hypothesis" than atheism, given the context of the scientific worldview. The epistemic risk involved in this is higher than for Pascal, who lived in a thoroughly Christian culture (or for earlier theistic voluntarists, of course).

There are still further issues regarding WB and the pragmatist theory of inquiry that need to be considered. In particular, *habits* and *habituality* are crucial in pragmatism, especially Peirce's. Generality, or the acknowledgment of "real generals" irreducible to their particular instances, is fundamental for Peircean pragmatism. Now, if one habitually forms beliefs about reality by relying on (something like) the WB method, then one perhaps exemplifies credulity. WB as such is not a vice, but its habitual application or employment may be. However, WB itself in a sense *precludes* its habitual employment: it is intended to be employed only in very specific and highly unusual, potentially life-transforming circumstances, that is, when there really is a "genuine option" at stake. These are always singular, unique, existentially "momentous" cases. *Could* WB ever even become a general habit? Among James's commentators, Gregory Pappas (1994) argues for a genuinely pluralistic ethics of belief appreciating individuals' concrete life-situations and the development of human character (comparable to virtue ethics and virtue epistemology). Thus, of course, Peircean-like generality is involved here, too. Again, this is a philosophical-anthropological issue, manifesting the contrast between continuity and uniqueness as features of human life.

It may, on the other hand, be seriously misguided to examine the issue in terms of habits in the first place – but then the WB method may be in tension with pragmatism more generally, because from the (Peircean) pragmatist point of view habituality and generality are fundamental to inquiry. However, Peter Hare (2015, 38) does emphasize this connection: "[. . .] the *will* to believe is [. . .] the deliberate acting-as-if which, carried through persistently enough, leads ultimately to belief itself, to *habits* of action."[31]

Does James replace epistemically constrained belief-fixation by practical (moral) considerations that may (in his view) in certain cases (i.e., "genuine options") legitimately influence our habitual belief-fixation processes? Remember that Clifford maintained that it is not only epistemically but also *morally* wrong to believe anything upon insufficient evidence. To be sure, it is epistemically wrong, too, but it is also morally wrong, according to his evidentialism. When reacting against Clifford, James defends both

---

[31] More complications result from the fact that, according to Hare (2015, 38), at least the following distinctions can be made: *will* to believe, *right* to believe, and *duty* to believe – but also *right* to *will* to believe, *duty* to *will* to believe, and so forth (when it comes to believing moral hypotheses, such as meliorism). Moreover, we may say that, for Jamesian pragmatism, *any* metaphysical hypothesis is ultimately moral (cf. Pihlström 2009; Kivistö and Pihlström 2016). This is, clearly, a kind of holism all over again.

our moral right and our intellectual (epistemic) right to voluntarily adopt beliefs in cases of "genuine options" that cannot be settled on purely intellectual grounds. Again, we should see the epistemic and the ethical as thoroughly, inseparably, intertwined here – characteristically for James's pragmatism as a whole. This, in my view, is the most important way in which holistic pragmatism is present in James – and present as a position in pragmatist ways of thinking about what we humans are like as the kind of creatures we are. Given the way we are, there is no principled dichotomy between the epistemic and the ethical. In particular, the central types of legitimate WB in "contribution" cases are moral, personal, and religious hypotheses (Campbell 2017, 105–106).

I propose to interpret this to mean that James is *deliberately* blurring the dichotomy between the epistemic and the ethical. This begins in the WB essays but continues more explicitly in the later pragmatist writings, which grow naturally out of the WB discussions in this respect. This leads to a tension within pragmatism more generally, because Peirce keeps these separate. If WB is a virtue or a vice, then it is *a holistic virtue or a holistic vice*: it concerns our lives in their entirety, the kinds of beings or individuals we are. This also entails that (according to James) whenever we discuss epistemic vices (or virtues), we are inevitably also discussing ethical vices (or virtues). Our epistemic and intellectual lives cannot be completely detached from our practical lives – especially in the case of religion, which may be a mixture of "recording" and "contribution" cases (in Campbell's terms). The claim they can amounts to what James called "vicious intellectualism", which is a false, and unethical, view of the human condition. Avoiding *such* intellectualism by an adequately holistic picture of human lives as both epistemic and ethico-existential, we may also take a Jamesian step toward reconciling individual sincerity with intersubjective pursuit of truth.

James is, as White also reminds us, right to maintain that "our view of what ought to be may sometimes legitimately determine our view of what is the case" (White 2005, 249) – and this, of course, is a key idea of WB.[32] For White, this point still remains primarily epistemological; as Hare (2015, 146) also notes, the "*ontological* dimensions of holistic pragmatism" are (so far) the weakest. Even so, one of the crucial steps in a holistic pragmatist articulation of WB is to acknowledge the *reflexivity* at work in

---

[32] For White's reading of James in the tradition of holistic pragmatism, see Chapter 2. As briefly noted above, WB in this sense is also at work, for example, in James's "The Dilemma of Determinism" (also in James 1979 [1897]), which argues for the reality of free will on broadly WB grounds. (Cf. further Gunnarsson 2020.)

James's holism regarding the need to (re)consider and adjust the epistemic status of the principles we both employ and simultaneously test (as noted in Chapter 2). Indeed, holistic pragmatism crucially contributes to understanding normativity itself as a pervasive feature of the human world – culture – that we inhabit (cf. Chapter 5).

4.5   Reflexivity

Recognizing that we can only normatively investigate what normativity is for us, and as our philosophy of culture is itself a cultural institution, we need to add some reflections on the concept of *reflexivity*, or self-referentiality. At the meta-level, endorsing the kind of Jamesian pragmatist WB position sketched in this chapter may (from the pragmatist perspective) be regarded as virtuous because it leads us to a thoroughgoing holistic morally relevant evaluation and critical assessment of our epistemic lives. For the Jamesian pragmatist, it is virtuous and pragmatically efficacious to maintain that our epistemic lives are never "merely" epistemic but always also ethical. (This could even be developed into a WB-based argument for WB itself.) Holistic pragmatism may, then, make the (Putnamian and Jamesian) entanglement ideas more precise: fact and value, or the epistemic and the ethical, are thoroughly intertwined. *This* in its own way "re-enchants" our epistemic relations to reality as thoroughly ethically structured (cf. also Pihlström 2009).[33] Even so, we may ask what the specific nature of the relevant relation of entanglement is. Is it metaphysical, epistemic, or conceptual? Or perhaps transcendental in a quasi-Kantian sense? These different forms of fact-value (factuality-normativity) entanglement may themselves be entangled, again reflexively, in a pragmatist construal of the "entanglement thesis".

Now, isn't holistic pragmatism itself a normative view *within* ethics, viz., a position that contains a significant ethical element, as a theory about what we can or should (legitimately) think or say about human cultural institutions? Aren't we, then, testing the whole conjunction of our beliefs, holistic pragmatism included (*if* it is among our beliefs), whenever holistically testing any belief, scientific or ethical (factual or normative)? We might also come up with the belief (or, perhaps, the moral feeling?) that, *pace* White, mere feeling is not an appropriate experiential back-up for

---

[33] Again, this broadly Jamesian idea connects with Joas's (2017) work: believers and secularists all have their own presuppositions that need to be reflexively and critically analyzed; there is no neutral "presuppositionlessness" (*Voraussetzungslosigkeit*) available in matters concerning religion or other existential and valuational questions (cf. Joas 2017, 28). James's WB is helpful for analyzing the existential significance of this presuppositionlessness, as is holistic pragmatism generally.

ethics, that is, that moral obligation transcends feelings of obligation. How can this feeling – stimulated, for example, by our experience of reading Kant – be accommodated within holistic pragmatism? Is the principle that feelings are central in ethics unsurrenderable in White's pragmatism? It definitely *shouldn't* be, given his general fallibilism and reflexively critical attitude. Should we, then, perhaps focus on values as cultural entities, instead of mere moral feelings, or more broadly on the valuational experience (feeling?) that, say, suffering cannot be justified?[34] Questions of this kind indicate the central significance of reflexive argumentation structure in holistic pragmatism.

White (2002, chapter 10) proposes that holistic pragmatism ought to be conceived as a normative (prescriptive) rule rather than a descriptive statement. The holistic pragmatist behaves like a legislator transforming a custom into a law when formulating the rule that no experience may disconfirm holistic pragmatism itself, as this is the method we should employ in testing all our beliefs. This saves the normativity of epistemology, including moral epistemology, within moderate naturalism. Yet, rules are not immutable, any more than legal statutes: "Resolving to accept holistic pragmatism does not mean that it can *never* be altered or surrendered, but it does mean that a very powerful argument would be required to effect either of those changes" (White 2002, 181). Holistic pragmatism itself is, in a genuinely holistic spirit, constantly tested when any hypothesis is tested according to its rule-like principles.

In addition to a more careful articulation of this meta-level reflexivity, the holistic pragmatist, arguably, needs a more metaphysical approach to the reality of values. Holistic pragmatism, just like Putnam's version of the entanglement thesis, may be argued to be *insufficiently metaphysical*: in addition to the epistemology of belief systems incorporating both factual and normative elements, the *reality* of values and norms ought to be pragmatically elaborated as well. Furthermore, the metaphysical dimensions of what it means to speak of "the whole man [person] in us" also need to be taken into consideration. Two candidates for such an approach (available to the pragmatist but not to be further discussed here, though) might be (i) *emergence* and (ii) *continuity*. Perhaps values in some sense emerge from facts, depending on them while being (ontologically) irreducible to them? Or, alternatively, perhaps values are ontologically continuous with facts (e.g., in

---

[34] See Kivistö and Pihlström 2016 for an argument for the view that the acknowledgment of the reality of meaningless suffering is a necessary precondition for the possibility of an appropriately ethical perspective on the world.

the sense of Peirce's "synechism")? Both are serious options in pragmatically naturalized metaphysics of value, and both would have to be considered in a more comprehensive holistic pragmatist exploration of the fact-value entanglement (see, for more detailed discussions, Pihlström 2010b). In the present context, there is no need to dwell on this matter further; it may here only serve as a reminder that such metaphysical issues need to be revisited when pursuing holistic pragmatism as an overall philosophical account of the human condition – and the possible pragmatist re-enchantment of our human world. The next chapter will make *one* move toward a transcendental (if not metaphysical) articulation of the place of normativity in the human world.[35]

4.6   Embedded Life: Persons, Habits, and Re-Enchantment

The opposition between *habituality* (invoking Peircean-like synechistic continuity, i.e., the idea that everything is continuous with everything else) and WB-type (Jamesian) *concreteness* and *uniqueness* can be seen as a key tension in the pragmatist conception of the human condition. This contrast is not irrelevant to the issues of individual sincerity and plurality tackled earlier (especially Chapter 2). Habit, of course, is one of the key concepts of pragmatism, frequently employed by all the pragmatist classics. Human action is not primarily viewed in terms of individual actions but in terms of habits and practices: generality and continuity are, from a pragmatist point of view, prior to particularity and discontinuity. Practices, moreover, may be understood as systematic, normatively governed, purpose-oriented, more or less institutionalized sets of interrelated habits. Therefore, personal and social *goals* are crucial in understanding and evaluating habits and practices. Habits and practices are inherently goal-directed; otherwise, they would be mere behavior that also mere animals are capable of. In this respect, pragmatism incorporates the Kantian emphasis on our necessarily "acting under the idea of reason". Habit is also a reflexive concept, because the habit of ameliorating our habits should be regarded as one of the most important habits we engage in.

Let us consider a WB-related practical issue of pragmatic world-re-enchantment: the interpretation of individual *vocations* as habits. A person's

[35] Furthermore, the entanglement thesis itself might, or perhaps should, also be understood as *transcendental*. Values are *necessarily* connected with facts and normativity in the sense that the very possibility of factuality presupposes normativity. As an analogy, we might compare this to the Wittgensteinian impossibility of private language. Again, this is a line of thought that cannot be pursued here.

vocation – their sense of a duty to be or become someone or something in particular in their life – cannot be based on an isolated individual act; generality is needed. The doubt-belief theory of inquiry, as developed by Peirce in "The Fixation of Belief" in the context of his analysis of the scientific method, is highly relevant here. We are familiar with the basic scheme:

belief → habit → action → surprise → doubt → inquiry →
(new or revised) belief → . . .

This is not a mechanical process but always incorporates normative elements. We must be able to interpret a surprising result *as* a surprise, contrary to the expectations of the habit in terms of which one initially acts. Beliefs, moreover, do not just give rise to but *are* habits of action, if we take pragmatism seriously; to believe something about the world is to be engaged in (possible) actions in the world, or to be a participant in normatively structured human practices. Fallibilism is also fundamental here: our human inquiries are always fallible, and any belief may need correction. Thus, our way of being in the world may always need revision. Indeed, revising belief systems amounts to revising one's life.

Just like the metaphysics of value cannot be left out of the holistic pragmatist picture of the fact-value entanglement, the metaphysics of habits needs to be taken seriously in this context. More specifically, Peirce's *extreme scholastic realism* is relevant right here: what Peirce called "real generals" (habits, laws, dispositions, possibilities) are to be distinguished from concretely existing particulars (cf. Pihlström 2003, 2009). The pragmatic method (Peirce's Pragmatic Maxim) itself is based on such realism about generality; this is because, when examining the pragmatic meaning of our concept(ion)s, theories, or ideas, we ought to, Peirce advises us, examine their *conceivable* practical effects. Accordingly, habit – in its generality – is a key notion in the pragmatic method of inquiry developed and employed by Peirce, James, Dewey, and their contemporary followers. The method might be applied very differently (as it is, e.g., by Peirce and James), but it is in any case ineliminably tied to the concept of habituality.[36]

---

[36] Peirce's key essays on realism about generality can be found in Peirce 1992–1998, ranging from the 1871 Berkeley review (in vol. 1) to late writings on pragmaticism (in vol. 2). I am not claiming that we *must* add the Peircean account of real generals and scholastic realism to the Jamesian and Whitean holistic pragmatism I have defended in this chapter. This is optional. My claim is, rather, that insofar as a more metaphysical dimension is necessary in the development of holistic pragmatism, a Peircean realism of generality is at least something that ought to be seriously considered. Conversely, its being able to enrich the rather thin holism we find in White might be a consideration in its favor. In any case, this is not the place to settle the issue either way.

We *are* the habits we have or engage in. We are not only what we have done but also what we tend to do, embedded in the habits and practices our actions embody. This yields a crucial holistically pragmatic kind of openness in our lives: habituality opens up entire *fields of possibility*, ways a person can be; the human person is never reduced to their actual concrete actions (individual or social) but is engaged in open possibilities. James's relational view of (personal) identity (cf. Chapter 1) is certainly relevant to this picture of the human condition and serves as an elaboration of his holism. According to James, nothing exists in a self-sustained manner, as individuals possess their identities only as parts of networks of mutual interdependence.[37]

Now, consider personal vocations, conceived as tasks or challenges of individual life. Vocations, understood as habits, invite issues in the metaphysics of *modalities*. Are they, for instance, "real possibilities" in a Peircean sense? One might, presumably, have a vocation that never actualizes due to various contingencies of one's life. Are there, then, also other non-actualized personal possibilities and interpersonal relations? Can there, in other words, be a habit with only one instance (can we have a habit of doing something and only do it once?), or even without any concrete action-instances at all? For example, one might have something like "the habit of escaping through the window when there is a fire in the house" – even when there is no fire during the person's life-time. Would it then be appropriate to call it a habit? There is inevitably some (deliberate) vagueness at work here. We live in and of our habits of action; we *are* to a large extent the habits we (so to speak) "inhabituate" as individuals-in-societies, constantly engaging in and (habitually) renewing habitual actions. Habits

---

[37] This interpretation of James has been forcefully defended by Jose Medina (2010), who emphasizes that in James's "radical empiricism" (cf. James 1977 [1912]) the human self amounts to a bundle of interpersonal relations of dependence. This has both metaphysical and ethical or political relevance. Even James's (1975 [1907], Lecture VI) pragmatist account of truth incorporates a version of habituality: true beliefs *tend to* produce good effects (see also Cormier 2001; Medina's relationalist reading of James's theory of truth was cited in Chapter 1). Practice-embeddedness, at any rate, is part and parcel of the pragmatist conception of inquiry. It may seem that, according to pragmatism, almost anything is practice-dependent, -laden, or -embedded: meaning (compare this to the Wittgensteinian principle, "meaning is use"); knowledge and cognition (epistemic practices); reality, existence (ontological practice-dependence); and so forth. Does this entail relativism or idealism? Does the pragmatist have to reject (ontological) realism? I have throughout this volume suggested (without being able to argue in any great detail) that there is no reason to think so, at least if one understands pragmatic practice-embeddedness analogously to Kantian transcendental idealism, which is compatible with empirical realism: "transcendental pragmatism", far from succumbing to any simple antirealism, in fact makes pragmatic realism possible (cf. Pihlström 2009, and Chapters 1 and 3). This amounts to what we may regard as transcendental meaning-constitution rather than any straightforward social construction of objects.

define and constitute us. We live, therefore, in a field of real possibility, again comparable to Peirce's "real generals". *Pace* Jean-Paul Sartre, we can never be reduced to what we concretely do or did; our habits are more than (though they might be argued to emerge from) our contingent individual actions.[38]

There is, it seems to me, a sense in which this understanding of vocations and habituality can again be seen as re-enchanting our *entzauberte* world. The world we live in becomes a field of significance and value, with (Jamesian-like) real risks, losses, and struggles, but perhaps real success and victories as well. However, mere possibility, even real possibility, is not enough. Concrete action is needed, too. James's WB could also be seen as reminding us that remaining at the level of *mere* potentiality or possibility amounts to inaction, to *not* making the choice one needs to make in a certain unique situation. *Existential decisions*, when sincere, also define who we are, and they can lead to establishing entirely new habits. Habits are, conversely, needed for WB type of "leaps" to take place at all; they cannot take place in a void. This leads to a deep tension within pragmatism itself, perhaps comparable to the realism vs. idealism tension, which arguably also structures the entire pragmatist tradition. We need *both* habits (possibility, continuity) *and* sudden, concrete, unique, particular existential decisions or choices (WB "leaps" *à la* James, analogous to "existential choices" *à la* Sartre); both need to be taken into account in a full-blown holistic pragmatism. These may run into conflict with each other, because WB leaps may require us to break out of our old habits normatively structuring our lives and establish new ones. Holistic pragmatism must accommodate *both* a kind of conservatism or continuity *and* concrete radicality, novelty, and breaches of our habitualities, merging everything into a holistic totality. Only then can our human world be properly speaking pragmatically re-enchanted, *wiederverzauberte*.

Is there a middle path, or a reconciliation, available? A healthy holistic pragmatism tries to make sense of both, to recognize the importance of real possibility (habits) as well as concrete action (WB "leaps", existential decisions) – just like, I would argue, a healthy pragmatism is (together with Kantian critical philosophy) both realistic and idealistic. It must be noted that, in existential decisions (i.e., in WB), the concept of *necessity* also plays a role. An existential decision may be "existentially necessary" for

---

[38] Real possibility, furthermore, is not to be conflated with mere imaginability (or logical or conceptual possibility). It is closer to, but perhaps not reducible to, metaphysical possibility. Vagueness prevails; no sharp dichotomies are available here.

an individual, that is, necessary for the identity of the subject in question, for that person to be or become "who s/he is" (constitutive of the subject in question). This is the sense of necessity we may experience in being guided by a personal vocation, and the related sense of anxiety we must struggle with when we need to existentially decide which vocation to pursue.[39] Such personal necessity is constitutive of what we mean by sincerity in our pursuit of truth.

A pragmatist way of keeping a kind of critical distance to excessive *Entzauberung* is to emphasize the sense in which the concepts of freedom and truth, in their "existential" employment, may be pragmatically articulated in such a manner that our world becomes partly re-enchanted, or disenchanted, in and through our existential considerations of who we actually are. We can, thus, use the WB strategy to make an existential decision – manifesting freedom and responsibility without claiming to solve the metaphysical riddles of the free will – about the inner "truth" or truthfulness of our own existence, about the kind of individual, person, or subject that we are. This is to freely pursue our own internal truth about ourselves, about the way we view and inhabit the world, irreducible to mere propositional truth about the way things are (hence perhaps closer to the concept of truthfulness or even sincerity than truth as such).[40] This is also to highlight the richness and existential depth of the pragmatist articulation of the close relation between the concepts of freedom and truth.[41]

These somewhat sketchy thoughts are closely related to pragmatic fallibilism (again). As noted above, the reflexive practice or habit of critically reflecting on and, if necessary, revising, transforming, and ameliorating one's practices and habits (and hence one's beliefs, including one's beliefs about the correct ways of fixing beliefs) is one of the most important

---

[39] A comparison to Sartre's (1946) example of Pierre readily comes to mind – and James is clearly a proto-existentialist in this sense. For a perceptive comparison between Sartre and James's WB, see Putnam 1992. It should be acknowledged, however, that vocational decisions may also be relatively everyday matters in comparison to the burning existential issues that WB considerations would typically address. It is a non-trivial task to distinguish between the exceptional existential cases where WB becomes relevant and the more ordinary cases where it (usually) won't.

[40] But recall that in Chapter 1 it was suggested that these notions are also constitutively entangled.

[41] Rorty (1989) rightly sees their connection but reduces both notions into something less existentially serious. We might even say that Rorty's conception of freedom and truth, as articulated in his 1989 (cf. Chapter 1), is a thoroughly *entzauberte* account of these notions. *Diese Entzauberung muss selbst entzaubert werden*, I would like to suggest. A (qualified) re-enchantment can be reached by means of the Jamesian WB: the individual existing subject freely chooses how to pursue their own "existential truth" (truth about who they are), to a large extent through *weltanschaulichen* WB decisions. This inner commitment to truthfulness is a kind of re-enchantment; yet, it must be constantly critically examined, and qualified re-enchantment certainly does not entail any uncritical attitude to how we make our WB decisions.

practices and/or habits we can have. A meta-level problem here is whether there are merely possible habits. What, in the end, is it for a habit to be real? Are there meta-habits with no actual instantiations as, or in terms of, "real" (first-order) habits? Presumably, a line must be drawn somewhere, so why not here: there are, let us stipulate, no merely possible habits, although habits themselves may accommodate merely possible actions. Otherwise we would have to postulate a truly unpragmatic ontology of ever new layers of meta-habits. Even so, the advancement of the melioristic critical meta-habit of revising one's habits is close to the advancement of the scientific rational attitude itself – and hence a cornerstone of critical pragmatic fallibilism in the pursuit of truth. Indeed, fallibilism and meliorism are integrated here: practices can always be ameliorated. So can persons and their personal responses to the world, that is, their goals and vocations, among many other things.

Meliorism and a certain kind of *negativity* are, finally, fundamentally connected. Insofar as habits and practices are to be ameliorated in a fallibilist spirit, we have to start from paying serious attention to what is *wrong* in them.[42] This is (as I have suggested elsewhere) pragmatism's *via negativa*: taking loss, failure, fragility, incompleteness, and finitude very seriously (see, e.g., Pihlström 2014a). In ethics, this also means taking evil and suffering fundamentally seriously as the starting point of any pragmatic reflection on the good life, or on how exactly to view the world "rightly" (see again Kivistö and Pihlström 2016; Pihlström 2020a). As argued in Chapter 3, pragmatism is thus ultimately a species of critical philosophy (cf. also Skowroński and Pihlström 2019), based on a pessimistic conception of humanity, and this should be particularly explicit in holistic pragmatism: pragmatic meliorism presupposes the idea of philosophy as a critical method of developing methods of criticism (and self-criticism), in Dewey's famous words, and of criticism in the Kantian sense of the reflexive turn of human reason (or, better, of "the whole man") toward a critical inquiry into its (her/his) own fragile capacities, conditions, and limits.

On the other hand, this also means that pragmatism, even when it seeks to make sense of, say, our practical vocations, is *not* to be equated with anything like "applied philosophy". Pragmatism (or *philosophy*, according to pragmatism) is relevant to human life in the way good literature is, not as an application of a theory that could even in principle be defended or even formulated in a "non-applied", practice-independent (non-embedded)

---

[42] Zackariasson's (2019) analysis of meliorism in relation to guilt is again highly pertinent here.

form, but as something that is always already engaged and embedded in our concerns of life.[43] There is no way pragmatism could prioritize practical applications to purely theoretical philosophical ideas, because the very identity of philosophical ideas is constitutively dependent on their potential (conceivable) practical results; by the pragmatic principle itself (i.e., what Peirce called the Pragmatic Maxim and James referred to as "Peirce's principle"), our philosophical ideas are the ideas they are only on the grounds of their possible significance in our experiential practices. Again, this constitutivity is, in our terms, transcendental.

4.7   Freedom and the Will to Believe: Advancing Pragmatist Humanism

While I have referred in passing to James's "The Dilemma of Determinism" (collected among the WB essays in James 1979 [1897]) and have repeatedly pointed out that the WB strategy can also be employed outside the philosophy of religion, for example, in a defense of human freedom, I have been unable to include any substantial examination of the issue of freedom vs. determinism in this chapter (or this book), let alone any scholarly study of James's own indeterminism. A few more words needs to be said about this topic, however, because it is central to our understanding of WB itself: we have to be able to *freely choose which live options to pursue*, and the very idea of sincerity in the sense sketched in the earlier chapters also presupposes a context within which we are free to sincerely make our epistemic, ethical, religious, and existential choices. The pursuit of truth is a free human pursuit, although we cannot just let truth take care of itself by taking care of freedom, as Rorty suggests (cf. Chapter 1). It could be even argued that freedom is a transcendental presupposition of the WB strategy itself: we can only "will to believe" something if we are free to make that choice at our own risk (even though there is also a sense in which genuine options are "forced" on us, i.e., unavoidable); and as we do at least occasionally exercise this will, freedom must be presupposed as a necessary condition for its possibility. It is, moreover, not far-fetched to suggest that, just as the idea of individual vocation discussed above is comparable to a Sartrean freedom to determine one's own identity, there is a kind of existential necessity in the freedom relevant to WB. We just cannot avoid pursuing the issues that are genuine

---

[43] In this sense, for example, James's concern with the problem of evil and suffering is very far from applied philosophy (or applied ethics) in any standard meaning of the term. See Pihlström 2005, 2019a.

options for us, be they religious, ethical – or metaphysical issues concerning freedom itself.

Up to now I have in this chapter already utilized the work of a number of philosophers inspired by and further developing Jamesian ideas, including White, Putnam, and Joas. Let me, before closing the chapter, offer two more excursions, this time to two interestingly different contemporary philosophers interpreting and further developing James's views on freedom, in particular.

I will first briefly comment on Rosa Calcaterra's elaborations of the WB idea. Calcaterra has for a long time been a careful and highly acknowledged interpreter of James and other classical figures of pragmatism (for her recent contribution to investigating James, see Calcaterra 2017). Here I only wish to draw attention to a somewhat earlier essay in which she makes an unusual comparison between James and the Finnish philosopher Georg Henrik von Wright (Calcaterra 1999). This comparative inquiry into pragmatist (or quasi-pragmatist) ideas on freedom and action perceptively notes connections between apparently rather different philosophical approaches that might easily go unnoticed, and thereby enriches our understanding of not only pragmatism but contemporary philosophy more generally.[44]

While Calcaterra's explicit comments on von Wright's views are relatively brief, she makes a very important point about von Wright's "clarification of the intermingling of social with individual factors of human behaviour" as an "integration of the jamesian [*sic*] discussion of free will" in the context of his "neo-Wittgensteinian" theory of action (Calcaterra 1999, 145). She argues that von Wright provides "an effective antidote against the risk that the notion of individual freedom – so dear to James – vanishes in a mere wishful thinking" by distinguishing between "internal" and "external" determinants of human action, thus appreciating the complexities of human motivation and "reinforcing the dynamic conception of rationality promoted by the pragmatists" (Calcaterra 1999, 145). According to Calcaterra, James's defense of free will is analogous to "the emancipation of the discussion about human freedom from traditional epistemological

---

[44] I find it particularly congenial to the pluralistic spirit of pragmatist to keep pragmatism open to philosophical ideas drawn from other traditions, including the analytic (cf. Pihlström 2015). I will, however, also have a minor critical point to make about Calcaterra's views on von Wright's (1974, 1980) allegedly "Jamesian" position. For my reading of von Wright in relation to pragmatism, see Pihlström 2014b, 2019d. As von Wright's theory of human action is, despite its enormous philosophical significance, only tangential to the concerns of this book, I only refer to him in the context of my dialogue with Calcaterra.

and ontological approaches" that we find in von Wright's logico-analytic theory of action, freedom, and determinism (Calcaterra 1999, 139). This is one clear indication of the fact that Jamesian (holistic) pragmatism should be considered relevant across the boundaries of philosophical traditions.

Analyzing James's views on rationality and freedom, Calcaterra describes how James challenges "both positivistic scientism and traditional metaphysics" by criticizing the concept of objective evidence in the WB essays (Calcaterra 1999, 139), drawing particular attention to "The Dilemma of Determinism", in which James views the choice between determinism and indeterminism as "personal" in contrast to an objectively resolvable question of metaphysics. Our reasons for rejecting determinism and defending free will are "practical" rather than theoretical or purely factual, as they are directly concerned with the ethical shape the world takes through our seeking to render our world-engagement as "rational" as possible through pragmatic involvement. Calcaterra (1999, 141) quotes approvingly James's (1979 [1897], 135) remark that "ethics and the ordinary attitude of acting cannot be understood 'without the admission of real genuine possibilities in the world'".[45] Thus, the issue of free will in James is "organised not in order to identify the ontological status of an assumed faculty or to provide an account of its definite function in man's life" but "rises from a description of the way in which individuals can make reasonable choices, provided that they wish to live up to certain standards" (Calcaterra 1999, 145).

We may say that James is a *pragmatist humanist* about freedom.[46] What is fundamental is not our rendering freedom scientifically or metaphysically acceptable as an element of a naturalized account of reality – just as such a scientific or metaphysical justification is irrelevant in the case of religious belief – but our being ethically and existentially committed to freedom (and its corollary, moral responsibility) as an ineliminable feature of our normatively organized form of life, that is, to viewing our lives as thoroughly structured by the concept of freedom, or again (in Kantian terms) "under the aspect of freedom". Crucially, there is no more fundamental level at which freedom could be secured than the discourse of

[45] In relation to the remarks on Peircean scholastic realism and Jamesian individualism above, I cannot avoid reading this in the context of Peirce's views on "real generals".

[46] Another defense of pragmatic humanism highly relevant to the discussion of the present chapter is Jung 2019. As I read Jung, he seems to be arguing that genuine options (in the WB sense) are *possible* for us only if we acknowledge human diversity and otherness. This insight in fact entangles the examination of WB (in this chapter) with the analysis of the Jamesian approach to diversity, pluralism, and the acknowledgment of otherness (in the previous chapters).

freedom and responsibility itself. As James memorably put it in a letter after his early mental collapse in 1870, "*My first act of free will shall be to believe in free will*" (quoted in Perry 1964, 121).[47]

It is this essentially non-metaphysical account of the problem of freedom vs. determinism that Calcaterra seems to believe von Wright shared with James. She closes her investigation by quoting a "paradigmatic passage by von Wright to which certainly James could have subscribed" (Calcaterra 1999, 145): "The 'freedom' or 'free will' of a man consists in the *fact* that he acts, one could say. [. . .] To deny that an *agent* is *free* is to commit a contradiction in terms. The 'mystery' of freedom, if there is one, is the 'mystery' of the fact that there *are* agents and actions." (von Wright 1980, 77–78) Indeed, von Wright also clearly rejects the picture – one that he finds speculatively metaphysical – of agency as a mysterious capacity that needs to be fitted into a natural-scientific conception of the world as a causal physical system. Such reductively naturalizing attempts – as well as attempts to respond to them in metaphysical terms – replace the humanist reflection on ethically engaged human freedom by metaphysical mongering that only leads us astray.

I entirely agree with Calcaterra that at this general level James and von Wright can very well be taken to share a humanist approach to the issue of human freedom. Moreover, von Wright is famous for (among many other things) his defense of the irreducibility of intentional explanations of human action (see von Wright 1971, 1974, 1980). There is no way in which intentionality or agency could be reduced to a naturalist-causalist picture of the world provided by, say, physics – or, more recently, by advanced brain research (see also von Wright 1998). To try to do so is to commit a kind of category mistake, to fail not just in the pursuit of truth but at a transcendental level (so to speak, though this is neither von Wright's nor Calcaterra's terminology) by being unable to account for the possibility of pursuing truth about the human condition. On the other hand, when metaphysics is understood in a properly pragmatic sense, I do *not* think that James's approach to the freedom vs. determinism issue, or any other apparently metaphysical topic for that matter, was thoroughly antimetaphysical – and this, indeed, is one of my primary reasons for invoking Calcaterra's comparison between James and von Wright at this point. For the Jamesian pragmatist, issues concerning the free will, the divinity, or fact and value are *metaphysical precisely by being ethical*. At least

---

[47] On James's views on freedom in the tradition of liberalism, see again Marchetti 2019 (briefly commented on in Chapter 1).

we should perceive that James's view is critical of speculative metaphysics in a sense different from von Wright's criticism.

von Wright was a leading representative of analytic philosophy at the peak of its flourishing. His reasons for opposing metaphysical speculation may not have been identical to, say, Wittgenstein's or the Vienna Circle logical empiricists' reasons, but they emerge from the same tradition. According to von Wright, causalist accounts of action and freedom confuse the logic or grammar of the language we use when speaking about agency and intentionality. James's (allegedly) non-metaphysical account of freedom is not logico-analytically grounded in the same sense. He is opposed to metaphysical theories of determinism (vs. indeterminism) insofar as they remain disconnected from ethics, but he *is* fully committed to a metaphysics of freedom insofar as it can be grounded in a pragmatic ethical articulation of our active engagement with the world we live in. This is, arguably, essential in the characterization of the pragmatic method (cf. James 1975 [1907], Lecture III): metaphysical problems must be considered pragmatically, that is, ethically (cf. Pihlström 2009, 2015). For James pursuing truth about the human condition is a thoroughly ethical project – a project in which WB can be legitimately employed – and the notion of freedom seems to be (transcendentally) presupposed by our very engagement in this normative and holistic inquiry.

It seems to me, then, that there is an important difference between Jamesian pragmatism and the kind of antireductionism about agency and intentionality that von Wright represents: the vocabularies or language-games that von Wright distinguishes and whose irreducibility he defends are *not* ontologically relevant in the same way as James's ethically grounded affirmation of freedom. While rational or intentional explanations of actions, referring to reasons instead of causes (von Wright 1998, 19–20, 38–39), can be said to be *epistemically prior* to behavioral and neural explanations, as mental (psychological) states are for us epistemically prior to neural (physiological) states, and while behavior in turn can be regarded as *semantically prior* to mental states, because the contents of mental states are available only through observations of external actions, neural processes within the organism are, von Wright admits, *causally prior* (and hence ontologically prior) to the behavior of the organism. An action, according to von Wright, *is* a bodily movement "*viewed under the aspect of intentionality*" (von Wright 1998, 142; original emphasis); the muscular activity and the intentional action share the same "*robust* reality" while being differently conceptualized within different language-games (von Wright 1998, 34–35; original emphasis).

Thus, there is a sense in which the contingent, factual neural processes giving rise to certain behavior are ontologically fundamental in comparison to anything else in human action and agency. The pluralism of conceptualizations and explanations von Wright espouses is not to be conflated with the genuinely ontological pluralism we find in James and other pragmatists. Unlike the von-Wrightian discourse of freedom, the Jamesian ethical need to admit "real genuine possibilities in the world", as quoted by Calcaterra, is in my view to be taken in a truly metaphysical sense – while remaining subordinated to ethics. Moreover, a key distinction von Wright (1974) relies on in his theory of causation, that is, the one between the *ontological order* of the world and the *conceptual order* of our descriptions of the world – a distinction manifested in his suggestion that while the concept of causation presupposes the concept of agency, causation itself, as operative in nature, is independent of actions and agents (von Wright 1974, 73–74) – is, for a pragmatist, a problematic assumption of metaphysical realism that leads to philosophical difficulties. Both classical pragmatists like James and neopragmatists like Putnam would argue that we can have access only to a world we have conceptualized from the perspectives of our practice-embedded frameworks.[48]

For these reasons, though I find Calcaterra's comparison between James's and von Wright's views on freedom highly illuminating and plausible, I believe we do need to add the qualification that these two great philosophers of human agency are not opposed to reductive naturalizations of agency and to metaphysical examinations of determinism for the same reasons. For the Jamesian pragmatist, it is the ethically engaged approach to metaphysical issues that must take priority over logical analysis, and the distinction between the ontological and the conceptual must accordingly be softened if not entirely abandoned. In a quasi-Kantian sense, theoretical reason can only be guided by practical reason – but in a Jamesian sense, these two are ultimately inseparable.

Logi Gunnarsson's (2020) more recent take on James is interestingly different, because he explicitly emphasizes the role played by our emotional or "passional" decisions in determining philosophical *truths* about matters such as freedom. In this sense, his reading of James is a mirror image to

---

[48] Cf. the brief remarks on Putnam's rejection of the fact/value dichotomy in the beginning of this chapter. For further reflections on von Wright's relation to pragmatism, see again Pihlström 2014b, 2019d.

Calcaterra's. While Calcaterra in my view goes *too antimetaphysical* in associating James's defense of freedom with von Wright's, Gunnarsson fails to take the crucial step to *truly pragmatist* metaphysics by merely emphasizing James's early discussion of the emotional basis of "philosophical truths". Let me explain.

Gunnarsson[49] in my view plausibly begins from the basic Jamesian contention that we have to philosophize as genuine human beings. This is definitely something I have also assumed in this inquiry, and sought to further elucidate. Philosophical theories are individual persons' attempts to live on in the world they find themselves in. We thus always encounter "the whole human being" in a philosophical work. "True philosophy" does not (at least not merely) consist of true theories but primarily of a correct philosophical way of living. For example, again, the question concerning free will (vs. determinism), as well as the meta-level one concerning compatibilism and incompatibilism, cannot be resolved purely theoretically but must be tested in one's life, with not only the intellect but emotions as well playing a crucial role in our evaluation of the potential solutions.

For a Jamesian-inspired pragmatist, it is relatively easy to agree with the main ideas proposed by Gunnarsson. What is more problematic is Gunnarsson's decision to restrict the discussion to the early James and to avoid James's later pragmatism, which, appropriately interpreted and developed, could actually render the basic position Gunnarsson develops even more plausible. His main sources are the essays collected in *The Will to Believe*, many of which were first published in the 1870–1890s, including "The Sentiment of Rationality", "Rationality, Activity and Faith", and "The Dilemma of Determinism" (see again James 1979 [1897]).

Gunnarsson repeatedly speaks about the "truth" of philosophical views. Philosophical theories or propositions ("*Sätze*") are said to be true ("*wahr*") or false; however, a "good philosopher" must also be a "true human being" ("*ein wahrer Mensch*") (Gunnarsson 2020, 19; see also, for example, 50, 79, 147, 218–219), and philosophical "truths" may thus be (partly) practical and emotional (Gunnarsson 2020, 77). These expressions suggest a play with the word "*wahr*", which could in some contexts be translated as "genuine"; in this sense, the German word behaves rather similarly to its English

---

[49] Gunnarsson's (2020) heavy volume on James is an unusual one, because it is set up as a fictional dialogue between two imagined characters, Bill Headstrong and Wilhelm Kornblum, who are planning to write a joint book on James. I will here ignore this frame of the discussion and will treat the views put forward by the two fictional figures as Gunnarsson's own, though there are clearly internal tensions within this position.

equivalent. So far so good. What troubles me is Gunnarsson's choice to resolutely avoid interpreting this in the sense of anything like the "pragmatist conception of truth". The truth the Jamesian "true human being" is seeking when pursuing philosophical truth (and philosophical life) is *not*, according to Gunnarsson, truth in the pragmatist sense – even though something like this was, presumably, James's more mature position.

Pragmatism, as well as other late works of James, is actually an extremely rich source of insights into what it is to be a "true human being" in a philosophical sense – and what it thus means to reach philosophical truths in the full-blown pragmatist sense. Many of the views criticized in *Pragmatism* (e.g., materialism, determinism, Hegelian idealism, theodicies explaining evil away) are arguably *pragmatically false* because they cannot in the end be held by a "true" human being.[50] Such philosophical theories cannot be sincerely held by us if we truthfully inquire into our human condition; this, in effect, could be a transcendental (yet pragmatic) result of our reflection on that condition "from within".

Nevertheless, what Gunnarsson says about the early James is important, and it should be admitted that pragmatism is only one of the potential outcomes of James's early thought (Gunnarsson 2020, 39). As philosophy is contingently embedded in human life, we should avoid reading classics like James teleologically, believing that their early views inevitably lead to their "mature" views. At the meta-level, however, I think James's position changed little: he seems to have maintained from early on that a "true human being" is presented with philosophical questions that need to be answered through that person's life, and that the point of philosophical systems is to answer such questions (Gunnarsson 2020, 25–26). Philosophy thus emerges as something like a vocation for a person living "truly".[51]

When justifying his restriction to the young James, Gunnarsson maintains that the claim that the answers to philosophical questions depend on emotional grounds is independent of the pragmatist theory of truth (Gunnarsson 2020, 47). This may be true, but due to the narrow focus on the early James, the exact sense in which the concept of truth is used remains less than fully developed and slightly obscure. Perhaps Gunnarsson just

---

[50] While I am not here investigating these views in any detail (as my discussion moves primarily at a pragmatic-transcendental meta-level dealing with the conditions for distinguishing between truth and falsity in relation to such philosophical or existential positions), my earlier discussions of, say, Jamesian antitheodicism (e.g., Pihlström 2020a) can, I suppose, be read along these lines.

[51] There is also a kind of melancholy – comparable to the notion of the sick soul in James's *Varieties* – almost inevitably attached to this philosophical life, and deep philosophical truths can be achieved only by going through such a melancholy (Gunnarsson 2020, 33–34, 79–80, 83). It seems to me that most of this is part and parcel of *Pragmatism*, too.

assumes the correspondence theory of truth or a non- or pre-philosophical "ordinary" notion of truth? But then again, James himself maintained in *Pragmatism* and elsewhere that his pragmatist conception of truth was a (pragmatic) way of making sense of the intuitive idea of truth as "agreement" with independent reality (see Chapter 1). It is, in my view, precisely pragmatic truth that can be seen as a relation of "agreement" between what a "true human being" is trying to do and the world that poses them philosophical questions.

Moreover, the idea that the grounds determining the correctness or incorrectness of philosophical theories are practical and emotional rather than purely theoretical (*"nicht rein theoretisch, sondern praktisch bzw. emotional oder empfindungsbezogen"*, Gunnarsson 2020, 48) sounds like a formulation of not only the WB approach but also of pragmatism, although the very distinction between the theoretical and the practical could be questioned. In my view, the pragmatist James, or the Jamesian pragmatist, here takes the further step of interpreting the "theoretical" as always already "practical".

For example, when Gunnarsson (2020, 127–128) suggests that, according to James, life can be worth living only if "pluralistic moralism" is "true" – that is, there is really good and evil in the world – this could be most plausibly understood in the sense of pragmatist truth. Similarly, the claim that optimism is made true by, or depends on, our subjective reactions (Gunnarsson 2020, 152) would be more natural to cash out in explicitly pragmatist terms. Alternatively, this could mean that we merely (epistemologically) use our emotions to test the truth of theories like optimism or materialism (cf. Gunnarsson 2020, 154), which are true or false independently of emotions, but this would be a relatively thin account of the "true human being". At any rate, both "early-Jamesians" and "late-Jamesians" can agree on the need to widen the scope of philosophical reason in truth-seeking from the allegedly merely theoretical area to a practical area taking individual temperament and emotions seriously. For example, the question concerning the truth of materialism cannot be distinguished from the question concerning our being able to live without objective normativity (Gunnarsson 2020, 168); our metaphysical views are thus not independent of our ethical orientation in the world we live in.

In brief, I believe it is problematic to isolate James's later pragmatism from the early writings Gunnarsson focuses on for at least two reasons. First, as I have suggested, the use of "true" and "truth" in the relevant contexts could be claimed to presuppose a pragmatist conception of truth – or to function as an early articulation of that conception – though this is explicitly denied by Gunnarsson. At least a pragmatist interpretation makes better sense of those contexts than, say, a standard realistic one (bearing in mind, however, the suggestion made in Chapter 1 to maintain realism and even correspondence truth within a more inclusive pragmatism). Secondly, more historically, James was, as we know, already in the 1870s deeply influenced by Peirce and the Metaphysical Club, within which pragmatism was emerging, even though the word was first used in print (by James) only in 1898 (see, however, Gunnarsson 2020, 167, 187–189).[52]

Even so, Gunnarsson's account of the young James – both philosophically and historically – *is* highly plausible. It is particularly important to understand James's spiritual crisis (ca. 1870) as a crisis concerning our philosophical search for the truth.[53] It is the pursuit of truth concerning freedom (vs. determinism) and, hence, the very possibility of morality that leads us to the philosophical, and melancholic, questions that brought James to the brink of collapse, and far from being able to resolve such issues by means of the kind of purely theoretical argumentation one encounters in the hundreds of volumes published on the problem of the free will, the Jamesian philosopher needs to face this crisis situation as an entire human being. In a sense, this crisis could also be seen as leading the Jamesian thinker to *critical* philosophy in a quasi-Kantian sense (though this, again, is not suggested by either Gunnarsson or James), because the basic worry concerns the inability of our philosophical use of reason to solve the problems our lives set us (see Gunnarsson 2020, 71).[54]

In the context of offering a painstakingly detailed interpretation of James's argument for incompatibilism (see Gunnarsson 2020, 327–331), illustrating the way in which James's "philosophy of philosophy" employs emotional reactions in the justification of philosophical theories, Gunnarsson argues that philosophical theories are objectively true or false – in a non-pragmatist sense – and the purpose of testing them in

---

[52] On the relation between Peirce and James in the formation of the pragmatist tradition, see Pihlström 2008a, chapter 1. Misak 2013 is one of the best general discussions of the development of pragmatism through these giants' (and their followers') work.

[53] More precisely, Gunnarsson distinguishes three periods in the development of the early James: the crisis phase (from the late 1860s to 1878), the creative phase (1878–1884, during which most of the papers addressing these issues were first written and published), and the reconsideration phase ("*Nacharbeitungsphase*", 1884–1896, when further contributions developing the same ideas, including most famously "The Will to Believe", were written).

[54] A quasi-Kantian aspect of James could also be easily emphasized when it comes to analyzing James's views on the conditions for the possibility ("*Ermöglichungsbedingungen*") of moral integrity and meaningful life (Gunnarsson 2020, 313).

practical life is to find out whether they are true or false; again, no
pragmatist theory of truth, or any other specific theory of truth, is ascribed
to James here (Gunnarsson 2020, 256–262). Emotions and subjective
reactions pertain primarily to the *grounds* ("*Gründe*") of philosophical
truths. Subjective emotions do not simply make such truths true, especially
not in any straightforward causal sense. There is, according to James,
a kind of "congruence" between our subjective contribution and the way
the world is, but this does not compromise the objectivity of philosophical
truth (see, e.g., Gunnarsson 2020, 279).

This discussion seems to oscillate, perhaps deliberately, between
a metaphysical dependence of truth on our subjectivity (on "life-reactions")
and a merely epistemic dependence of our reasons for believing truths on our
subjectivity. The great value of a fully developed pragmatist account of truth is
precisely to run these together, and this is particularly important, I think, in
the WB type of cases concerning, say, freedom – in short, cases that may lead
us to crises of life coloring our entire pursuit of truth. In addition, James's later
pragmatic pluralism is in my view also a development of the early position,
rather than something to be rejected in order to maintain the objectivity of
philosophical truth (cf. Gunnarsson 2020, 289–290).[55]

Gunnarsson not only seeks to motivate a certain reading of James but
also aims at showing that a carefully articulated version of the Jamesian
position is actually correct (for a summary of the metaphilosophical theses
defended, see Gunnarsson 2020, 374–375). Here the notion of truth is
brought onto a metaphilosophical level: "*Wir wollen vor allem die Wahrheit
in James' These ausarbeiten, dass der ganze Mensch über die Wahrheit
philosophischer Theorien entscheidet. Ist diese These richtig?*" (Gunnarsson
2020, 337) Does it follow that the concept of truth can equally well be
applied at the metaphilosophical level to the theses and theories put
forward in Gunnarsson's work – or this book, for that matter? Or is the
choice of the word "*richtig*" here a signal of some uncertainty regarding this
point?[56] Again, a pragmatist conception of truth would offer a smooth way
of handling the matter. Gunnarsson repeatedly reminds us that the pragmatist theory of truth is *false* (see, e.g., Gunnarsson 2020, 408) – whatever

[55] Here it is impossible to comment on any further details of Gunnarsson's interpretation, but a critical
reader might also ask, for instance, what exactly it means to speak of grounds that constitutively
explain ("*konstitutiv erklären*") truths (e.g., Gunnarsson 2020, 284, 297, 335, 360). Is this "truthmaking" (cf. Gunnarsson 2020, 357) in the realist philosopher's sense, or something else? This notion of
explanation (see also Gunnarsson 2020, 352) must presumably be something different from, say,
scientific explanation.
[56] Toward the end of Gunnarsson's volume, both truth and rightness are ascribed to philosophical
theories (e.g., 2020, 343–344).

this exactly means for him. In contrast, I have suggested that the pragmatist conception of truth (suitably interpreted) is itself pragmatically true, enabling us to deepen our understanding of our practices of pursuing the truth.

Gunnarsson's Jamesian project is not only directly relevant to the treatment of the pursuit of truth I have undertaken here but also highly ambitious and bold in its thoroughgoing reflexivity: whatever it means to speak about truth in philosophy, we have to extend this discussion to the philosophical and metaphilosophical truths we pursue in seeking the right kind of attitude to philosophizing in our lives. In this sense, his investigation is really about what it is to be a "true human being". This also means that metaethical theses must be investigated with reference to ethical views and emotions (cf. Gunnarsson 2020, 373). While Gunnarsson does not develop his ideas in these terms, it could be suggested that he ascribes to the early James (and, possibly, to himself) a version of holistic pragmatism: our theoretical and practical, including ethical, beliefs are "in the same boat" and form a "seamless web" tested as a totality in the course of our lives, and feelings of ethical obligation may in some cases legitimately lead to a revision of what seem to be purely factual beliefs about the way the world is. If this is the case, then, despite my disagreement with him concerning pragmatism and truth, his overall position may be regarded as an ally to my appropriation of James.

4.8   Holism, Ethics, and Existential Choices

Let us take stock. It is important to emphasize, again, that holistic pragmatism can be used to articulate and ameliorate processes of inquiry in, for example, general considerations of the normative and the factual (overcoming at least naïve versions of Hume's Guillotine), interdisciplinary studies of various cultural phenomena (beliefs and/or theories within different disciplines forming a single "web"), philosophy of culture and cultural institutions, metaphilosophy (entangling historical interpretations and systematic ideas or arguments), and many other clusters of philosophical issues concerning the human condition and its normative structures. Again, all these are value-embedded, normative inquiries into values and normativity in different areas of human culture. Holistic pragmatism can also be employed to formulate and elaborate on the kind of position we just saw Gunnarsson develop: philosophizing – making commitments to the truth of philosophical ideas, theses, or theories – is a process involving "the whole person", and in assessing the truth of a philosophical view we are in a sense also assessing the "truth" of the person her-/himself maintaining that truth-commitment in her/his belief system (which, of course, in pragmatist terms "translates" into a set of habits of action).

One of the fundamental pragmatist principles (famously due to Peirce) is that one should never "block the road of inquiry". Holistic pragmatism should always keep the path of inquiry open. This entails necessary revisions to the WB idea that James developed. In particular, Peirce's *abduction* is certainly preferable to WB when it comes to scientific inquiries: arriving at a possible explanation or hypothesis, not to be *believed* but to be merely (e.g.) "pursued", taken seriously in the interest of critical testing, does not need a WB-type adoption of the corresponding belief.[57] Generally, James is

---

[57] For a major recent contribution – historically learned and systematically exact – to the theory of abduction in a broadly Peircean spirit, see Niiniluoto 2018. Another question (again not to be settled here) is whether the Peircean "hope" that scientific questions can be rationally answered (cf. Hookway 2000, as well as the critical discussion in Cooke 2006) could be reinterpreted as a kind of WB; this presumably depends on how exactly the distinction between belief and (mere) hope is construed. On Peirce and WB, see also Gavin 1980, as well as Hookway 2000, 13–14. Incidentally, it may be pointed out that Hookway is one of the few commentators on Peirce and James to have also significantly contributed to the discussion of transcendental arguments (see his essay in Stern 1999, as well as Chapter 3). I have earlier (Pihlström 1998) speculated with the idea that the Jamesian WB and the pragmatized conception of transcendental argumentation (as very briefly elaborated on in Chapter 3) share at least one important point of departure: both seek to understand our entitlement to philosophical or existential commitments from within a practice (e.g., inquiry or a religious form of life) made possible by those commitments. Here I cannot develop this analogy further; I must admit it remains speculative and perhaps merely intuitive. Let me add a brief comment, though. We may suggest that the kinds of reasons we may have for our beliefs within our various pragmatic frameworks come in different types: for example, our pragmatic reasons for embracing (or continuing to maintain) a religious belief may be based on a Jamesian-like "passional" WB argument, but pragmatic reasons may also be based on (quasi-)transcendental conditions we find necessary for the functioning of our practices. Arguments seeking to understand the conditions for the possibility of things we take for granted in our epistemic, ethical, and other practices are standardly referred to as transcendental arguments (cf. Chapter 3), and there are, indeed, few commentators apart from Hookway who have fully appreciated the significance of both transcendental and WB arguments in their work. In a holistic assessment of the practices of providing and defending pragmatic reasons for our beliefs, we may draw attention to the relation between, and the possible entanglement of, pragmatic reasons of these two types, viz., the WB type and the pragmatic-transcendental type. The kind of holistic pragmatic analysis I have undertaken in this chapter, drawing inspiration from White, is useful to highlight this point. What such an analysis may yield is the following: when you are already in a situation in which you have "genuine options" in James's sense, you are, according to James, entitled to employ a WB argument in order to arrive at (or stick to) a hypothesis that cannot be settled by purely intellectual means; however, in order to ascertain that you indeed *are* in such a situation – that you have the genuine options you do have and that the WB strategy is thus at your disposal – it may be suggested that you need to engage in a transcendental consideration of what necessary conditions make it possible for you to be, or remain, committed to your practices of thought, inquiry, and belief-fixation in the first place. Accordingly, the employment of Jamesian WB may depend on the results of a prior transcendental argument (or at least transcendental reflection or consideration, if not strictly speaking an argument); conversely, however, you might also need to resort to a WB argument in a situation in which your transcendental argument does not seem to enjoy the apodictic certainty that Kant himself, the father of transcendental arguments, required such arguments to have.

not at his best when it comes to the philosophy of science; pragmatist philosophy of science or theory of inquiry is more systematically developed by Peirce and Dewey (and, of course, White). Yet, in "existential" and *weltanschaulichen* matters James certainly cannot be overlooked. In order to distinguish WB from the pragmatist theory of inquiry and philosophy of science, it might have been better for James not to speak of "hypotheses" at all but of (holistic) life options, or perhaps even (as we have done above) vocations and changes of habit, as well as (as he did in *Pragmatism*) individual temperaments.

So what should we now say about moral realism, with which we started this inquiry, or more generally about normative realism? From a pragmatist perspective, there is a certain kind of *plurality* inherent in our realisms themselves: scientific realism, commonsense realism, theological realism, and moral realism (among many others) all need to be explored in their relevant contexts (cf. Pihlström 2020a). Different human practices yield different pragmatic realisms. Value realism could be thought of in terms of an analogy to realism in art and literature (rather than science). It amounts to understanding the (in Putnam's words quoted in the beginning of this chapter, "messy") "reality" of human life, especially its violations of what we find valuable (e.g., human suffering, evil, humiliation, non-acknowledgment), as real phenomena of the human life-world and its practices. Insofar as holistic pragmatism enables us to articulate a plausible version of such realism, we may again say that it also provides a certain kind of re-enchantment, or at least a disenchantment of the scientistic project of thoroughgoing disenchantment.

Someone might ask whether there can be anything like *ethical progress* according to holistically formulated pragmatic moral or normative realism. Does the ethics–science continuum in the sense of holistic pragmatism entail that insofar as there is scientific progress there is also ethical progress? Critical self-renewal is certainly a task fundamentally important in ethics, just as it is in science. Ethics and metaethics need to be pragmatically (not essentialistically) distinguished, however. We may say that James's WB functions at a metaethical level (e.g., as a response to the question whether we are living in a "moral or immoral" universe), though it is indistinguishable from moral reflection itself. As Gunnarsson (2020) and many others rightly emphasize, James's leading question is whether morality makes sense at all – as a human practice or perspective on reality – or whether it is an illusion. In "first-order" ethical reflection or moral inquiry James is, again, a holistic pragmatist, with the "cries of the wounded" functioning as ethical "evidence" used in testing ethical "hypotheses". On the other hand, the religiously believing (or potentially believing) subject of James's WB can be compared to the Kierkegaardian or Sartrean existential subject making a risky, or even absurd, "leap" toward a religious, ethical, or political view and/or action.[58]

Arguably, then, James's basic message is not only holistically pragmatist but also *existentialist*: we are ultimately ourselves responsible for the kind of (holistic) doxastic life we choose to lead – without any higher court of appeal – and we are responsible for cultivating whatever epistemic and/or ethical virtues (or vices) we may find relevant to such a life. There is no firmer guarantee or any metaphysically secure ground for such existential responsibility – nothing over and above our lives themselves.[59] This call to responsible life in general could itself be seen as a (meta-level) vocation. It is only within such overall responsibility that we can make sincere vocational choices, or any other choices for that matter. Accordingly, pragmatism and existentialism are close philosophical relatives here – though this connection needs further exploration. In any event, James's WB is clearly "more existential" than White's holism, which remains relatively epistemology-centered – central in the epistemology of ethics (metaethics) but perhaps not as strongly as WB in existential moral reflection itself. It is in this sense, again, that the dis-disenchantment available *via* WB is also more thoroughgoing than White's.

Finally, any existentialism worthy of the name should find reflexivity a major issue (as indicated above). Can, thus, WB be *self-applied*? Could we apply the WB strategy to adopting the WB strategy as our habit of belief-fixation (regarding specific existential "genuine options")? Is this a vicious circle? Or is it, rather, a self-strengthening one? A comparison to the problem of freedom again invites itself. The freedom of the will (as analyzed by von Wright and Calcaterra; see above) is, arguably, needed as a background assumption of WB, but our commitment to freedom may itself need WB, as suggested in "The Dilemma of Determinism" by James. Is there in the end any other coherent defense of the WB method than a self-applied WB-based adoption of the method (insofar as employing it *is* a "genuine option" for us in the first place)? Clearly, no evidence can fully settle the legitimacy of WB – or our commitment to finding ourselves free.[60]

---

[58] For an existentialist reading of the WB argument, see again Putnam 1992; cf. Putnam and Putnam 2017.

[59] Compare this to Wittgenstein's comment on language-games just being there, "like our life".

[60] A question that will still remain open even at the end of the present inquiry, is, however, whether WB in the end presupposes too strong doxastic voluntarism (either at the "first-order" level or the meta-level). Excessive voluntarism might render dis-disenchantment problematic to begin with. However, even when inquiring into this issue we need holistic pragmatism, reflexivity, and possibly WB itself.

Reflexivity is vitally important for James at different levels. WB needs to be defended by means of WB; pragmatism works pragmatically, or is (only) pragmatically true; there is a pragmatic plurality of pluralisms available (cf. Chapter 2, as well as Pihlström 2013); and we may be "blind" to our own "instinctive blindness" to others' experiences of significance and value.[61] We may be, or become, deaf to our own claim to listen to the cries of the wounded. This is all comparable to the role played by reflexivity in pragmatism generally. We may adopt pragmatism for pragmatic reasons, because it "works" in our philosophical practices as the commitment to reflexively reflect on the roles played by reflexivity in our ethical-cum-epistemic lives. Holistic evaluation, furthermore, focuses on how holistic pragmatism itself "works" as an element of our entire system of beliefs. A theory of re-enchantment itself contributes to the process of *Entzauberung entzaubern*. Having vocations, or being open to novel vocations, may itself be a vocation. And so forth.

The Jamesian pragmatist who has digested the outcome of Chapter 3 and is prepared to interpret their pragmatism in terms of the Kantian vocabulary of transcendental philosophy may easily view this reflexivity as analogous to the transcendental reflexivity of human reason in Kant: we need a critique of reason guided and conducted by nothing else than reason itself. Moreover, in its guiding role our reason is never merely neutral instrumental reason but always already ethically oriented. Hence the fundamental significance of sincerity and truthfulness in the very articulation of pragmatism. In this sense, the pragmatist analysis of the WB strategy and holism in this chapter has implicitly continued the transcendental reconceptualization of pragmatism, and if my admittedly complex elaboration is on the right track, the reflexivity at work here lends holistic support to the entire system of transcendental pragmatism accommodating WB, holism, and a Jamesian account of individual sincerity in our practices of pursuing the truth.

---

[61] In terms of James's 1899 essay, "On a Certain Blindness in Human Beings" (James 1962 [1899]), analyzed in Chapters 2 and 3.

CHAPTER 5

How Is Normativity Possible?
A Holistic-Pragmatist Perspective

The pursuit of truth (and truthfulness), as well as our personal existential responses to both ethical and epistemic challenges of human life analyzed in the previous chapters, unavoidably occur within a normative context of both individual and social commitments and principles. So far I have more or less taken for granted the irreducible normativity of our human practices in my pragmatist investigation of the practice-embeddedness of philosophical notions such as truth, sincerity, and belief. It is now time to focus on the nature of normativity itself.

The philosophical question concerning the very possibility of normativity captures an essential puzzlement about what it is or means to be human – inherited into our contemporary discussions all the way from Plato's and/or Socrates's criticism of Thrasymachus in *The Republic*[1] – and in my view it does so more deeply than, for example, the question concerning the nature of consciousness. The problem is as old as the Greeks' distinction between *fysis* and *nomos*; however, it is not solved by merely claiming that normativity is based on, or arises from, human convention, social negotiation, or something similar. That is merely to restate the issue. The problem is that such conventional practices already presuppose a normative context. We are thus dealing with a problem of infinite regress or circularity, while on the other hand we may also ask – analogously to the issues of reflexivity we just encountered in the Jamesian WB context in Chapter 4 – whether the relevant kind of circularity is vicious or perhaps rather beneficial. In fact, recognizing its *inevitability* is part of my pragmatist reaction to our issue in this chapter. In a sense, the question about the possibility of normativity may have no "solution" at all; what needs to be done is learning to live with it.

This topic is particularly important for the pragmatist, because, as we have seen, pragmatist accounts of truth, truth-seeking, belief, and inquiry

---

[1] See Plato, *The Republic*, Book I.

144

tend to invoke the normativity of our practices of pursuing the truth. It is through such a pragmatist conception (or, perhaps rather, assumption) of irreducible normativity that we are naturally led (again) to a transcendental way of asking the question about the conditions for the possibility of the kind of normativity that holistically needs to be presupposed in order to make sense of any of our practices. The pragmatist simply cannot get rid of the philosophical issue of normativity – also because some way must be discovered to account for the possibility of normativity that does not sacrifice the general (non-reductive) naturalism that pragmatism, even transcendental pragmatism, is committed to.

5.1 Racism, Sexism, and Misogyny

Before investigating how holistic pragmatism views the relation between the normative and the natural, I will introduce the fundamental (transcendental) issue of this chapter by means of a case study on the normativity vs. naturalism issue hopefully making my later pragmatist treatment of these concepts sufficiently concrete.

In a chapter of her book, *The Monarchy of Fear: A Philosopher Looks at Our Political Crisis* (2018), aptly titled, "A Toxic Brew: Sexism and Misogyny", Martha Nussbaum revisits the theme of political emotions, which she has examined in a series of publications spanning several decades. One of her novel ideas is that *fear* – a humanly natural and often also highly useful emotion – makes many other emotions, such as anger and envy, "toxic" in our political life. It has of course been pointed out by many others that fear is easily used by political populists – and has indeed been in the past, as we know from cases like the rise of Fascism and Nazism in the 1920s and 1930s – but Nussbaum analyzes this phenomenon in a contemporary political context with her characteristic sharpness and philosophical perceptivity.[2]

She distinguishes three different – often entangled and mutually reinforcing – dynamics of hostility toward women, all primarily driven by fear but in different ways. First, the "fear-blame" dynamic seeks to put women back in "their place", blaming them for taking "our" (male) possessions (such as leadership roles). Secondly, "fear-disgust" focuses on female corporeality and sexuality, while, thirdly, "fear-envy" is based on the fact that women

---

[2] While it must be hard to write with respect and acknowledgment about people – such as Trump – who say horrific things about other people, Nussbaum sincerely tries to understand the emotional forces that drive Trump supporters. Fear, she argues, plays a fundamental role here, typically in conjunction with other emotions.

are "enjoying unparalleled success" in many spheres of life, in both the United States and elsewhere. (Nussbaum 2018, 169) In addition to discussing each of these three "dynamics" in detail,[3] Nussbaum provides us with accurate conceptual observations, especially regarding the distinction between sexism and misogyny. While sexism, she maintains, can be understood simply as a set of beliefs, often held with considerable uneasiness and uncertainty, about women's inferiority to men – of their being naturally "less fit for a variety of important functions", including employment and political ones – misogyny is "an enforcement mechanism, a set of behaviors designed to keep women in their place", in short, a "determined enforcement of gender privilege" and a "determination to protect entrenched interests". (Nussbaum 2018, 172, 177) It is hardly inaccurate to summarize the distinction by saying that sexism is a *theoretical* (ideological) attitude while misogyny represents the more *practical* determination to do something about certain social developments.[4]

Misogyny is, Nussbaum reminds us, often taken to be justified by sexism, even though sexism has little evidence to back it up (Nussbaum 2018, 177).[5] Following John Stuart Mill, she points out that there is a tension between sexism and misogyny: if women really *are* inferior, then there is hardly any need to go into much trouble in keeping them "out" (Nussbaum 2018, 174). Therefore, using sexist beliefs in support of misogyny may be problematic for misogynists themselves, and hence they typically do not rely on such beliefs too much. This is an important

[3] One of the truly important points Nussbaum (2018, 182–186) makes in discussing the "fear-blame" dynamics is that the attempt to keep women "in their place" often goes together with the claim that the more women pursue independence and career, the less they care for home and children, which allegedly results in social problems. This response, she argues, obscures our attention to real social problems such as poverty and workplace inflexibility. It is these latter problems, instead of women's independent career pursuits, that often lead to children suffering from the lack of sufficient parental care, for instance. She also offers an interesting analysis of "fear-disgust" (Nussbaum 2018, 193–196), reminding us that Trump's disgraceful comments on women "appeal above all to disgust". The main point here seems to be that the kind of misogyny related to disgust, or fear-disgust, is ultimately based on the fear of *death* and "mortal embodiment". This kind of fear arises from the idea that women (in some sense different from men) are not just life-givers but "dirt and death". In what sense exactly are women closer to death than men? Is it simply because they are closer to birth, or is it perhaps because this closeness to birth, actual or potential, somehow brings them closer to the natural cycles of bodily and vulnerable human life generally? This is only one example of the intriguing issues Nussbaum's discussion raises. For the significance of the problems of death and mortality in pragmatism, see Pihlström 2016.

[4] In this context, Nussbaum cites Kate Manne's highly relevant discussion of misogynist logic in *Down Girl* (Manne 2017).

[5] Nussbaum also maintains, accurately as far as I can judge, that Trump and Trumpists can be much better described as misogynists rather than sexists – and so can, unfortunately, Rousseau (see Nussbaum 2018, 177–178, 181). She usefully notes that misogyny has some leftist history as well; it is by no means a mere right-wing, nor a mere working-class, phenomenon.

observation, because in popular discussion sexism and misogyny are often confused. Indeed, sexism can be *refuted* by evidence – and has been. The real problem is different: it is the determination by a sufficient number of men to maintain the "old order" – a "purely negative" strategy that is predominantly, she argues, driven by fear (Nussbaum 2018, 176–179).

Why have I paraphrased Nussbaum's discussion about sexism and misogyny, especially as there is nothing that I particularly disagree about in her findings? I consider the analysis compelling and highly informative. The reason for raising the issues here is that, at a more philosophical level, I still wonder how exactly we should analyze the relation between sexism and misogyny – and this worry is profoundly related to both the (obvious) pragmatist habit of questioning any sharp dichotomies between the theoretical and the practical and to the upcoming discussion of recognition and normativity later in this chapter. I do find Nussbaum's distinction important, but let me pose the following question, based on the idea that sexism is the theoretical counterpart of the practical (action-related, discriminatory) attitude of misogyny.

Suppose sexism were *not* refuted by evidence but were, rather, supported by evidence (*horribile dictu*). Or suppose, more strongly, that sexism, in some standard formulation, were true (assuming it makes sense to suppose a view like that can be true, or can be claimed to be true even for the sake of argument). If sexism can, even in principle, be used to justify misogyny, and if it in a way even makes sense, in some sense of "makes sense", for some sexist-misogynist men to try to do so, would the truth of sexism then really justify misogynist attitudes and practices? I am posing a kind of *modal* (though of course also moral) question here. If we so much as admit that there is a *possible* justificatory relation between sexism and misogyny (or at least gender-based discrimination), how should we react to such discrimination in a possible world in which sexism *were* true or justified?

Consider, in comparison, *racism*. I recall a dinner conversation at a conference many years ago with a world-famous philosopher (I am not going to tell you who he is, but yes, it's a "he"). If I recall it correctly, this person said that *if* racism were (theoretically, objectively) true (which of course he didn't believe to be the case), *then* racially discriminatory practices could be ethically and politically justified. I was, and I still am, convinced that there must be something very seriously wrong in this argument, and I hope the pragmatist analysis of normativity and recognition I will engage in later in this chapter might help us settle the case. To anticipate, it could be suggested that the rejection of racism – and the related affirmation of the fundamental equality of human beings – is such a key assumption in our argumentation for *anything* whatsoever, and in any sincere pursuit of truth possible for us within what we recognize as a shared human form of life, that it makes little sense to rationally consider how we ought to view racially discriminatory practices in the imagined case that racism were true. If we actually did believe in the truth of racism, or even in its being justified or justifiable by evidence, we would step outside the normative sphere of argumentation based on an equal recognition of all human beings as potential partners in dialogue, conversation, and argumentation. No normatively grounded claim about the inferiority of "lower races" would be *available* to us, if we were committed to the truth of racism, because honoring normativity already presupposes honoring something like *human dignity* as a structural feature of the form(s) of life within which (only) it is possible to argue and inquire at all.[6]

I would thus be willing to suggest, at least tentatively, that the rejection of racism is comparable to a *transcendental condition* for the possibility of ethically appropriate discourse in general, including any discourse of, or inquiry into, racism and anti-racism (cf. Chapter 3). We cannot engage in any argumentative conversation about anything whatsoever, including racism and its alternatives, if we endorse racism, however "theoretically". (Would it be possible to be a "merely theoretical" racist? Does this even make sense?) Our subscribing to racism would disqualify us from making any judgment about the justifiability or unjustifiability of racially discriminatory practices, or any other practices for that matter. The norms of inquiry that need to be recognized for us to be able to seriously argue for anything already preclude racism as a serious candidate of approval.[7] Our recognizing such norms presupposing non-racism – and non-sexism – cannot itself depend on empirical evidence; nor can it depend on mere psychological acts of recognizing (see below). It is possible only in a normative context already pregnant with such irreducible normative structures as our commitment to human equality and dignity. There is an analogy to this argument available in the area of sexism and misogyny. We might say that at the quasi-transcendental level of constitutive norms of inquiry, our being committed to the truth of sexism would disqualify us from the practices of justifying, or standing in any normatively placed attitude to, anything whatsoever, including misogynist practices themselves.

---

[6] There is, perhaps, a structural analogy here to the argument by means of which Putnam (1981, chapter 1) once tried to show that we cannot possibly be "brains in a vat": if we were, we could not refer to brains and vats, or anything else for that matter, given the way reference functions (according to his theory). Paradoxically, what I am suggesting comes close to the claim that if racism were true, we could not (sincerely) be racists, given the way normativity functions in our practices of maintaining any genuinely held beliefs about the world.

[7] In the Jamesian terms of Chapter 4, racism cannot be a "genuine option" for us – nor, however, a view we could choose to endorse on the basis of evidence.

The question I am trying to raise is ultimately a question about the modal status of our denial of views such as sexism and racism. Are we, when defending, say, anti-sexism, just dealing with beliefs concerning contingent matters of fact that could be otherwise but fortunately aren't – that is, facts about there being no empirically justifiable factual differences in what women and men are capable of, for example, in terms of intellectual or professional achievements? Or are we dealing with a more fundamental (even transcendental, in a pragmatically "naturalized" sense) principle according to which the equality between women and men (and other genders), just as the equality between members of the human species with different skin colors or different ethnic and cultural backgrounds, is, *for us*,[8] such a basic starting point for any discussion or argument concerning anything whatsoever, including the relations between women and men, that there is no way *we* (from within the cultural context in which we are investigating these matters from within our norms of inquiry and argument) could really conceive the matters to be otherwise? If the latter, then we might even say that the opposition between sexism and its denial is not an opposition between different sets of empirical beliefs concerning contingent factual matters but an opposition between profoundly different frameworks for thinking about human life in general. And if this is the case, then our commitment to rejecting sexism may be much deeper than a mere empirical theory-choice based on the strongest available evidence. It could be closer to an existential – or essentially pragmatic – choice between different holistic frameworks enabling us to evaluate any empirical evidence, or any considerations regarding the justification of our beliefs and practices. It is *constitutive* of the normative framework we must already presuppose in order to engage in any debate over sexism and racism.[9]

---

[8] A lot depends on this "us", on who "we" are. In my vocabulary, transcendental inquiry is historicized and practice-embedded (cf. Chapter 3, as well as, e.g., Pihlström 2003); thus, it is compatible with what I am suggesting that anti-sexism and anti-racism did not *always* define our norms of inquiry, even if they must do so for us now (and we are responsible for being committed to *this*). A related issue is whether this "we" should include non-human beings: could specism be as problematic as racism or sexism? I do *not* think so – and I will (again) get back to the significance of a certain kind of pragmatist humanism in due course.

[9] It is compatible with this transcendentally pragmatic commitment to anti-racism and anti-sexism as constitutive of our practices of inquiry to continue to self-critically inquire into the various implicit tendencies to racism and sexism that our lives and practices may manifest. Such a critical inquiry is analogous to the Kantian investigation of the (unavoidable) transcendental illusions of reason. When suggesting that racism and sexism should be rejected for transcendental-constitutive reasons, I am not suggesting that it would be easy to get rid of them. On the contrary, exorcizing these illusions of thought (and action) requires the heavy artillery of Kantian (yet pragmatic) transcendental critique (without neglecting, of course, the significance of first-order empirical research and political debate on these matters).

Our commitment to avoiding sexism and racism is, then, a fundamentally normative matter concerning the choice of frameworks (e.g., sexism vs. feminism) through which we ought to view our lives with other human beings, rather than a purely naturalistic issue about what the world, independently of human conceptualization and categorization, is like. I would like to suggest that emphasizing the emotional level of fear – in combination with such emotions as disgust – in Nussbaum's way might bring us too close to naturalizing such normativity and thus slightly eclipse the crucial sense in which we are dealing with a problem concerning the thoroughly normative holistic frameworks we operate in when examining matters like this.[10]

Note, finally, that my suggestion does not entail, absurdly, that everyone who engages or has ever engaged in ethical (or generally normative) discussion, such as the great moral philosophers of the past, would necessarily be non-sexists and non-racists. Indeed, many of them have in fact been both sexists and racists. What I am defending is a transcendental consideration regarding *our* commitment to the normative sphere we operate within and have a responsibility to maintain and further develop. It amounts to the meta-level proposal that *we* cannot continue moral discussion about anything, including sexism and racism, unless we are sincerely committed to steering clear from sexism and racism. Maintaining this stance requires constant pragmatic and critical vigilance – it is unending, as the Kantian critique of reason is.

It has taken centuries of serious thinking and conceptual discovery for us to get to this point – creative "redescriptions" and new "vocabularies" to put it in Rorty's (1989) terms – and certainly we will need to open up further normative contexts in order to inquire into these developments. Moreover, these historical developments are themselves normative all the way down (in a sense not, I think, adequately appreciated by Rorty,[11] who ultimately seems to reduce the relations of our language-games or "vocabularies" to the flatly causal level): it is not without normative reasons that people have gradually come to think that women (among others) have

---

[10] This could, furthermore, be something that a *pragmatist* feminist might suggest – or a *quasi-transcendental* feminist, for that matter. I can also foresee the criticism that such a view might seem to mystify both sexism and feminism and that there would then be a price to be paid for the deeper modal level at which the matter is considered. The sexism issue would then in a sense be placed beyond reasonable empirically based criticism (and so would the racism issue, for that matter). Perhaps we should not want to go that far, even if we want to avoid viewing the choice between sexism and its denial as a mere empirical issue, either. This, I think, is a genuinely philosophical issue to be explored, entangled with the problem of normativity we will further discuss in this chapter.

[11] Again, see the brief critical discussion of Rorty in Chapter 1.

rights, even though such changes in our ways of thinking are of course historically contingent. But those reasons are not being simply tested along with empirical beliefs – at least not by us. Rather, for us today, they constitute the framework within which test our beliefs. Insofar as they are "tested", as any beliefs and convictions must always be, according to a critical pragmatic fallibilist, they are tested, and further developed, in the holistic sense of inquiry sketched in White's holistic pragmatist terms, as discussed in the previous chapter (and to be returned to in a moment). Of course there are also all kinds of empirical beliefs, including scientific ones, entangled with the normative beliefs here – but the very point of holistic pragmatism is that we are pragmatically evaluating this totality as a whole.

5.2   Transcendental Inquiry and the Negative Method

The case study inspired by Nussbaum's considerations should make us receptive to the idea that a normative context seems to be already presupposed in attempts (at least any sincere attempts) to account for the nature and possibility of normativity. We should therefore begin our more theoretical reflections on normativity in the context of holistic pragmatism from the conviction that we need to develop a genuinely transcendental inquiry into normativity. Such inquiries include, in my relaxed pragmatic sense (cf. Chapter 3), not only Kant's theory of the categories of the understanding and the moral law[12] but also classical pragmatists' like Peirce's and James's views on habits of action, human practices, and constructive purposive activities, as well as the later Wittgenstein's philosophy of language-games, forms of life, and rule-following.[13] These transcendental yet pragmatic conceptions of normativity are to be distinguished from non-transcendental *metaphysical* theories[14] of the grounds of normativity based on ideas such as

---

[12] Indeed, normativity is at the core of Kant's projects both in theoretical and in practical philosophy; cf. also Chapter 3.

[13] I am not including Hegel into this camp, as I believe the transcendental philosopher of normativity should follow Kant rather than Hegel, but I will comment on the concept of recognition, a concept with a strongly Hegelian history, in what follows. While I won't be able to discuss their work in this chapter, my approach comes closer to the broadly Kantian analysis of the "sources of normativity" by Korsgaard (1996) than, say, Taylor's (1995 [1992]) more Hegelian position. (For my brief reading of Korsgaard's project and her notion of practical identity, see Pihlström 2005, chapter 3.) On the other hand, Taylor's (1989) notion of "strong evaluation" is not far away from the idea of the transcendental constitution of irreducible normativity.

[14] But keep in mind that transcendental philosophy, including transcendental idealism, need not be non-metaphysical but can be put in the service of pragmatist metaphysics (see Chapter 3 and especially Pihlström 2009).

emergence, Peircean continuity ("synechism"), and naturalizing reductions, all of which seem to try to account for normativity from an "external" rather than reflexively "internal" perspective (but cf. Pihlström 2010b). In brief, a transcendental philosophy of normativity seeks to understand and further articulate our commitment to normativity from within a framework (practice, form of life) already defined by such a commitment. It may thus seek to offer a transcendental "deduction" in the Kantian sense of rendering our commitment to norms *legitimate*[15] – rather than a scientific or empirical explanation of how or why the norms we do commit to have arisen.

For the same reason, transcendental investigations of normativity also need to be distinguished from the mainstream approaches of social ontology. A key concept often employed in social ontology that we will, however, examine in some more detail in this context is *recognition*. I think of contemporary recognition theory as lying somewhere between transcendental and non-transcendental approaches to normativity. While recognition is still *contingent* in a way a fully transcendental ground of normativity cannot be (or so I will argue), it can be claimed to be *constitutive* of social facts and institutions, or even human personhood. From the perspective of the present inquiry, an essential question is whether the relevant kind of constitutivity is metaphysical in a non-transcendental sense or transcendental in a (quasi-)Kantian sense. I am not going to return to Kant's own views here any more (cf. again Chapter 3, however), but we should recall the idea, strongly albeit somewhat implicitly present in the First Critique, that the categories of the understanding are constitutive of all humanly possible experience and its objects by providing *normative requirements for what it is to be an object for us*. I will try to explain why I am not convinced that the kind of normativity that recognition brings to our social world could operate at the same transcendentally constitutive level.[16]

---

[15] The analogy, of course, is to the *de jure* question Kant (1990 [1781/1787]) poses in his transcendental deduction of the categories of the understanding.

[16] As an approximation of our main issues in this chapter, it might be noted that the United Nations Declaration of Human Rights mentions, in §6, the right to recognition before the law – something comparable to what Hannah Arendt called "the right to have rights" (cf. Bernstein 2018). Such rights, I will argue, cannot be the *source* of normativity, as they are only possible in a context that is already normatively structured. These fundamental philosophical issues become strikingly practical as soon as one notes that, for example, the situation of former Isis women and children at refugee camps or of the Guantanamo prisoners can be seen as a state of "rightlessness": these unfortunate people, for various reasons (for which they are not innocent), have ended up in circumstances in which they do not seem to be recognized by any normative system, or to have even the right to have (e.g., legal) rights. For a very important contribution to the relation between rights and recognition (especially in the context of race issues), see Darby 2009.

I have elsewhere recommended, especially to pragmatists, a *negative method* for various philosophical purposes of pragmatically elucidating what certain concepts mean for us in our lives (cf., e.g., Pihlström 2014a); in the present case, such a method would urge us to take a serious look at various (actual and possible) violations, eliminations, or reductions of normativity in order to understand and appreciate what normativity (positively) is. These may include, for instance, reductionisms of various stripes (e.g., attempts to reduce humanly distinctive normativity to, say, brain activity or evolutionary processes, or both);[17] populist politicians' (e.g., again, Trump's) tendency to step out of normative contracts in international relations, preferring something like a Thrasymachian politics of force; or, to take a timely local example, a Finnish MP's comparing (in 2019) Israel (an internationally recognized state, however problematic) to Isis (a generally non-recognized terrorist network). I find it a horrible mistake, especially for someone in a politically powerful position, to confuse or even overhastily compare states (however cruel), with their in principle (prima facie) legitimate normative structures, to (for instance) criminal terrorist groups that enjoy no normative legitimacy whatsoever. This is a serious misunderstanding of what is distinctive in the human form of life, because to be human is to live in a normative "space of reasons" that cannot be simply replaced by non-normative structures, even by structures manifestly performing similar actions.[18]

For the same reason, human dignity cannot be grounded in recognition, or any other contingent attitudes, and morality cannot be reduced to brain activity, for instance. The attempt to base "nice" and positive humanly natural emotions such as empathy on our evolutionary history and the development of our brain, and the further attempt to build an ethical theory on these grounds, are unfortunately examples of a similar reductionist tendency that is at work in, say, populists' campaign of deconstructing international norm structures. A philosophical analysis of normativity is thus more widely relevant than it might initially appear. Its significance

---

[17] Something like this may also seem to take place, for instance, in the attempts to ground morality in the humanly natural tendency to feel social emotions like empathy. For a criticism of empathy-based moral philosophy (with both historical and contemporary discussions), see Pihlström and Kivistö 2021. Analogous criticism should be directed at attempts to reduce political normativity to something non-political; the autonomy of the political – and more generally normative – sphere is to be acknowledged. For example, when radically right-wing "ethno-nationalist" populists emphasize the genetic similarity among those belonging to an *ethnos* (e.g., the Finns), they are reducing the normative (nationality) to the natural (genes). But so are those friendlier people who emphasize empathy – in contrast to, say, duty – as a foundation for ethical and political virtue.

[18] On the other hand, there are obviously much more extreme cases, especially Nazism, where this will not hold (cf. below).

ranges from daily phenomena of interpersonal encounters to extremely complex political processes, and beyond.

A "negative" investigation of normativity involves, moreover, a *self-criticism* of our normative form of life analogous (again) to Kant's analysis of the illegitimate transgressions of human reason manifested in the transcendental illusions he analyzes in the Transcendental Dialectic of the First Critique. For example, what I am calling "naturalizing reductions" of normativity can be readily compared to such illusions. There may even seem to be a kind of unavoidability inherent in them comparable to the unavoidability of transcendental illusion: it might seem that norms just *have to* be grounded in natural facts, even though in a sense they *cannot* be so grounded, more or less as it might in the Kantian context seem to us (i.e., our human reason) that, for instance, the world as a totality must have spatio-temporal limits while at the same time it cannot have such limits.[19] Naturalizing reductions (in a broad sense) thus tend to replace the philosophical (transcendental) question about the very possibility of normativity by an empirical and/or causal explanatory question about the emergence and development of normativity, and while there is of course nothing wrong with the latter kind of question as such, the replacement tendency leads us seriously astray – or so I will argue. It leads us astray in a way analogous to the problem I identified in Nussbaum's analysis of the relation between sexism and misogyny. The pragmatist, in particular, ought to appreciate the relevance of empirical research to philosophical and conceptual issues, while avoiding the reduction of the transcendental to the empirical.

The investigation of the possibility of normativity in the remainder of this chapter thus hopefully further articulates what kind of transcendental reflection is available to the pragmatist seeking to understand the commitments defining and structuring our practices of truth-seeking and personal existential commitments "from within".

5.3 "Human Nature": Normativity as a Philosophical-Anthropological Issue

The issue we are exploring goes back to the problem of "human nature", or *philosophical anthropology*.[20] In terms of Heikki Kannisto's (1984) highly

---

[19] Clearly, no detailed interpretation of Kant's investigation of the antinomies of reason is possible here.
[20] Cf. Kannisto 1984; Pihlström 2003, 2016; as well as, for an indication of the current recovery of philosophical anthropology, especially in relation to debates over various forms of naturalism, Honenberger 2016.

useful fourfold classification of the "ideal types" of philosophical conceptions of humanity, we may (in a simplified way) pose our basic question in
this form: do we as human beings belong to an objective, autonomous,
cosmic normative order (*essentialism*), are we placed outside or living
without any such order (*naturalism, existentialism*), or are we creators of
our own cultural normative order(s) (*culturalism*)? How, moreover, can we
decide between these alternatives?

Following Kannisto's terminology, we may say that reductive naturalism "factualizes" any normative order we might take ourselves to be
inhabiting by reducing the classical essentialists' (e.g., Aristotle's) postulation of cosmic teleological normativity into mere nature, that is, contingent and fully natural matters of fact, and thereby moves human beings out
of any distinctive normative space of reasons to the realm of natural law,
which no longer provides us with a fixed essence but merely a contingent
matter-of-factual nature. Such naturalism may at least in its reductive
forms be argued to be problematic precisely because of its inability to
account for genuine normativity, but on the other hand it has at least since
the Enlightenment plausibly questioned the classical essentialist postulation of Platonic or Aristotelian cosmic normativity beyond our concrete
and contingent human activities (as well as Christian or other theological
variants thereof).[21] In contrast to both naturalism and essentialism, culturalism may be argued to be a more plausible way of accounting for
normativity: our normative sphere is humanly constructed; it is, for us,
fully real, but it does not emanate from any Platonic or other transcendent
sources beyond our human forms of life themselves.[22] Moreover, for the
culturalist, normativity always comes in the plural: human beings create
a diversity of such orders (cf. also Chapter 2) in the different cultural
surroundings they inhabit.

However, precisely due to this pluralism, there is a problem analogous to
naturalism within culturalism itself, because, ironically, *cultural relativism*,

---

[21] Another line of argument critical of classical essentialism is existentialism, according to which
human beings have no ahistorical metaphysical essence but individually create their own lives and
normative principles in the contingent (absurd) situations they happen to find themselves in. Due to
its radical individualism, existentialism might also lead to a fragmentation of normativity, though
for reasons different from naturalism. Cf. Chapter 4 for brief remarks on James in relation to
existentialism.

[22] This can be regarded as, essentially, a Kantian-cum-Wittgensteinian framework for philosophical
anthropology, with the world-constituting activity of the Kantian transcendental subject reconcep-
tualized as a Wittgensteinian normatively structured form of life. Pragmatist versions of culturalism
could include, for example, the Rortyan conception of philosophy as cultural politics (Rorty 2007)
and the Whitean holistic pragmatist conception of "philosophy of culture" as an inquiry into the
nature of our normative institutions (cf. Chapters 2 and 4).

an arguably natural articulation or development of culturalism, may be just another way of "refactualizing" the normative order into mere contingent matters of fact.[23] While culturalism emphasizes that human beings live in a normatively structured human world that is largely of their own making, rather than being placed within a pre-established teleology and cosmic normativity in a classical (e.g., Aristotelian) sense, this idea rapidly collapses into relativism as soon as we admit that any such structuring of normative frameworks takes place within specific and spatio-temporally localized historical cultural spheres.[24] The challenge for a culturalist philosophical anthropologist is to maintain as much irreducible normativity as possible without postulating any Platonic or Aristotelian essentialist normativity that cannot be grounded in any natural processes. This is the traditional issue of nature vs. culture all over again, with broadly culturalist approaches ranging from Kant's distinction between theoretical and practical reason (with their specific normative tasks) to Dewey's (1986 [1929]) analysis of "experience and nature" and Wittgenstein's (1953) claim to study "the natural history of human forms of life" when investigating the necessary grounding of linguistic meanings in normatively structured yet historically changing and contingent language-games.

It is, in my view, exactly this challenge that pragmatism – speaking of pragmatism generally as a philosophical orientation from Peirce and James to Rorty and Putnam, and beyond – has seriously aspired to meet.[25] One reason why I have always found pragmatism one of the most promising

---

[23] My worries here concern only the most radical forms of relativism. There are certainly responsible moderate forms around. For example, the relativism often associated with "Wittgensteinian" philosophers such as D. Z. Phillips is a case in point. In an illuminating recent essay, Koistinen (2019) analyzes Phillip's views and the charge of relativism in the context of exploring the methodology of both moral philosophy and the philosophy of religion, defending Phillips's "contemplative" Wittgensteinian approach against the standard accusation of relativism. Citing Phillips, he points out that in the Wittgensteinian sense "practices" are not simply systems of beliefs or even grounded in beliefs; they are, rather, contexts within which beliefs are expressed and can be judged as true or false (Koistinen 2019, 168). From the pragmatist perspective, I just want to add that beliefs can still play a central role in any human practices, but beliefs themselves must be understood as habits of action and as, hence, irreducibly practice-embedded and practice-involving (cf. Chapter 4). In this respect, it seems to me that there is no major disagreement between, say, (Jamesian) pragmatist philosophy of religion and the Wittgensteinian approach exemplified by Phillips. Rather, Phillips (as interpreted by Koistinen) is an example of a philosopher often seen as a relativist yet not obviously guilty of the kind of refactualizing cultural relativism I am worried about here. I think this reading is reconfirmed if one compares Phillips's (e.g., 1986) views with pragmatism.

[24] Putnam, in a famous essay, "Why Reason Can't Be Naturalized" (in Putnam 1983), also aptly suggests that cultural relativism ought to be understood as a species of (reductive) naturalism. Both are, in short, haunted by the loss of normativity.

[25] I try to offer a pragmatist yet transcendental philosophical anthropology (with special emphasis on the problem of death and mortality) in Pihlström 2016.

philosophical approaches in this particular discussion is that it takes seriously both non-reductive naturalism and irreducible cultural normativity.[26] Instead of continuing to dwell on pragmatism in any detail, I will here shortly turn to the concept of recognition, however (returning to holistic pragmatism in a later section of this chapter). Could recognition theory, we may ask, also be employed to make sense of the emergence of the normative order as such? Or does it already presuppose a normative order? Is there a "first" recognition act upon which the normativity of our social world could in principle be based? These are among the questions that need to be addressed by anyone taking seriously the task of bridging the gap between naturalism and culturalism, and it might be tempting to think that recognition theory could resolve this issue.

Without claiming that contemporary recognition theorists are actually in the business of doing so, it might seem natural to view recognition as a way of accounting for the possibility of normativity. Thus, normativity would be grounded in *acts of recognition*. In a sense this goes back to Hegel's dialectic of the master and the slave. But is there, then, an "original" – and hence natural – situation with no recognition acts in place yet? There would, ideally, have to be something like that, if recognition were to offer a ground for normativity in the sense of (miraculously) turning initially natural facts into normative statuses. If so, then *how* does, or how did, normativity emerge from such a situation? From recognitions of normative statuses perhaps? But then how do we know (or how did the "first recognizers" know) to whom, or to what, such recognition acts should, or even could, be directed? If we all suffer from what James called our "blindness", how does the first flash of recognizing vision emerge? Let me re-emphasize that I find these much more important – and more human – questions than the allegedly deep question of how, say, consciousness emerged, or emerges, from non-conscious matter. The questions concerning recognition and normativity are presumably also less prone to lead to postulations of mysterious qualia or other strange non-natural entities that may not seem to fit into the scientific worldview.[27] The Kantian issue of legitimacy,

---

[26] More generally, we may say that the three *critical* (transcendental) philosophies of normativity that I am trying to understand and develop further both in the present discussion and earlier (e.g., Pihlström 2016) are Kantianism, pragmatism, and Wittgensteinianism. Obviously their relations cannot be explored here at any length; however, as this chapter (and this book) as a whole is crucially informed by a pragmatist approach to normativity, my transcendental discussion of normativity is one more attempt to demonstrate the crucial link between transcendental and pragmatist inquiries into the human condition.

[27] Putnam (1999) persuasively argues that there is something seriously wrong in the temptation to think of the mind in terms of a (quasi-)scientific mystery in the first place. I agree, though I am not

or entitlement, cannot be settled by focusing on any quasi-scientific factual question.

Let me illustrate our problem with reference to the very distinctive horrors brought into our social and cultural world by Nazism. What is relevant here is, arguably, the *Nazis' destruction of (almost) all normative* (ethical, political, legal, etc.) *statuses of the victims*, or most of them at least (cf. Snyder 2010, 2015). Ironically, the Nazis of course did have their own "laws" and a "*Volksgericht*" delivering legal judgments within their bizarre society, but these perversions of normativity were ultimately based on a thoroughly biologistic doctrine of *Lebensraum* and racism; accordingly, the normativity at work in the Nazi system was, arguably, almost entirely reducible, and indeed rather literally reduced, to both the victims' and the perpetrators' racial and biological contingencies, such as the Germans' allegedly natural need for *Lebensraum* and the fact that the non-Aryan "lower races" of the East were on the way. As Holocaust writers like Primo Levi forcefully testify, the Nazis largely succeeded in reducing the Holocaust victims into mere beasts, not merely by what they concretely did to them but also by using the kind of non-humanizing language they used (cf. Levi 1988 [1986]), while in a sense remaining human themselves, because remaining guilty and responsible for what they did. This reduction of human beings to mere animals is carefully analyzed in Holocaust literature, including Levi's compelling work.[28] But it required a philosophical-political analysis of the magnitude of Hannah Arendt's to show what novel kind of crime the Nazi crime was. In Arendtian terms, the elimination of human spontaneity in totalitarianism (see Arendt 1976 [1951]; cf. Chapter 2) can be seen as a version of the reduction of normativity into mere natural factuality, or even non-human bestiality.

The alarming observation now is that the allegedly "positive" natural capacities we have do not necessarily fare much better. For example, empathy as the ground of morality doesn't make the problem easier: we are, according to empathy-grounded ethics, ultimately animals with our contingent natural reactions, such as empathy or compassion, however

investigating the mind here, except perhaps in the extremely broad sense that normativity (naturally) requires mental or psychological creatures.

[28] On Levi's importance in the acknowledgment of the meaninglessness of suffering, see Pihlström 2020a, chapter 6. In a Wittgensteinian analysis of Levi, Sparti (2005) argues that acknowledging others as humans, or the lack thereof, needs a form of life as its context – and my argument in this chapter comes close to this line of thought. However, Sparti speaks about our *responsibility* of acknowledging others; again, the question is how (and when) such a normative responsibility arises. Doesn't it already need a normative context to be so much as possible? For an insightful analysis of the way in which the horror of the Holocaust moves us beyond language and the normative, see Cavarero 2018.

benevolent.[29] This moves us out of the normative sphere into mere nature, too. While we nowadays hear *ad nauseam* that we should develop our "skills for empathy" and bring compassion to workplaces, for instance, in times like ours we should, rather, emphasize *the irreducibility of our normative order*: duty, law, reason. Unreflective emotionalism naively plays into the hands of the reductionists willing to exploit our natural non-normative tendencies.[30] It is the task of the philosopher focusing on normativity to maintain a critical distance to such developments in our societies. Our problem in a nutshell, then, is that normativity is *irreducible but not non- or supernatural*. In our philosophical-anthropological efforts to understand the normative structuring of our practices, it is crucial to avoid both "bald naturalism" and "rampant Platonism", as John McDowell (1996 [1994]) aptly calls them, and this needs to be done across the philosophical board from logic and epistemology to ethics and political philosophy.[31]

5.4 Recognition

Let us now move on to a slightly more detailed discussion of recognition as a ground of normativity. Obviously, I am not seeking to offer any comprehensive account of contemporary recognition theory; my remarks may be understood as critical suggestions that would, I think, have to be addressed by anyone who proposes recognition as a "natural" (socio-)psychological ground of normativity, but this is compatible with acknowledging that contemporary recognition theorists themselves would only rarely do so.

[29] I am not here attributing this conception of ethics to any particular philosopher. The tendency to base morality on natural emotions of sympathy is certainly there in the tradition of moral philosophy at least since Hume, with a number of different variations.

[30] Therefore, while the form of pragmatism primarily defended in this volume has been the Jamesian one, we should be wary of its tendencies toward too simplified emotionalism – not in order to deny the obvious significance of emotions in human life, including its normative practices, but in order to put them in their proper place within the "whole man in us", rather than letting them govern the normative realm as such (cf. also Chapter 4).

[31] McDowell's (1996 [1994]) notion of "second nature" might also be helpful here (cf. Pihlström 2003, 2005), but if so, it must, for my purposes, be *transcendentally* (and pragmatically) articulated, with normativity naturally based on (but not reduced to) our on-going critical self-reflection on our constant failure to follow the norms and rules governing our lives. (A "via negativa" method is at work here, again.) This approach parallels Korsgaard's (1996) Kantian account of procedural normativity. Having dealt with McDowell's (and, briefly, Korsgaard's) views earlier (Pihlström 2005, chapters 2–3), I won't dwell on this issue any further here, while I warmly agree with his understanding of the ethical as "a domain of rational requirements" to which we are "alerted" by acquiring appropriate conceptual capacities through enculturating upbringing (see McDowell 1996 [1994], 82), and with his antireductionist view that nothing non-normative can ground or justify the normative.

My worry with the notion of recognition in this context, as already hinted at above, is that it may be too psychologizing and, hence, also too naturalistic and "factualizing" a concept to be able to account for the possibility of normativity in a sufficiently deep transcendental sense.[32] In its own way, recognition theory may seem to reduce normative structures to our *acts* of recognition, that is, something that we as contingent psychological and social individuals "naturally" do (or fail to do). As a further approximation of our problem, consider this question: could there be a *duty* to recognize (say, someone as something) if one just doesn't "feel" the compelling demand coming from the other's point of view, such as their request for recognition, as already binding in any sense? The vocabulary of duties, it seems to me, would come too early here. The mere availability of such a question shows that recognition cannot be the ultimate ground of moral duty, or any duty. Or consider, again, this: if there was a *first* act of recognition, was it an idealization like the Hobbesian sovereign rising from the state of nature, or Rawlsian justice emerging from an original position behind the veil of ignorance? Such an idealized postulation would in my view put the cart before the horse precisely because recognition is too contingent to account for the possibility of normativity as such at a transcendental level, or for the grounding of the normative order in our natural psycho-social characteristics and (merely factually conceived) human nature. The same holds, *mutatis mutandis*, for any other psychological or natural, or generally non-normative, attempts to account for the grounding of normativity.

A practice of recognition is, indeed, a *practice*. We need a well functioning set of already normatively structured and established human practices at work in order for there to be acts of recognition at all. Systematic recognition theory (cf., e.g., Koskinen 2017, 2019, 2020) analyzes those practices and the concepts they invoke in great philosophical detail and with admirable sophistication, but as far as I can see it cannot *ground* the

---

[32] Someone might wonder why I am including pragmatism in my relaxed articulation of transcendental philosophy (or transcendental inquiry into normativity) while excluding recognition theory, which might seem to have a much more intimate connection with German idealism and therefore also with the transcendental tradition. One key reason for this is that I see recognition theory as, *qua* Hegelian, giving up at least one basic idea of transcendental inquiry, i.e., transcendental idealism, while I see pragmatism as a fundamentally Kantian approach precisely in its attempt to rearticulate transcendental idealism in a "naturalized" and historicized fashion. (The same could be said about the later Wittgenstein as a kind of transcendental pragmatist thinker; see Pihlström 2003, 2012a.) Moreover, my critique of recognition theory is restricted to understanding recognition as basically psychological and socio-psychological action; insofar as this perhaps overly psychologistic characterization of the theory is inaccurate, I am of course pleased to welcome recognition theory as a contribution to the (quasi-)transcendental inquiry into the possibility of normativity.

normative order as such (nor is it, I suppose, necessarily taken to, though, unless recognition is proposed as *the* fundamental concept in social ontology).[33] Yet somehow norms undeniably *do* arise out of our natural ways of doing things. I would be inclined to analyze this phenomenon in terms of our "naturally" occupying or engaging in always already (for us) irreducibly normative forms of life (Wittgenstein), or practices (pragmatism). But the question remains: *how* do these forms of life or practices get their distinctive normativity? From something like recognition acts perhaps – but by whom, and based on what?

In a sense, recognition shares the problem of naturalism and cultural relativism; that is, the worry is that it ultimately amounts to a "refactualization" of the normative order. It functions very well as "social glue" and is arguably *ontologically* constitutive of the social world as we know it, but it cannot *transcendentally* function as the necessary condition for the possibility of normativity. This is because there must already be a rich context of normative statuses at work in order for any act of recognition (i.e., recognizing, or failing to recognize, such statuses) to be so much as possible. This is once again something that can be explicated by means of transcendental argumentation. In order for us to be able to recognize, or fail to recognize, anything whatsoever, in any sense stronger than a mere natural reaction (in principle available to "mere animals"), as having a normative status of any kind, we must already live in a normative order, a space of reasons. This is comparable to the way in which we, according to Kant, need a system of categories already in place for us to be able to have cognitive experience of any object or event – rather than a mere Humean "rhapsody" of sense impressions. Recognition can no more ground the possibility of normativity than the Kantian categories (as normative requirements for objecthood) can be grounded by or derived from (Humean) experience, or Wittgensteinian rules of using language within a language-game from mere marks and noises. Any theory finding recognition foundational for morality and normativity is therefore, in an extremely broad sense, "Humean" rather than Kantian.[34]

Let us elaborate on the problems and prospects of the notion of recognition in this context by taking a slightly more detailed look at a recent

---

[33] Let me again emphasize that my criticism is not primarily directed at contemporary recognition theory as such – which might indeed have received sufficiently transcendental elaborations by some of its practitioners – but at a (potential or actual) philosophical *temptation* to employ this theory in an attempt to ground normativity in contingent acts of recognition.

[34] In addition to being Hegelian, of course. There is a sense in which my discussion here parallels Kantian criticisms of Humean accounts of ethics based on sympathy. Cf. again Pihlström and Kivistö 2021.

investigation of the topic developing and applying the original insights of
Axel Honneth (2005 [1992]) and other pioneers of the theory. In their
editorial introduction to the valuable recent volume, *Recognition and
Religion* (2019),[35] Maijastina Kahlos, Heikki J. Koskinen, and Ritva
Palmén emphasize the relevance of recognition theory to the issue of
normativity by reminding us that in contemporary recognition theory,
recognition in its most relevant sense means that "to recognize someone is
to grant another human being a positive normative status based on her
personhood" (1). "On the most general level", therefore, a recognition act
"means taking and treating the other *as a person*" (Kahlos et al. 2019, 1;
original emphasis). When this is specified, "particular aspects of personhood" are brought into the picture, and then we can, following
Honneth's seminal theory, distinguish between respect, esteem, and
love (focusing on general human dignity, specific identities, and unique
individual personhood, respectively) as the main dimensions of recognition (Kahlos et al. 2019, 1–2).

The editors continue to label recognition "a fundamental normative
phenomenon" and to suggest that it "constitutes an adequate *response* to
specific aspects of personhood" and may even play a crucial role "in the
very *constitution* of general personhood, as well as more specific aspects of
it" (Kahlos et al. 2019, 2; original emphases). While the paradigmatic case
of recognition is "a mutual granting of positive statuses between individual human persons", recognition extends to social groups as well as
"normative entities quite generally" (Kahlos et al. 2019, 2). Fortunately,
the three editors also point out that although recognition is generally
positive and a "vital human need", it has a "darker side" due to misrec-
ognitions, power relations, and the need to "struggle" for recognition (cf.
again Kahlos et al. 2019, 2). They also take what we may call a "realistic"
attitude to recognition by claiming that though it was Hegel whose work
signals a turning point in the development of recognition theory, "the
phenomena themselves were already present before their conceptual
articulation by Hegel", because recognition is, indeed, a "basic human
need" and presumably even constitutive of human persons and their
identities (Kahlos et al. 2019, 4).[36]

Given the task of this chapter, we need to ask *how* "fundamental",
exactly, recognition is as a normative phenomenon. One obvious question

---

[35] This book is a rich collection of essays ranging from various historical explorations to theological and
philosophical analyses of recognition phenomena in different historical and systematic contexts.
[36] Saarinen's (2016) historically detailed study also emphasizes that in theological and religious
contexts recognition has in interesting ways been conceptualized a long time before Hegel.

related to this general issue is how far the recognition theorist needs to go in the direction of realism. Would it be possible to maintain that recognition "phenomena" are, though "real", themselves something constituted (e.g., by further recognition acts)? They are themselves social phenomena, after all. This is a more general question regarding realism about the normative (as well as about historical social facts and institutions).[37] In this context, however, a possibly more serious philosophical question can be formulated on the basis of the overview of normativity sketched above. No matter how "fundamental" recognition is as a "normative phenomenon", it can be claimed that it is only *possible* within a context that is itself already richly normative. Perhaps the recognition theorist seeks to emphasize such irreducible normativity by suggesting that social reality is constituted by recognition acts, but my transcendental worry about this is that the very identity of those acts as recognition acts (rather than acts of some other kind), or even as *acts* at all, already presupposes a normative context.[38]

Another issue the above-quoted comments raise is related to the strong emphasis on personhood among many recognition theorists. Does the world, we may ask, somehow divide itself up to, for example, persons and non-persons already prior to recognition acts? Or do those acts (as is occasionally suggested) *constitute* persons (etc.) in a strong ontological sense?[39] But then how is it determined what kinds of things *can* through recognition acts be turned into persons? Some kind of "pre-recognition" must arguably have taken place for *relevant kinds of beings* to be even potentially recognizable as persons rather than something else. This, in turn, presupposes criteria of relevance that must, again, already be regarded as irreducibly normative. Therefore, there just is no way to ground normativity in mere psychological acts of recognition, or contingent psychological acts of any kind. In terms of the case study of the first section of this

[37] The realism issue can also be raised with respect to the more specific forms of recognition such as the trilateral, mediated, and transitive ones carefully distinguished by Koskinen (2019) in his systematic taxonomical paper (in Kahlos et al. 2019, chapter 2).
[38] The force of this argument depends on how strictly we require that a foundational "beginning" of recognition acts would have to be presupposed. Clearly, our practices of recognition and their normative contexts can develop together over time. This may be compared to Peirce's argument (in his 1868 essay, "Questions Concerning Certain Faculties Claimed for Man", in Peirce 1992–1998, vol. 1) for the absence of any "unmediated cognition". In any case, we are not here dealing with any temporally identifiable "first foundations" of recognition; I am merely suggesting that, at any time, our being so much as able to engage in recognition acts presupposes that we are already situated within normativity.
[39] Would our recognizing another as a person constitute their personhood also if we (or just I?) recognized animals, machines (artificial intelligence, robots), Martians, or the replicants familiar from Ridley Scott's 1982 science fiction film *Blade Runner* as persons? Where would, or could, we draw the line?

chapter, we cannot even begin to consider whether (and how) to recognize, say, the equal rights of women and men (or other genders), and people with different skin colors, if we start from an allegedly neutral context within which it is not yet clear that sexism and racism are to be rejected; the context within which appropriate acts of recognition are possible must already have set views like sexism and racism aside as non-starters.

Recognizing other human beings as persons, Koskinen (2019, 36) notes, involves acknowledging "their normative status as persons".[40] Koskinen also refers to Robert Brandom's notion of "robust recognition", "the practical attitude of recognizing another as a simple recognizer", "as itself the kind of thing for which things can have a specifically normative significance" (Koskinen 2019, 40). However, as recognition theorists like Koskinen of course acknowledge, the normative form of life we share with other human beings may require (or even normatively obligate) us to recognize human beings for whom things do not, and cannot, have any normative significance because they lack the capacity to attribute such, or any, significance to anything. When Brandom and Koskinen characterize interpersonal recognition as an act of "[t]aking something to be subject to appraisals of its reasons, holding it rationally responsible" and thus of "treating it as some*one*: as one of *us* (rational beings)" (Koskinen 2019, 42; quoting Brandom, original emphasis), the immediate issue that arises is how we should account for our recognizing human beings who are *not* persons, and not, except perhaps potentially but (tragically) not actually, among "us", such as the permanently ill or severely mentally disabled?[41]

---

[40] This may be, for instance, more general normativity than something associated with one's being a person of a certain kind – for example, in Koskinen's example, a theist or an atheist. Even if the theist and the atheist do not recognize, qua rivals, each others' views, they may recognize each other as persons (Koskinen 2019, 38–39) – and this observation helps us appreciate the significance of what Koskinen calls "mediated recognition" (see also Koskinen 2017, 2020). But how about recognizing the other as, say, rational, or as an inquirer committed to the norms of inquiry? This might be a specification of personhood (or an extension of it) leaving the mutual recognitive attitudes of the theist and the atheist somewhat unclear. If the disagreement is deep enough and concerns the others' commitment (or lack thereof) to fundamental norms of inquiry, for instance, there must at some point be a limit to one's recognizing the other as rational at all, or perhaps even as a person.

[41] In recently established terminology, recognition theory tied to the idea of personhood might be problematically "ableist", denying recognition (of a certain kind) to those lacking certain relevant capabilities. On the other hand, it must be acknowledged that recognition theorists like Koskinen do not simply endorse any straightforward "rationality criterion" for the kind of "respect-recognition" they take all human beings (or persons) to deserve. (Thanks are due to Dr. Koskinen for several conversations on this issue.) However, *some* ontological criterion needs to be presupposed in any case, for example, based on the metaphysics of personhood, sentience, or some other feature of the beings that are to be recognized. From the point of view of the transcendental considerations of this discussion, *any* such fundamentally ontological criterion is problematic insofar as it aims at grounding the ethical relation of recognition at an allegedly more basic level.

It is, I would like to argue, only within an always already normative context guided by something like (among others) the idea of human dignity – or some suitably general and irreducibly normative equivalent – that we can so much as *ask* whether, and how exactly, our various acts of recognition, or our failures to commit such acts, are appropriate or inappropriate, acknowledging or constituting relevant normative statuses. Though it remains only loosely employed here, the concept of dignity is transcendentally presupposed by any consideration of recognition as contrasted to non- or misrecognition. It is, in short, only within a human form of life that is already thoroughly ethical and normative that we can discuss whether, and how, to recognize someone or something as something (and why). If this is the case, the human form of life in its normative dimensions *just cannot arise from (mere) recognition*. We must already be human in order for us to be able to engage in recognition acts.[42]

In my view, these remain open issues; this chapter admittedly raises more questions than it provides answers to. It is, at any rate, unclear to what extent recognition is (or is even claimed by recognition theorists like Koskinen to be) a "fundamental" normative phenomenon in the sense that it could be taken to ground the normative order we live in, or the human form of life in general. I have suggested that contingent recognition acts are less fundamental than our already finding ourselves committed to and guided by normativity, because we need to so conceptualize ourselves in order to be able to engage in any such acts in the first place. Therefore, normative statuses cannot be ultimately constituted by such recognition acts. But I also acknowledge the possibility that recognition theory might actually seek to express the kind of notion of irreducible human dignity I am invoking, because the affirmation of dignity as normatively fundamental (and thus non-naturalizable) may itself be regarded as a recognition act. If so, then recognition theory would already presuppose normativity more or less along the lines suggested in this chapter – in which case my transcendental criticism would lose at least some of its relevance.

Be that as it may, recognition is, at least, somewhat less fundamental than one might be tempted to think, but we should remain open to elaborations of recognition theory that render it closer to the transcendental requirements of "grounding" I have emphasized here. Furthermore, one

---

[42] "Let us be human", Wittgenstein once wrote (1980a, 36), perhaps indicating that being human is already a task, something that normatively challenges *us* (as humans) only from within a human form of life – otherwise the encouragement would hardly make sense. (This phrase, like many Wittgensteinian ones, is thus arguably much more complex than its apparent simplicity might lead us to think.)

might, in Wittgensteinian terms, argue further that recognition acts are always (for better or worse) somehow "reasoned" or "ratiocinated", while our being committed to normativity in general is, rather, based on "blind" rule-following, on our being "naturally" (though obviously not in the sense of reductive naturalism) engaged in the kind of practices within which our language-games find their homes.[43] An explicitly pragmatist (Peircean) version of this criticism would emphasize that particular recognition acts presuppose a wider context of habituality that is, again, already normatively structured. Once again, as suggested in Chapter 4, pragmatism needs to recognize an active interplay and mutual dependence of contingent particularity and genuine habituality.

An argument parallel to the one I have sketched here can be plausibly formulated in a Wittgensteinian context.[44] Thus, I am very much in agreement with Martin Gustafsson (2019, 183) about the need to avoid dichotomous oppositions such as "the priority of practice over intellect" that some pragmatism-inspired interpreters of Wittgenstein may have read into Wittgenstein's (1953) rule-following considerations. A truly pragmatist picture of Wittgenstein would, indeed, find practice and intellect mutually interdependent instead of conceiving their relation in terms of any priority claim (Gustafsson 2019, 184), in addition to overcoming a number of other unpragmatic dichotomies that may lead Wittgenstein interpreters astray in a variety of ways (see also Pihlström 2012a). In the context of this general (pragmatist) context of understanding Wittgenstein, Gustafsson offers us a penetrating analysis of what Wittgenstein famously says about "blind" rule-following at §219 of the *Investigations*. Blind obedience in rule-following is not merely a "brute reflex response" but requires a "background of established linguistic practice mastered both by speaker and hearer" (Gustafsson 2019, 187). This is something that I would be willing to consider a transcendental condition necessarily required for the possibility of any meaning, rule-following, or normativity, although I of course understand that many readers of Wittgenstein, presumably including Gustafsson, are not entirely happy with bringing such Kantian transcendental terminology into this Wittgensteinian context.

In any event, Gustafsson succeeds in articulating what is essential in a pragmatic transcendental reading of Wittgenstein when arguing that the presence of a "background linguistic practice" is required even by immediate,

---

[43] "Language did not emerge from some kind of ratiocination", Wittgenstein (1969, §475) maintains.
[44] See, again, Koistinen 2019 for a Wittgensteinian (more specifically, Phillips-inspired) engagement with relativism that I find parallel to pragmatism; cf. Pihlström 2012a.

unreflective ("blind") obedience; indeed, "the possibility of obedience goes hand in hand with the possibility of critical reflection and disobedience", as we can "obey unreflectively" only if we can also "reflect, criticize and disobey" (Gustafsson 2019, 188). This I take to be an exemplary pragmatic-cum-transcendental analysis (without using those terms) of presuppositional relations and necessary conditions needed for the possibility of the kind of activities we regard as linguistic, or generally normative – or human. These reflections can also be used to illuminate what has been called the "contingency of necessity" in Wittgensteinian contexts: it is a contingent fact about our practices and forms of life that orders are "by and large" obeyed (cf. Gustafsson 2019, 189), but this fact makes the very *concepts* of order and obedience (and thus the modal structures of rule-following) possible. As Gustafsson suggests, the classical pragmatists might have more or less agreed about this picture of practices, obedience, and critical reflection (Gustafsson 2019, 190) – and I entirely agree, even though I cannot develop the comparison between the pragmatist and the Wittgensteinian perspectives in any detail in this volume. Arguably in the Wittgensteinian framework as much as in the pragmatist one, mere natural recognition is, then, insufficient to yield the modal structures necessary for a transcendental account of the possibility of normativity.

5.5 Dignity and the Threat of Refactualization

In contrast to any position that defends human equality (understood as ethical and/or political or more generally normative) or basic human rights on the basis of merely natural and contingent facts about human beings – facts we could appeal to as pieces of evidence in support of non-sexism or non-racism, for instance – I want to propose that the basic category of the human being, and the related category of human dignity, should be treated as more foundational than the category of the person, or the concept of "human rights", or any other concept whose applicability specifically depends on contingent acts of recognition.[45] I have argued above that our moral and generally normative reality cannot be transcendentally (regarding the conditions of its *possibility*) grounded in our acts of recognition even if such acts are constitutive of the normative and the social (and of personhood) in an ontological sense. In order for such acts themselves to be *possible*, we must, I have suggested, live in a thoroughly normative

---

[45] I am here drawing inspiration from Veikko Launis's (2018) recent work on human dignity. His comprehensive discussion of the topic is, however, available only in Finnish. On the irreducible significance of the notion of the (other) human being in our lives, see, for example, Gaita 2000.

sphere in which we, for instance, evaluate our morally relevant acts and uses of language, including our recognizing behavior, in terms of our being *already* responsive to human dignity. This normative sphere is not reducible to contingent recognitions of personhood based on natural capacities, and it also invokes a notion of humanity wider than the category of the person, because we need to treat with dignity also those human beings who clearly lack the rational, emotional, and possibly other capacities of persons (e.g., deeply mentally disabled individuals). Our responsibility of treating others with dignity does not arise from our psychology or brain structure (e.g., empathy) or from the contingent falsity of sexism and racism. It is, as Wittgensteinians might put it, *there* – "like our life".[46]

Acknowledging such transcendentally constitutive structures of the practices we are committed to requires that we are willing to develop pragmatism in a Kantian critical manner. The Rortyan neopragmatist might interpret this talk of dignity as an appeal to a historically contingent "final vocabulary" (cf. Chapter 1), and certainly it *is* historically highly contingent that we do have the practices and conceptual frameworks that we do. The transcendental necessity of there always already being normative conceptual structures underlying our human practices is a presuppositional necessity identifiable only from within those very practices themselves.

Commenting on the case of sexism (in dialogue with Nussbaum 2018), I also suggested that we are not here merely dealing with factual beliefs that can be confirmed or disconfirmed by empirical evidence; we are dealing with more basic pragmatic-cum-transcendental commitments enabling us to normatively engage in argumentative relationships in the first place. Just as our acts of recognition already require a normative framework, these argumentative relationships presuppose a normative context within which no argument for or against sexism or racism could even get off the ground.

A problem that now rearises is whether our transcendental notion of human dignity, or any other normative notion we might use in a comparably fundamental (transcendental) normative role, is just a contingent cultural specificity based on particular recognition acts we commit in our local cultural surroundings. Is it (especially from a pragmatist point of view) merely a local cultural practice, ultimately reducible to mere facts about what we in this specific culture do, to treat other human beings as equal in

---

[46] Cf. Wittgenstein 1969. In this sense, Sparti's (2005) way of speaking about the "responsibility" for acknowledging as more fundamental than acknowledging itself sounds somewhat problematic (and, despite his Wittgensteinian approach, curiously non-Wittgensteinian).

the sense of rejecting, say, racism and sexism?[47] This question brings us back to the issue concerning the relation between normativity and "human nature". Is there a kind of normativity already in place that enables us to ask the question whether it is our moral duty to avoid sexism or racism, or does our contingently recognizing the normative statuses of (say) women and people representing "other" ethnic backgrounds create any normativity there is in matters like this? We are back in basic issues of philosophical anthropology all over again.

Returning to Kannisto's (1984) scheme briefly introduced above, we may recall that cultural relativism is a "natural" development of culturalism, with the alarming tendency to "refactualize" the culture-specific normative order that culturalism had "re-established" on the ruins of classical essentialism. Even if "we" in our culture *do* recognize women and non-white people, for instance, as fundamentally equal to white men, and even if we propose this recognition as a universal model to be carried over into other cultures as well, are we still only dealing with a local cultural specificity that can ultimately be reduced to a mere contingent fact about how we behave and how we contingently happen to think others ought to behave, too? (Rorty would be happy with this, I guess.) How exactly should the relation between the natural and the cultural (or the contingently factual and the normative) be understood?

Pragmatism, as should be obvious by now, is an attempt to bridge the gap between the natural and the cultural, and therefore we must, before concluding the chapter, more explicitly return to a promising pragmatist way of dealing with normativity – viz., holistic pragmatism, already discussed and employed a number of times during this inquiry.[48]

---

[47] This could be taken to be a problem analogous to the issue of epistemic and/or scientific norms of rationality being based on the contingent reasonings by scientists and other inquirers in specific historical contexts. I am not planning to open *this* can of worms here. For a pragmatist discussion, see Pihlström 2008b.

[48] A relevant pragmatist approach *not* to be explored further here would obviously be Rorty's *ethnocentrism*, according to which we just have to "start from where we are", that is, where we contingently find ourselves, and develop our "vocabularies" with the "ironic" awareness of the contingency of that starting point. We should not, I think, assess Rorty's pragmatism purely negatively; his emphasis on the historical contingency of our most fundamental normative frameworks is, I think, to be taken very seriously. I am, however, looking for a pragmatist account that would be reconcilable with a transcendental inquiry into normativity, and here Rorty seems to be of little help – a form of pragmatism more responsive to the transcendental "vocabulary" is needed. (Cf. Chapters 1 and 3.) In fairness to Rorty, it must also be noted that his view does not collapse into simple relativism. While our norms are culturally and historically relative in the sense of having developed within a particular culture, it does not follow (even according to Rorty) that their reach would be similarly relative. Our holding that racial discrimination is wrong has a cultural history but reaches wider than the culture within which this norm developed; indeed, we take this wrongness to

5.6   Holistic Pragmatism and Normativity

One plausible suggestion for a way of developing a pragmatist philosophical anthropology entangling naturalism and normativity is, again, White's
(1956, 2002) holistic pragmatism, which, as we have seen, is basically an
epistemological position but can be extended to a more general account of
the "human form of life" (cf. Pihlström 2011b, 2015; see especially Chapter
4). Like his long-time friend and colleague Quine, White follows the anti-
Cartesian and more generally anti-rationalist line of pragmatist thought,
abandoning any "first philosophy" (White 2002, 3–5). This makes him
a moderate philosophical naturalist, but his naturalism takes seriously the
task of accommodating irreducible normativity into our holistic belief
system. While both Quine and White begin from a firm rejection of the
analytic/synthetic distinction and from the holistic idea that our beliefs (or
sentences we assent to) are not tested individually but "face the tribunal of
experience" in corporate bodies (see Quine 1980 [1951]), they draw quite
different morals from this picture, as was already explained above.

Whereas philosophy of science was, for Quine, "philosophy enough",
White recommends that we extend the kind of holistic approach Quine
preferred in the philosophy of science into a philosophy of culture,
accounting for not only science but also other normative practices, such
as religion, history, art, law, and morality (White 2002, x–xi). This "cultural philosophy" covers philosophy of science as one of its subfields –
science, of course, is part of culture, something that human beings "culti-
vate" – but White insists that other cultural institutions require empirically
informed philosophical scrutiny no less than science does (White 2002,
xiii). Holistic pragmatism says that "philosophy of art, of religion, of
morality, or of other elements of culture is in great measure a discipline
that is epistemically coordinate with philosophy of natural science" (White
2002, 66). Quine's way of restricting his philosophical concerns to science
should be abandoned as an unfortunate and by no means necessary
remnant from logical positivism (White 2002, 3). The idea that ethics, in
particular, may be viewed as "empirical" if one includes feelings of moral
obligation as well as empirical experiences in the "flux" of experience
employed in the on-going critical testing of one's beliefs (cf. Chapter 4)
has been strongly present in White's writings from an early stage to the
present (see White 1956, 1981, 2002). White is thus one of those

be universal. (I am grateful to one of the anonymous reviewers for pressing me on this point.)
However, I still wonder how this view can ever get its normative force within Rortyan pragmatism,
which ultimately seems to reduce all normativity to mere causal clashes between vocabularies.

philosophers who can be read as having defended a pragmatic form of moral and generally normative realism (cf. Pihlström 2005).

Quine took his famous holistic step by arguing that even logical truths are not immune to revision, because they are tested along with factual claims as components of larger conjunctions of statements (White 2002, 71). No general analytic/synthetic division can be drawn, as statements about, say, the synonymity of terms are ultimately empirical statements describing the contingencies of factual language-use (White 2002, 71, 73). Despite this fundamental agreement with Quine, White argues against Quine that "observation sentences" (e.g., "That's a rabbit") and ethical sentences such as "That's outrageous" cannot be sharply separated from each other any more than analytic and synthetic statements can; their difference is a matter of degree, not a difference in kind (White 2002, 154–155, 160–163). The ethical sentences at issue are, moreover, genuinely normative:

> Avoiding the view that ethical sentences are synonymous with sociological or psychological sentences, and being impressed by the failure of reductive phenomenalism as well as the power of holism to bridge the traditional epistemic gap created by the distinction between the analytic and the synthetic, I propose a nonreductive version of holism in order to bridge the gap between the moral and the descriptive [. . .]. (White 2002, 157)

That is, descriptive statements and normative ethical principles form conjunctions that are tested holistically, just as Quine had argued that empirical and logico-mathematical beliefs in science are. Logic, science, and ethics form a unified whole, a holistic web without epistemic dichotomies. Moreover, as logical principles *may*, by Quinean lights, be given up in the face of sufficiently recalcitrant experience, descriptive statements *may* be denied in order to preserve a normative principle we do not want to give up (White 2002, 159), although such situations may be rare. White's point, then, is that ethics is not inferior to science, or immune to empirical evaluation, because feelings of obligation together with sensory observation link ethical sentences to the natural world. It is a "soft science" rather than a "hard" one but hardly any softer than Quine's own naturalized "epistemological science", the branch of psychology studying human cognition (White 2002, 161–162). Furthermore, "feeling sentences" anchoring ethics to experience are fallible and can also be surrendered when a conjunction is tested (White 2002, 166). Both ethics and science are, hence, corrigible yet cognitive elements of normatively structured human culture that in the end constitutes a holistic totality instead of any compartmentalized group of distinct areas with definite boundaries. Knowledge and morals, as White himself put it many years ago, form a "seamless web" (White 1956, 287). As analyzed in the previous chapters, there is, at least potentially, an endless process of mutual holistic normative adjustment of beliefs and evidence at work whenever we need to examine a normative argument with factual premises – like in any empirical inquiry, yet extending to the fully normative sphere.

Now, in comparison to the holistic argumentation explored in Chapter 4, consider this very simple argument: (1) Racism (sexism) is true. (2) If racism (sexism) is true, then racial (or gender-based) discrimination is justified. (3) Therefore, racial (or gender-based) discrimination is justified. In order to reject (3), we need not necessarily find purely theoretical or evidential reasons to reject (1). We may reject (1) because (3) cannot ethically *work* as an element of our overall holistic system of belief within the human form of life we find ourselves to be inhabiting. Or better, no such system – no such life – can "work" if it contains a conclusion such as (3). Our reason for rejecting a factual belief like (1) may be thoroughly normative, and holistic pragmatism makes sense of this. Indeed, in the racism and sexism discussion earlier in this chapter I argued more strongly that racism and sexism must be rejected for any argumentation to be so much as possible within our practices of pursuing the truth. Thus, the critical holistic pragmatic argument against such positions would eventually take place at a meta-level in relation to the kind of highly simplified "first-order" argument imagined here.

I would be happy to construe these ideas somewhat more metaphysically as yielding the claim that there are, for us, no "value-neutral" facts at all (see Pihlström 2005, 2010b), though I doubt that White himself ever intended them in such a metaphysical sense.[49] In any case, as already suggested earlier, White's holism may and should be extended from the epistemic justification of different kinds of statements (sentences) or beliefs to the critical evaluation of entire cultural practices and normatively governed institutions. A continuous

---

[49] See again Chapter 4. White, like Putnam (2002), is strongly opposed to any metaphysical ("inflated") version of the fact-value entanglement. *This* might be seen as a remnant of logical positivism, too. A critic might ask here whether the defense of irreducible, non-factualizable normativity in this chapter runs into a conflict with the Putnamian pragmatist conception of the fact-value entanglement (briefly defended in Chapter 4). I do not think so, because I am certainly not denying the fact that the normative structures we find ourselves living within are always, despite their irreducibility, in a naturalized and factual sense related to or emergent from entirely natural ontological structures; what I am denying is that it would even be possible for us to be *committed to* them, or to a life guided by normativity at all, on reductively naturalistic grounds. In fact the defense of irreducible normativity goes very well together with the defense of the fact-value entanglement, provided that both are conceptualized in a properly pragmatist manner. In other words, in order to adequately account for the place of normativity in our lives and our world, we cannot just focus on a metaphysical theory of its (natural) emergence (nor can we simply reject metaphysics, though) but must continue to explore it in intimate relation to our pragmatist account of the practices of belief committed to normative structures, including truth-seeking.

critical (re)consideration of the normative structures that constitute our (thoroughly and irreducibly normative) form of life is precisely what holistic pragmatism calls for, and indeed makes sense of.

Another extension of holistic pragmatism is also needed because White's version is, arguably, *too thin* not merely with regard to the lack of metaphysical account of value (cf. Chapter 4) but also regarding the nature of moral obligation, as characterized by White. Mere *feelings* of obligation are, again, just natural and contingent. Normative commitment to feeling-transcendent rational duty (in a quasi-Kantian sense) needs to be built into the idea of the holistic assessment of our normative-cum-factual pursuit of truth. Moral emotions and even "mere" feelings do have a role to play in such a holistic practice, but they cannot alone act as the epistemic ground for our moral commitments. And the same goes for more general normativity. Furthermore, it can be suggested that holistic pragmatism, applied to the issue of normativity and its factual "grounding", comes very close to what is known as the method of *reflective equilibrium* (see Goodman 1954; Rawls 1971).[50] Yet, even that method hardly yields a "grounding" of normativity in a sense that would not already presuppose normativity. We must operate within a normative structure in order to employ the method of reflective equilibrium itself. Even when we (following Goodman 1954) reflect on the equilibrium of our rules of inference and the particular inferences we actually make, we can only do so within a framework that already presupposes *some* contextually valid rules – hence normativity. There is no "reflection" or "reflectivity" that would not already be normatively guided.

In terms of Chapter 3, we may say that all this means that the pragmatist cannot go "around Kant" but must work their way to holistic pragmatic adjustment of beliefs and evidence right through Kant.

5.7 Humanism

Holistic pragmatism is of course only one suggestion designed to meet our needs of defending the normative human form of life against reductively naturalizing (or "factualizing") tendencies, just as recognition theory has above been examined only as an example of an approach we might be tempted to employ in an attempt to ground normativity in our natural human capabilities and actions. In addition to "positive" suggestions

---

[50] See also White's (2002) own discussions of Rawls and Goodman; clearly, White recognizes the affinities holistic pragmatism has with the method of reflective equilibrium.

seeking to articulate a pragmatist philosophical anthropology integrating (soft, antireductionist) naturalism with culturalism, it is at least equally important to engage in a "negative" critical examination of well-intended yet (in my view) insufficiently deeply normative proposals such as recognition theory – also here illuminated through the case study on sexism and racism we started out from in this chapter. Let me now close the chapter with brief general remarks on the kind of *humanism* that I think the holistic pragmatist needs to embrace in order to be able to account for the possibility of normativity.

A defense of the irreducibility of our normative orders is – as my frequent references to the human "form of life" might also suggest – also a defense of humanism, even rather traditional Enlightenment humanism, with a kind of reincarnation of the transcendental subject at its center, a subject self-reflectively examining its own capacities and limits. This defense operates at a transcendental meta-level. I find the currently popular variants of anti-, trans-, and post-humanism basically human beings' attempts to reflect on their relation to pre-established social and cultural hierarchies, to non-human nature, to animals, to intelligent machines, etc. – to something non-human. They cannot escape our humanistic predicament, nor fundamentally challenge it. Something we may label transcendental humanism, I would like to argue, thus ultimately prevails (see also Chapters 3 and 6), because any such criticisms of traditional humanism (just like any acts of recognition or arguments concerning whom to recognize, as what, and why) must inevitably take place within a space of reasons and thus within the human normative order. Only transcendental humanism makes empirical anti- or posthumanisms possible, analogously to the way in which for Kant it is only transcendental idealism that can make empirical realism possible.[51] Moreover, it is precisely on the basis of transcendental humanism that we can see the issue of normativity as inescapably – and holistically – intertwined with the philosophical-anthropological question about what the human being is like.

I have in this chapter argued for these conclusions by employing a negative philosophical method. In a more comprehensive examination, it would be important to analyze critically not only the horrible cases of the elimination or reduction of normativity to mere nature, such as the Nazis'

---

[51] For these same humanistic reasons, I do not think the transcendental argument against sexism and racism considered above extends to, say, non-human animals. But as our form of life changes, we might have to redefine what counts as "us", or even as humans. Even then, this would be a human change, and a human redefining process, in principle to be accounted for in terms of transcendental humanism.

reduction of the Jews to stateless and normless animals, to a kind of dehumanized indifference (cf. Cavarero 2018), but also more "positive" reductionisms, such as the tendency to see the basis of morality in natural phenomena like emotions (e.g., empathy) and the temptation to defend equal human rights primarily (or merely) on the basis that there is no empirical evidence for, for example, racism or sexism. Rejecting racism and sexism is, I have suggested, more fundamental for our normative sphere than any evidence we could have against them.[52]

The rejection of racism and sexism (etc.), the affirmation of human equality and equal dignity, is thus more fundamental than any contingent natural reactions (such as empathy or recognition) or any empirical evidence for or against contingent states of affairs (e.g., empirical evidence against racism and sexism). The commitment to valuing dignity constitutes the normative sphere within which (only) we can engage in the practice of discussing *anything* ethically or normatively at all.[53] Hence, it cannot be defended (or criticized) by means of empirical evidence; it is more fundamental (like religious belief is for some Wittgensteinian philosophers of religion), albeit not in principle non-revisable or infallible. Thus, we could definitely end up in a dystopic world rejecting human dignity, though it would be difficult for us to

[52] According to Nussbaum (2018), as we saw, we should recognize women as equal to men because sexism is empirically false. In my view, our living in a normative order presupposes that we treat all human beings with dignity, and it is only in this context honoring human dignity that anything can be empirically true or false for us at all. (Nussbaum is a non-transcendental thinker.) Furthermore, I would also suggest that analyses of the Nazi tendency to destroy the human (and thus normative) status of their victims, such as Cavarero's (2018), would benefit from an explicitly transcendental approach. For example, the very unforgiveability of the Nazi crimes may be seen as a transcendental insight into what the Nazis did: "Wherever the human is injured, human beings can neither forgive nor punish this radical offense to the human as such." (Cavarero 2018, 139) It is self-evident that the Nazis had their own normative system, but a transcendental analysis may point out how deeply they were engaged in the dehumanizing project of destroying their victims' normative statuses – including the language in terms of which their human form of life had been meaningful to them. (For transcendental engagements with the problem of suffering, see Kivistö and Pihlström 2016.)

[53] This could be regarded as a reformulation of what I have elsewhere called "pragmatic moral realism" based on a transcendental argument (Pihlström 2005). Again, the recognition theorist could respond that making *this* claim is itself an act of recognition. There is no need to deny this, but one way of rephrasing my point might be to suggest that the "always already" presupposed acknowledgment of normativity as a transcendentally pervasive feature of the human world may (when analyzed from an external perspective such as the one provided by recognition theory) be "realized" as empirical (factual) acts of recognition, just as our transcendental self can be seen as identical to our empirical psychological self (i.e., not as an ontologically additional entity on top of the natural world). Cf. again Pihlström 2003, 2016; on the transcendental self, see especially Carr 1999. The concept of "realization" here could be regarded as analogous to the conception invoked in the philosophy of mind of mental states as always being realized in physical states (not taking any stand to the accuracy of that view, though).

(now) include ourselves in that potential "we" that would have lost the transcendental framework of dignity inescapably characterizing our form of life. Conversely, if we were hopelessly confined to what James labeled our "blindness" toward others, we could not compare our situation to that of those better versions of ourselves that would have seen the normative light. To be aware of the kind of blindness James is worried about – or to recognize evil as a radical inclination in us *à la* Kant – is to be already placed in a normative world in which it is possible, though not easy, to liberate oneself from that blindness. To be a Kantian-cum-Jamesian humanist is to be committed to trying to do so within the normative framework we cannot opt out from. There is no *natural* cure for Jamesian blindness or for the Kantian *Hang zum Böse*.

Moreover, holistic pragmatism reminds us that the boundary between the natural and the normative is itself constantly holistically tested and may historically change. Nothing, not even our normatively structured form of life conceived as a holistic totality, is permanently beyond pragmatic critical transformation. This critical fallibilist spirit is itself inherent to humanism and to the normative framework that humanism defines.[54] Transcendental pragmatist humanism is deeply committed to the practice of constantly transcending itself – of transforming its contents and transgressing its boundaries – insofar as such critical self-renewal amounts to an amelioration of that practice. Whether it does is again a matter of holistic pragmatic inquiry.

Furthermore, it may also be acknowledged, at the meta-level, that transcendental inquiry into normativity is in an important sense *optional*; one *can* avoid it and engage in what I have called "naturalizing reduction" (or, less reductively, recognition theory) instead. In a sense this would, if my argument is on the right track, be like living in a transcendental illusion. Yet, such an illusion is visible *only from within*, that is, only when we have made a transcendental turn and committed ourselves to an "internal" analysis of normativity as constitutive of our lives. So whether the transcendental perspective *is* optional or not is a question receiving different answers depending on whether we have adopted that perspective or not (or, in pragmatist terms, whether or not we have chosen to operate within a practice colored by our having adopted that perspective). This reintroduces

---

[54] It in this spirit that we also need to continuously examine the meta-level question of whether the holistic-pragmatist model of belief revision is itself normatively binding for us, or merely a factual account of our procedures of reasoning. I am here putting it forward as a self-reflective norm that is itself in principle testable and revisable on its own holistic-pragmatist grounds. See Chapter 4 for more reflection on this issue.

the relativism and refactualization issues all over again: our adopting the transcendental perspective is itself historically contingent, a local fact of the matter concerning our de facto processes of inquiry.[55] And so it goes: the transcendental inquirer cannot avoid working within a kind of endlessly reflexive spiral. Transcendentally, there is no way for us to *access* any non-normative "foundation" upon which we could, from within our form of life, build this normativity we are committed to. This might, I suppose, be read as *a* formulation of "transcendental pragmatism".[56]

A final note is needed. The transcendental problem concerning the very possibility of normativity is, we should admit, a philosophical mystery deep enough to make it understandable (albeit not for that reason justifiable) that some of us may think it cannot be solved without reference to something *transcendent*.[57] However, the transcendental humanist maintains that even by making such a move we cannot get rid of our inescapably human starting point. Even theism would not liberate us from the *burden* of humanism and the puzzlement about normativity. Normativity is an enigma *for us*. In philosophical-anthropological terms, a culturalist (humanist) view of the irreducible normativity of the human world, as well as its pragmatist articulation along the lines proposed in this chapter, is in a constant danger of collapsing into either cosmic transcendent teleology (classical or Christian) or refactualizing naturalism and/or cultural relativism, or the individualist contingencies of existentialism.[58] A transcendental humanism is needed at the meta-level to guide our search for plausible accounts in this field defined by these open issues, and especially to guard us against too easy solutions.

---

[55] The Rortyan would say that in this book more generally I have just contingently chosen to put forward a transcendental vocabulary of pragmatism clashing with a naturalistic one. From Rorty's own perspective, he is right – but then again, his position lacks the normative force or legitimating authority that would compel me to turn to it and out of mine. Ultimately, he can *merely* put forward his own vocabulary clashing with mine. At the meta-level, I do not see any (normatively!) good reasons to maintain such an overall position that hinders, instead of enhancing, the possibility of normatively structured philosophical debate and dialogue.

[56] The transcendental vocabulary in my view also usefully highlights the *presuppositional* character of the necessity we attach to normativity as a condition for the possibility of human practices. *Of course* normativity is entirely contingent – as everything in our human world is. Yet, insofar as there is any such human world at all – viz., any human practices – as we presumably have to assume there is, then there is also, *per* transcendental necessity, a normative structure for them as their inescapable presupposition.

[57] Taylor (1989), for example, ultimately places his account of "strong evaluation" in a theistic context; cf. Pihlström 2011a for some critical remarks on the relation between the transcendental and the transcendent.

[58] I examine these issues in more detail in Pihlström 2016. A Jamesian pragmatist may be tempted by all three, but s/he should also be able to maintain a critical distance to all of them.

CHAPTER 6

Pragmatic Agnosticism – Meaning, Truth, and Suffering

We have in the previous chapters been concerned with "existential" matters from a pragmatist perspective. In addition to the pursuit of truth as a general philosophical topic, we have drawn attention to individual commitments to truthfulness and sincerity, as well as to our ability to make pragmatic ("will to believe") decisions in existential and/or religious contexts. The possibility of normativity, as presupposed by such explorations, has also been extensively discussed.

In this final substantial chapter, I will take a further meta-level step to investigating the proper pragmatic attitude we should adopt to actually embracing or endorsing, rather than merely sincerely considering, existential positions in pragmatist contexts of inquiry, especially when it comes to dealing with issues in the philosophy of religion. Perhaps somewhat surprisingly, I will end up defending a kind of *agnosticism* – even though it might not sound as a choice a Jamesian pragmatist would be willing to make. While I have defended sincere individual commitment, I also want to carefully maintain a critical distance to recommending full-blown commitments that may turn dogmatic.

6.1 Varieties of Agnosticism

Agnosticism is usually understood as an *epistemic* position. In the philosophy of religion, agnosticism is typically characterized as a view that avoids taking any firm stand in the metaphysical and theological debate between theism and atheism by maintaining that we do not, or cannot, know – or that we do not, or cannot, justifiably believe – anything regarding whether God exists or not. There is, according to the agnostic, no way for us to rationally decide the matter either way. We are not, and perhaps can never be, justified in believing that we could finally settle the theism vs. atheism dispute in one direction or the other.[1] The agnostic may add to this basic formulation some plausible explanation for this lack of knowledge and/or epistemic justification; for instance, the spatio-temporally restricted human cognitive apparatus may be constitutively incapable of reaching any justified beliefs about the transcendent – or, conversely, about there being no transcendence at all.

Thus formulated, agnosticism could be taken to be a form of *skepticism* regarding the question about God's existence, analogous to, say, external world skepticism, which sets into doubt our capabilities of knowing anything about the existence of a reality external to our mind and thought. The relation between agnosticism and skepticism would obviously have to be spelled out in more detail, but that is not my aim in this chapter. Nor am I suggesting that agnosticism is a brand of skepticism. Here it is sufficient to note that *if* it is understood as a form of skepticism, it is a *local* variant of skepticism, focusing on our knowledge about God (and, possibly, by extension about other religiously relevant topics, such as the reality of afterlife), rather than on knowledge in general. Moreover, and more importantly, it must not be confused with what is known as "skeptical theism", because the skeptical theist does not subscribe to skepticism regarding their theistic commitment but only regarding to, for example, how the theistic God can be claimed to morally justify the reality of evil and suffering, or divine hiddenness (i.e., how God might, for all we know, have good moral reasons beyond our understanding to allow apparently innocent suffering). The skeptical theist may be locally agnostic about the way in which the problem of evil, for instance, ought to be resolved, but this does not entail agnosticism about the reality of God; therefore, skeptical theists are not agnostics about God's existence.

Both theists and atheists may (and often do) maintain that agnosticism is a cowardly middle-ground position not worthy of serious consideration.[2] One should bravely embrace either theism or atheism, they might argue,

---

[1] In a sufficiently broad construal, atheism might also cover at least some forms of agnosticism, if the former simply amounts to the lack of belief in God's existence; cf. Martin 1990. Usually interesting forms of atheism place the doxastic operator differently: the atheist believes that there is no God, rather than just failing to believe that there is. For a lucid discussion of the relations between (various forms of) atheism and agnosticism, see Draper 2017. Following Draper (among others), we may also distinguish between agnosticism as a mere *psychological* state (involving actual disbelief, or contingent lack of belief, in both theism and atheism) and agnosticism as a *normative* commitment to the proposition that neither God's existence nor non-existence is, or can be, known by us. See Draper 2001 for his reflections on his own agnosticism. Continuing the discussion of Chapter 5, the entire examination of agnosticism in this chapter should be understood as normatively framed, though (as I will explain in a moment) I will not focus on epistemic agnosticism.

[2] For a critical analysis of this line of argument, see Yoder 2013.

instead of suspending the judgment. I will try to show, in contrast to such accusations (also typical among Jamesian pragmatists), that agnosticism deserves much more serious consideration than it often gets. It need not at all amount to giving up the pursuit of truth, as it may often be portrayed. This may sound surprising, given my emphasis on the importance of making sincere individual commitments in existential matters (cf. especially Chapter 4). However, the kind of agnosticism I am primarily interested in here is not of the standard epistemic kind.

In this chapter, I will suggest that we may, in addition to received epistemic accounts of agnosticism as a non-committal position between theism and atheism, apply the general idea of agnosticism to a somewhat different issue in the philosophy of religion. I will propose that we consider *meta-level variants of agnosticism.* Such forms of agnosticism are not positioned on the scale between theism and atheism, but they are rather applied to the availability of that scale for our epistemic consideration. More specifically, a form of agnosticism directed to the question concerning the cognitive meaning of religious language will be investigated (and, with some qualifications, defended). While I cannot provide any comprehensive argument in this chapter for the meta-level meaning agnosticism I will outline, I do wish to propose it as a candidate for serious consideration by the pragmatist philosopher, a useful tool for understanding the normative structure of our sincere pursuit of truth (particularly in the philosophy of religion but by extension across a range of subject-areas). Agnosticism should be particularly relevant to pragmatist philosophy of religion, because some of the best-known arguments against agnosticism have been presented by one of the greatest pragmatists, James; nevertheless, what I will call meta-level *meaning agnosticism* can, I will suggest, be itself understood as a pragmatist position.[3]

In principle, one could be "locally" agnostic not just about the theism vs. atheism debate but also about various other issues in the philosophy of religion, such as, say, the evidentialism vs. fideism dispute in the epistemology of religious belief, or the variety of approaches that have been proposed to deal with the problem of evil. In these cases, the agnostic would claim that we do not, or cannot, know how to resolve those debates

---

[3] In a more detailed investigation, an analysis such as this ought to be integrated with a more detailed and comprehensive pragmatist philosophy of religion (cf., e.g., Pihlström 2013); in this context, my discussion of meta-level agnosticism should be primarily understood as a case study continuing the pragmatist reflection on what it means for us to be committed to – and thus to care for – the sincere pursuit of truth, even in borderline cases, such as religion, where we cannot be certain about our really being able to engage in such a pursuit.

either way. One might even be an agnostic about the theodicism vs. antitheodicism opposition in the problem of evil and suffering (to be revisited toward the end of this chapter).[4] I will in the following first focus on meaning agnosticism and will return to the problem of evil and suffering only later, also showing how a pragmatist approach in the philosophy of religion should take agnosticism more seriously than pragmatists (including the most important pragmatist philosopher of religion, James) have usually done.

Standard formulations of agnosticism as an epistemic position start from the assumption that it is *meaningful* to claim God to exist or fail to exist. The statement, "God exists" (or "There is [a] God"), is either true or false, depending on the way the world is, that is, depending on whether God actually exists or not. This statement is thus purportedly factual, and we can judge its epistemic credentials by considering what kind of evidence can be provided *pro et contra* the statement and/or the belief it expresses. It is to these epistemic credentials that standard agnosticism focuses. Let me now suggest meta-level formulations of agnosticism that transfer the debate over agnosticism and non-agnostic positions to the context of the cognitive and/or factual meaningfulness of religious language – formulations, that is, that do not just uncritically presuppose that the statement about God's existence is determinately either true or false independently of us and our practice-embedded language-use.

6.2 Meta-Level Meaning Agnosticism

Most of the different rival views in the philosophy of religion today presuppose that it makes sense, cognitively, to speak about God and God's existence (and, *mutatis mutandis*, about other religiously relevant matters, such as the reality of afterlife). The strengthening of this assumption, of course, marks a major turn in the philosophy of religion after the mid-1900s.[5] While early analytic philosophers found religious language the main problem in the

---

[4] As I have suggested elsewhere (Kivistö and Pihlström 2016; Pihlström 2020a), the opposition between theodicism and antitheodicism should be understood as the choice between those approaches to the problem of evil and suffering that consider it a normative requirement for the discussion to deliver a theodicy and those that do not. Accordingly, both theists maintaining that a theodicy can be delivered and atheists denying this (while expecting theists to deliver one) are theodicists in my sense, while antitheodicists reject this way of setting the dispute in the first place by criticizing (e.g., for ethical reasons) the theodicist expectation or requirement itself.

[5] It might be suggested that the move toward theological realism (and out of antirealist or non-cognitivist views) in the philosophy of religion is parallel to the emergence of scientific realism in the philosophy of science (cf. Pihlström 2020a).

field, more recent philosophers exploring issues in religion and theology
hardly doubt the cognitive significance of our statements about God but are
happy to move straightforwardly into considerations about the rationality
(vs. irrationality) of maintaining, say, that God exists. In the simple case of
theism vs. atheism, the theist indeed believes that God exists, while the
atheist denies this. Both, in any event, presuppose that the statement, "God
exists" (or "God is real"), makes sense, that is, that it is cognitively meaningful and has a truth-value. In terms of standard bivalent truth-conditional
semantics, this presupposition simply means that "God exists" is either true
or false depending on whether its truth-condition, the fact of God's existing,
obtains in the mind- and language-independent world. Another way of
putting the matter is to say that both theists and atheists are committed to
realism regarding religion and theology. They conceive of religious discourse
about God as truth-apt: the concept of truth can be applied to religious and/
or theological statements about the divinity (as well as, again analogously,
other religiously relevant parts of reality, such as, perhaps, the soul and its
postmortem existence), and therefore such discourse is to be treated as (in
principle) cognitively meaningful (see also Chapter 2).

An *antirealist* and/or *non-cognitivist* about religious discourse denies
realism and/or cognitivism, maintaining that religious expressions such
as "God exists" are not properly speaking cognitive statements at all. They
are not in the business of stating facts that would obtain in the world if the
statement were true. They are not made true (or false) by anything in the
language-independent world. They are, rather, expressions of emotions, or
perhaps implicit prescriptions recommending a certain way of life or
expressing one's participation in certain ritual practices.

While this approach was popular among early analytic philosophers, the
contemporary versions of such views include the *expressivist* positions
defended by Huw Price (2011) and many others. In the context of the
topics investigated in the previous chapters, it may be noted that Jonathan
Knowles (2019) takes up the complex relations between pragmatism,
naturalism, and realism by comparing Price's "global expressivism" to
the attempt to develop pragmatism as naturalized form of Kantian transcendental philosophy (i.e., the kind of attempt I have engaged in in this
book, too).[6] We may admire the complicated argumentation developed by
philosophers like Price and Knowles who wish to defend pragmatism and

---

[6] Knowles questions my earlier "dissatisfaction" with Price's proposal to maintain a naturalized and
deflationist pragmatism without any Kantian idealism or other forms of antirealism (Knowles 2019,
72). I suppose one potential disagreement between us could concern the notion of antirealism:
Knowles claims that even Peirce's conception of truth as what would be believed at the end of inquiry

realism without representationalism,[7] opting for some form of (global or local) expressivism instead. However, my basic worry is that, as far as I can see, we cannot coherently – thinking *from within* our use of language in the context of our forms of life – *just drop* the idea of language as representing an extra-linguistic reality (insofar as that idea can be given a pragmatic, rather than metaphysically-realistic, meaning). Conceptual (or pragmatic) pluralism can perhaps be fitted into this account, Knowles suggests (2019, 80), but I have argued in the previous chapters that even pragmatic pluralism needs to be given a transcendental interpretation.

From the Kantian point of view, however, the very idea that human cognition represents, or at least can represent, objects that are (empirically speaking) external to it – or the pragmatist version of that idea, with cognition understood in terms of practices of inquiry – cannot be easily replaced by an antirepresentationalist account.[8] On the other hand, the fact that it cannot be *easily* replaced or abandoned does not entail that a serious consideration of agnostic views about whether it can or should would not be an important element of a pragmatist account of language and reality. While global expressivism or antirepresentationalism is, I think, implausible as a general conception of language and reality, it does not follow that carefully considered suspension of judgment concerning the truth-aptness of a particular discourse could never serve the practices of truth-seeking. Hence, while a tentative conception of pragmatist truth and the truth-aptness of religious discourse (in an inclusivist framework) was established in Chapter 2, we now need to take a step back to examine whether our meta-level attitude to such truth-aptness is not overly confident.

The expressivist line of thought, or something very close to it, was adopted both by the logical positivists (who were mostly harshly critical of religion, rejecting religion and theology precisely due to the alleged cognitive meaninglessness of religious discourse) and early analytic philosophers of religion such as Richard Braithwaite (1955), as well as already before him, in his distinctive way, John Wisdom (1945). There is also a sense in which a version of this non-cognitivist approach was continued

---

is antirealistic (Knowles 2019, 70), but this is precisely where I think the Kantian pragmatist should carefully distinguish between transcendental idealism and antirealism, maintaining that pragmatism is committed to empirical realism instead of (any) antirealism. (This is, admittedly, partly a terminological matter, but I have always believed such matters to matter, as our terminological choices shape our philosophical discourses.)

[7] See also Rydenfelt 2019a for a careful argument along these lines.

[8] I surely have my doubts about antirepresentationalism, but I also agree with Knowles that pragmatist antirepresentationalism (when articulated, e.g., along Price's lines) need not share all the problems that, say, Rorty's version suffers from. On Rorty, see Chapter 1.

in the Wittgensteinian tradition, even though Wittgenstein himself cannot be clearly classified either as a non-cognitivist or as anything else. Incidentally, it can be claimed that most Wittgensteinian philosophers of religion have hardly simply suggested that religious discourse lacks cognitive meaning but that different language-games establish different criteria of meaning, and the kind of meanings that a properly religious use of expressions like "God" – or even "exists" – may have in religious contexts must not be conflated with non-religious, for example, scientific, usages of such expressions.

Now, what I wish to suggest is that we may apply the general idea of agnosticism to the debate over the cognitive meaningfulness of religious statements. Instead of either affirming (with cognitivists and realists finding religious discourse truth-apt and purportedly factual) or denying (with non-cognitivists and non-realists finding such discourse lacking in cognitive meaningfulness and not being in the business of stating facts at all) this cognitive and factual meaningfulness, or the truth-aptness of religious discourse, the agnostic at the meta-level maintains that we do not, or cannot, know (or justifiably conclusively determine) whether religious discourse is cognitively meaningful, purportedly factual, and/or truth-apt. Or at least there is no way we could rationally resolve the matter either way. We should, in other words, remain "meaning skeptics" about religious discourse. We cannot, when engaging in religious discourse or when examining it philosophically (or theologically), know, or perhaps even justifiably believe, that it makes sense, cognitively speaking, but neither can we know that it doesn't. Perhaps somewhat surprisingly, I will try to argue in what follows that this is a line of thought that a pragmatist philosopher of religion may be particularly well equipped to adopt.[9]

Admittedly, the pragmatist (as well as the non-pragmatist, for that matter) could argue that it becomes problematic for us to actually view ourselves, with full confidence, as participants in religious practices and discourses, if we adopt meaning agnosticism. However, this is one reason why agnosticism is a potentially pragmatically valuable position. It makes sense of our participating in religious discourse and religious practice without full cognitive access to the ways we are, or are not, able to "make sense" of our own language-use within such discourses and practices. This

---

[9] The pragmatist philosopher of religion may of course also question (e.g., on Jamesian grounds) what exactly it means to claim religious discourse to be "truth-apt" and may propose, as I did in Chapter 2, a pragmatist conception of truth, integrated with the ethical notion of truthfulness, for a further elaboration of this idea. On the other hand, this pragmatist attitude to truth may itself be a reason to consider the kind of agnosticism I am proposing.

position might be regarded as a kind of meaning skepticism, but there is a sense in which it definitely is not a skeptical view; the agnostic is not simply denying our being able to know that we can, or cannot, make sense by using religious language. On the contrary, our adopting an agnostic stance enables us to occupy an open space of philosophical (and, as the case might be, theological) reflection that is better equipped to acknowledge the distinctive character of religious ways of using language than any dogmatic commitment to straightforward forms of realism or cognitivism about religious discourse, or the denials of such commitments, ever can. (I will return to this issue concerning the meta-level significance of agnosticism toward the end of the chapter.)

There might, indeed, be some obvious attractions in an agnostic view concerning the cognitive and/or factual meaningfulness of religious statements. One would not, for instance, have to take any firm stand in the debates between realists and non-realists.[10] I suppose many of us may find it very difficult to arrive at any clear conclusion here, so agnosticism might, just as in the theism vs. atheism case, *prima facie* be a way of maintaining a critical middle path, while actively keeping the issue open – without just *leaving* it open in the sense of failing to care about pursuing it further. Moreover, just as the meta-level agnostic need not settle the realism vs. antirealism issue one way or the other, s/he presumably will not have to settle the evidentialism vs. fideism issue, either. Nor will the agnostic have to worry too much about the fact that realism about religious discourse (understood as truth-apt) may seem to entail a form of religious exclusivism, which we might be ethically and politically motivated to criticize quite independently of the realism controversy.[11] Agnosticism may thus help us get rid of a wide variety of troubling and unwelcome philosophical complications – in this case at the meta-level rather than at the "first-order" level of the theism vs. atheism dispute. Indeed, if it turned out that agnosticism is necessary for developing a plausible version of religious inclusivism (cf. Chapter 2), then we would have all the more reason to embrace agnosticism.

Even so, the kind of agnosticism I am (tentatively and with qualifications) defending here is an attitude of active critical inquiry rather than an

---

[10] In a more comprehensive examination of realism regarding religion and theology, a distinction between non- and antirealism would also have to be made (see, e.g., Pihlström 2020a, chapter 1). Here I won't dwell on that issue, as religious and/or theological realism in its multiple forms is not my main topic in this book but is only tangentially related to my pragmatist elaborations.

[11] For the argument that (strong) realism entails exclusivism, according to which at most just one religion is true (either in a straightforwardly propositional sense or in a more theologically pregnant soteriological sense), see Chapter 2, as well as Pihlström 2020a, chapter 4.

attitude of mere passive and uncritical relaxation or quietism. We can never be sure that we can continue to rest content with our decision to avoid taking a stand. Agnosticism does not mean that we should cease to inquire into the issue about which we are (at the moment) agnostic.

6.3   Non-cognitivism about Religious Language

In order to add some concreteness to the proposal to develop a meta-level meaning agnosticism regarding religious language, let us consider the view propounded by one of the very few logical empiricists who actually entertained religious ideas, Richard Braithwaite. His 1955 lecture, "An Empiricist's View of the Nature of Religious Belief", deserves a brief exposition, as it explicitly takes up the issue concerning the cognitive content of religious language.

Braithwaite points out that the philosophy of religion at the time of his writing had made decisive progress precisely by turning its attention to the nature of religious and theological language: "until recently the emphasis has been upon the question of the truth or the reasonableness of religious beliefs rather than upon the logically prior question as to the meaning of the statements expressing the beliefs" – "as if we all knew what was meant by the statement that a personal God created the world" (Braithwaite 1955, 3). It seems to me that this is precisely what contemporary analytic philosophy of religion seeks to do, having returned to questions of truth and reasonableness and leaving behind the "logically prior question" concerning meaning, and therefore a healthy dose of meta-level agnosticism would in my view serve the field rather well, also in a pragmatist framework.[12]

Just as Wisdom (1945) had suggested in his famous essay, "Gods", Braithwaite argues that the hypothesis that God exists cannot be empirically refuted. He takes it as obvious that "most educated believers" do not think of God as being "detectable" and "hence do not think of theological propositions as explanations of facts in the world of nature in the way in which established scientific hypotheses are" (Braithwaite 1955, 6). This is in striking contrast with, for example, the current science vs. religion debates, in which various cosmological explanatory attempts to use theism precisely in that way seem to be the rule rather than an exception. However, Braithwaite moves from this critical account of the cognitively nonsensical character of religious statements

---

[12] The mainstream contemporary theistic philosophers mentioned in Chapter 2, Plantinga and Craig (among others), are good examples of the way of thinking that takes religious language to be truth-apt, in addition to being problematically committed to the exclusivist view that *they* have found religious truth in their language-use.

to a comparison between religious and moral statements. Referring to Wittgenstein's *Philosophical Investigations* – at that time a recently published posthumous work – he appeals to the "use principle" of meaning, according to which "the meaning of any statement is given by the way in which it is used", and reminds us that moral statements "have a use in guiding conduct" (Braithwaite 1955, 10). The problem of religious belief therefore becomes an empirical problem concerning the use of religious statements to express religious convictions (Braithwaite 1955, 11).[13]

Braithwaite does not subscribe to the standard logical positivist account of moral language as "emotive"; rather, he finds it "conative" and views moral assertions as commitments to policies of action (Braithwaite 1955, 12–13). It is through this analogy to moral statements that he arrives at his solution to the problem of the nature of religious belief:

> That the way of life led by the believer is highly relevant to the sincerity of his religious conviction has been insisted upon by all the moral religions, above all, perhaps, by Christianity. 'By their fruits ye shall know them.' The view which I put forward for your consideration is that the intention of a Christian to follow a Christian way of life is not only the criterion for the sincerity of his belief in the assertions of Christianity; it is the criterion for the meaningfulness of his assertions. Just as the meaning of a moral assertion is given by its use in expressing the asserter's intention to act, so far as in him lies, in accordance with the moral principle involved, so the meaning of a religious assertion is given by its use in expressing the asserter's intention to follow a specified policy of behaviour. [. . .] it is the intention to behave which constitutes what is known as religious conviction. (Braithwaite 1955, 15–16)

This could be read as a commitment to a certain kind of pragmatism about religious belief – specifically, about *sincere* religious belief. Jamesian pragmatists, after all, have also repeatedly quoted the Biblical phrase, "by their fruits ye shall know them". Indeed, it is no wonder that pragmatist philosophy of religion is often neglected by the analytic mainstream today: it might be taken to be basically just logical empiricism, only less formal and, hence, less clear. Conversely, however, the pragmatist may find many valuable insights in Braithwaite's somewhat untimely meditations.

Indeed, Braithwaite seems to subscribe to a pragmatic holism not very different from the one espoused by Morton White (see Chapters 2, 4, and 5). Just as scientific hypotheses need to be understood not in isolation but

---

[13] Let me note that I am not taking any stand on whether Braithwaite's account of Wittgenstein's "meaning as use" idea is correct (i.e., I remain agnostic regarding the accuracy of his reading of Wittgenstein).

in relation to the "whole system of hypotheses", we also need to consider "a system of religious assertions as a whole" and the way this whole system is "used" (Braithwaite 1955, 17). This leads him to perceive a very intimate connection between religious and moral principles – both are ultimately principles of conduct (Braithwaite 1955, 18). Indeed, the following could be read as a formulation of the pragmatist maxim or principle better known from Peirce and James: "The way to find out what are the intentions embodied in a set of religious assertions, and hence what is the meaning of the assertions, is by discovering what principles of conduct the asserter takes the assertions to involve." (Braithwaite 1955, 18)[14]

Toward the end of his essay, Braithwaite arrives at his characterization of what religious assertions are: "A religious assertion, for me, is the assertion of an intention to carry out a certain behaviour policy, subsumable under a sufficiently general principle to be a moral one, together with the implicit or explicit statement, but not the assertion, of certain stories." (Braithwaite 1955, 32) Like moral beliefs, understood as intentions to behave in a certain way, religious beliefs are such (moral) intentions to behave, "together with the entertainment of certain stories associated with the intention in the mind of the believer" (Braithwaite 1955, 32–33). This also, in his view, makes religious beliefs open to reasonable critical discussion, as the practical consequences of behavioral principles can obviously be rationally discussed and compared (Braithwaite 1955, 34).

I have not quoted at length from Braithwaite's examination of religious belief in order to endorse his views, which I admit remain too closely stuck with the strict empiricist criteria of meaningfulness set by the logical empiricists. I do think, however, that Braithwaite's assimilation of religious beliefs to moral principles deserves much more serious attention than contemporary analytic philosophers of religion, or even most pragmatists, would be prepared to grant them. Among other things, they carry certain extremely important themes from Kant (religion can rationally and legitimately only be based on morality) and classical pragmatism (the meaning of a concept or statement is ultimately based on its potential practical

---

[14] Braithwaite's analysis continues by the observation that religious stories play a crucial role in shaping the practical attitudes of conduct that the religious believer is committed to. Such stories do not have to be interpreted as empirically veridical (Braithwaite 1955, 27); rather, the religious person may pragmatically interpret them "in the way which assists him best in carrying out the behaviour policies of his religion" (Braithwaite 1955, 29). This may sound too straightforwardly instrumentalistic even for a pragmatist taste, but the basic idea of entangling religious language-use very closely together with moral conduct is something that Braithwaite shares not only with the pragmatists but also with Kant, for whom religious concepts like God and the immortal soul were, famously, only available to us through the use of practical reason (cf. Chapter 3).

outcome), as well as the later Wittgenstein ("meaning is use") to the philosophy of religion – via logical empiricism, to be sure, but without succumbing to the simplified scientistic repudiation of religion and theology that movement is famous for.[15]

The purpose of my discussion of Braithwaite in this section should now be clear. What I am proposing is not that we endorse the view formulated by him but that we *consider* adopting an agnostic stance to the question concerning the rational justifiability of his position in contrast to the realist-cognitivist one. We may be well advised to suspend judgment regarding the rational decidability of this meta-level linguistic issue either way. (It might be added that the agnostic might also insist on remaining agnostic about agnosticism itself and avoiding any final commitment even here, though.) This meta-level meaning agnosticism, at any rate, provides us with an open space for critical inquiry into the problems and benefits of both realism/cognitivism and antirealism/non-cognitivism concerning religious and theological language. We may, as *pragmatic* agnostics, find a view like Braithwaite's to be *available* to us in a sense different from the rather dogmatic neglect of such positions especially in the metaphysical mainstream of analytic philosophy of religion today (but obviously also in Braithwaite's own account, which by itself is not agnostic but resolutely non-cognitivist).

6.4   The Pragmatic Meaning of Meaning Agnosticism

Agnosticism has of course been criticized for many reasons – for example, for the reason that it allegedly fails to care about continuing the inquiry into the matter that is left open – but here it is particularly interesting to note that it has sometimes been taken to collapse (back) to atheism. This is, at least from a pragmatist perspective, a much more interesting criticism, as agnosticism certainly does not need to entail an uncritical dismissal of inquiry. It may, on the contrary, be understood as a way of keeping the path of inquiry open.[16] But the collapse to atheism only concerns epistemic agnosticism.

---

[15] Certainly Braithwaite's view does not deserve the brief dismissal by William Hasker (2005) as a mere surrendering of the cognitive content of religious belief "in the interest of defending its personal and ethical significance in the life of the believer", because with a suitably pragmatist reinterpretation, the latter kind of practical significance might actually be regarded as the source of any content a belief might have.

[16] See Yoder 2013 for a highly relevant critical discussion of how both atheists like Richard Dawkins and philosophers sympathetic to religion like James have argued against agnosticism.

In James's "The Will to Believe", agnosticism figures as an inherently unstable position: if you postpone your decision concerning the "live option" of whether or not you should commit yourself to the theistic belief, suspending judgment in the hope of acquiring more reliable evidence for either theism or atheism later, then you will, James argues, practically speaking live the life of an atheist, failing to take the practical step of believing in God. Thus, agnosticism is pragmatically equivalent to atheism. This could also be regarded as an application of the pragmatic method, as spelled out in James's *Pragmatism*, in particular.

Recall, again, how James (1979 [1897], 14–15) characterizes what makes an option "genuine": it has to be "live" in the sense that both of the rival hypotheses are "live" ones for the subject; "forced", that is, the decision cannot be avoided, as we cannot refuse to face the issue and there is no "third way"; as well as "momentous", that is, a unique, highly significant, non-trivial chance (cf. Chapter 4). Crucially, suspending judgment – that is, remaining agnostic – may be equally risky as believing, or refusing to believe. Even if agnosticism were a reasonable choice "in theory", in our practical lives it would take us no further than atheism.

However, it may be argued that this pragmatic reduction of agnosticism to atheism does not similarly work at the meta-level. Even though we may (I think) agree with James that agnosticism – when seen as a possible position within the theism vs. atheism debate – is unstable and at least runs the risk of collapsing to atheism (or perhaps even directly so collapses), and that therefore from a pragmatist point of view there is no clearly discernible difference between atheist and agnostic positions regarding God's existence, this conclusion may not hold at the meta-level. That is, a meta-level agnosticism about the cognitive and factual meaningfulness of religious belief, for example, an agnosticism regarding the question whether to embrace Braithwaite's position in contrast to the mainstream analytic philosophers' of religion firm commitment to realism, may not be similarly reducible to either non-cognitivism (anti- or non-realism) or cognitivism (realism). This is at least partly because the WB argument in the Jamesian style does not similarly apply at the meta-level, as our "live" *weltanschaulichen* options hardly include abstract meta-disputes such as the one between cognitivism and non-cognitivism.[17]

---

[17] On the other hand, I do maintain that the WB idea can in principle be applied in very different contexts, including meta-contexts. In a sense, I here wish to remain agnostic regarding the actual scope of applications of the WB principle. It should not be dogmatically maintained that meta-level disputes can never become genuine options available to WB considerations. Cf. further Chapter 4.

At least I cannot find in Jamesian pragmatism any obvious reason for rejecting meaning agnosticism right away. On the contrary, agnosticism, as suggested above, may enjoy several interesting benefits. Instead of hindering our pragmatic commitment to critical inquiry into how exactly we in our religious or non-religious language-use live amidst the questions concerning whether our expressions make sense, and (if they do) what kind of sense, agnosticism, when adopted at the meta-level, may actually be a pragmatic attitude of the critical inquirer who needs to keep the matter open precisely in order to continue investigation.

The kind of meaning agnosticism I have sketched may, hence, even have the benefit of serving some humanly vital purposes and being therefore pragmatically highly significant. This is particularly because it may be taken to play a very important role in acknowledging the kind of *unease* we may experience regarding our religious (and non-religious) views about the world. We may, simply, be sincerely puzzled about whether or not such views, or our attempts to express them in religious language, make sense at all. Therefore, meaning agnosticism needs to be considered precisely because it may enhance our commitment to the sincere pursuit of truth and truthfulness (see Chapter 1). Religious meaning agnosticism might be regarded as an attempt to acknowledge (some) religious believers' (the possible inappropriateness of the word "believer" here notwithstanding) puzzlement about whether they are so much as able to make sense by using their religious expressions. They may not be willing to simply deny such sense-making, but it would also be a violation of the depth of their religious convictions to maintain that their religious language-use simply unproblematically makes factual and/or cognitive sense, as that would bring it on a par with everyday or scientific discourse concerning tables, trees, and viruses – which could even be regarded as blasphemous by some religious people. Therefore, there could be *theological* reasons for religious meaning agnosticism. There may also be *humanistic* reasons: agnosticism can, precisely due to its refusal to take a determinate stand on whether our religious language "makes sense", seek to make sense – at a meta-level – of our human condition itself and the inevitable fragility of its (our) sense-making activities.

It may, then, be pragmatically extremely important for us – it may play an existential role in our lives as well as a normative role in our practices of pursuing the truth – *not* to take a firm stand on whether our statements are cognitively meaningful or not when we utter religious expressions. Therefore, views such as Braithwaite's need to be kept on the agenda of philosophers of religion even today. And therefore agnosticism is a meta-level stance worth maintaining. It plays a vital pragmatic role in our on-going consideration of how to respond to the challenge of speaking about matters that religiously matter. Or, to put it more mildly – more agnostically – we cannot be certain that it does not play such a role.

6.5   Antitheodicism and Agnosticism as Humanism

I have argued that focusing on religious language enables and motivates a deeper, more interesting and more exciting form of agnosticism – an agnosticism about the meaningfulness of religious language – than the more straightforward agnosticism that simply advocates epistemic neutrality or suspension of judgment regarding the standard apologetic opposition between theism and atheism. Agnosticism about religious meaning may take us deep into the problem concerning what religious language-use is and hence into a reflection on what it means to live one's life as a believer engaging in such language-use (or, conversely, what it means, pragmatically, not to live such a life). It is a form of agnosticism that enables us to avoid the apologetic alternative between pro- and anti-religious metaphysical worldviews. It therefore serves the pragmatist commitment to sincerity and truthfulness by questioning any simple assumption of truth-aptness.

One might even suggest that the meta-level form of agnosticism I have recommended is not only the attitude of pragmatic critical inquiry but also a more humanistic form of agnosticism than the typical epistemic types of agnosticism (though not "humanistic" in the sense of being committed to a "secular humanism" opposed to any religious outlook): focusing on religious language, and especially on the thin line separating the critical views propounded by the logical positivists from the more religious-friendly views espoused by thinkers like Wisdom and Braithwaite (and, of course, the Wittgensteinians), entails focusing on the role played by this distinctive and problematic discourse in our human practices and forms of life. This is a focus clearly shared by classical pragmatism, too, albeit not as narrowly confined in linguistic analysis. In contrast, the theism vs. atheism controversy today often remains stuck in the context of something like natural theology and its rejection, with cosmological and design arguments (in their classical and updated versions) flourishing. Such a metaphysical orientation is a return to something pre-Kantian. The foundational insight of early analytic philosophy of religion – without specific references to Kant – is that we have to start examining religion and its place in our lives and worldviews by first critically investigating how we structure our world in terms of religious discourse. This fundamentally Kantian approach ought to be shared by pragmatism as well (cf. Chapter 3), and in these terms both Kant's critical philosophy and pragmatism may be seen as sharing a meta-level agnosticism, too.

Various further applications of meta-level agnosticism may also be proposed. They might include agnosticism about theodicies and antitheodicies, for instance. I have argued on a number of earlier occasions (e.g., Pihlström 2020a) that we should embrace an antitheodicist position for ethical reasons, in order to avoid instrumentalizing other human beings' meaningless suffering in the service of some "overall good" – that is, rendering it allegedly meaningful in some more comprehensive sense. But it also seems to me that theodicism threatens to come back in an antitheodicist context, because even when formulating antitheodicies in contrast to theodicies we seek to view the world harmoniously and "rightly" in an ethical as well as epistemic sense (see Pihlström 2020a, chapters 5–6). At the meta-level, it may therefore be advisable to suspend any final judgment regarding the ultimate philosophical success of antitheodicism. This agnostic attitude might even play a role in the attempt to acknowledge the kind of puzzlement about our meaning-making capabilities suggested above, this time in the context of our attempts to philosophically deal with the evil and suffering around us. It might be religiously and theologically relevant for our forms of life or religious practices to maintain that we, as limited human beings, are not in the position to rationally determine whether we can attach cognitive meaningfulness to our religious language-use, and as an element of this suspension of judgment we may maintain that we cannot ultimately settle the philosophical issues concerning meaningless suffering and evil.[18]

This "dialectics of antitheodicism" should in my view be taken very seriously, and one way of formulating this seriousness is precisely by applying agnosticism at the meta-level to the question concerning the rational resolvability of the problem of evil and suffering.[19] I could still be firmly committed to promoting antitheodicism for pragmatic and ethical reasons, but I could maintain intellectual humility by acknowledging that there is no way I can argumentatively or theoretically fully resolve this issue either way. Its theoretical irresolvability could indeed be an element of its being a pragmatic and essentially ethical or existential

---

[18] Again, let me note that I am neither defending nor attacking any religious outlook here. My criticism of theodicism, as well as any agnostic view on the outcome of this critique, is also intended to cover the secular versions of theodicist "meaning-making".

[19] Another meta-level question is, of course, what should be meant by the rational resolvability of this, or any similar, issue.

issue: our taking a stand on this question defines, in practical terms, who we are. However, we need to dwell on the idea of antitheodicism, and its dialectics, a bit more in order to fully appreciate the strength of the (meta-level) agnosticist option in this context. We need to explore this idea particularly in the interest of elaborating on the idea of agnosticism as a form of pragmatic humanism. It is a key idea in my meta-level meaning agnosticism that we ought to take very seriously our fragile and insecure human predicament, our never being fully confident about our abilities to make sense by participating in the religious discourses and practices we (may) participate in, as well as the more specific discourses within those discourses, such as the theodicism discourse in particular.

6.6   The Dialectics of Antitheodicism, Agnostically Analyzed

Let me, thus, in order to elaborate on this humanistic dimension of agnosticism in some more detail, add a brief excursus to the theodicism discussion, which can obviously only very summarily be taken up here, despite its overall significance to Jamesian pragmatist philosophy of religion (cf. again Pihlström 2020a).

Consider first an example of antitheodicist argumentation. Hans Jonas, a celebrated Jewish philosopher who started his career as one of Martin Heidegger's students, delivered his seminal lecture, "Der Gottesbegriff nach Auschwitz" ("The Concept of God after Auschwitz"), in München in July 1984 (reprinted in Jonas 1996). The lecture powerfully articulates Jonas's idea of a processual, finite, and suffering God. The only divinity we may, morally speaking, be able to believe in "after Auschwitz" – after the devastating catastrophe of the Holocaust, which functions as a metonymy for unspeakable evil and suffering in general – is, Jonas argues, a God of "contraction, withdrawal, self-limitation", that is, a God who "renounced his being, divesting himself of his deity" in order to allow human life (and death) to emerge in the world (Jonas 1996, 134–135, 142).

Jonas, of course, is not alone in proposing an ethical rethinking of God in response to the ethical need to come to terms with evil and suffering. I have suggested on an earlier occasion that his account can be usefully compared to what James had to say about the concept of God several decades earlier (see Pihlström 2014a). Jonas comes from an entirely different tradition, but his conception of the divinity as "involved" and as "run[ning] a risk" (Jonas 1996, 138) is strikingly parallel to James's idea of a "finite God", which James (e.g., 1975 [1907], Lecture VIII) set against the theodicist views propounded by his Hegelian absolutist contemporaries (such as F. H. Bradley).[20] What is crucial for this comparison between two otherwise very different thinkers is the fact that both James and Jonas based their metaphysics of the divinity on *ethical* considerations. Both were prepared to revise the traditional metaphysically realistic picture of an absolute, atemporal, and infinite God in response to concrete temporal and historical events, and especially the uncompromising reality of human suffering such events manifest. Both for a pre-Holocaust thinker like James and for a post-Holocaust one like Jonas, the inescapable ethical need to recognize the suffering other – especially the meaninglessness of their suffering that cannot be fitted into any allegedly purposive divine plan, or any secular teleological (e.g., Hegelian) proxy thereof – yields an ethical demand to adjust the concept of God (insofar as one employs that concept in the first place) in such a way that any theodicies seeking to justify suffering from a divine perspective are rejected as immoral (cf. Bernstein 2002; as well as, again, Kivistö and Pihlström 2016; Pihlström 2020a). We might say that in making their proposals Jonas and James did not *merely* pursue the truth about God's reality in a metaphysically realistic sense but were engaged in an ethical and existential pursuit of truthfulness in the pragmatic sense articulated in Chapter 1.

I believe we need to follow Jonas and James in maintaining that one's individual ethico-existential commitment to a truthful and sincere exam-ination and transformation of personal ethical convictions and ideals in varying historical contexts – such as one's attempt to desperately come to terms with the irrevocable historical fact that the Holocaust did take place – may legitimately lead to even rather fundamental revisions of one's metaphysical and theological ideas, including those concerning the reality (or unreality) of God. James and Jonas share with Kant the convic-tion that ethics must not and cannot be based on religion or theology, but in a quasi-Kantian sense religion and theology need an ethical grounding (cf. Chapter 3), to the extent that nothing, not even our account of the divinity, can be immune to critical ethical reflection. Indeed, the moral necessity of revising our theological picture of the divinity is arguably one instance of the broader moral necessity of rejecting all (explicit and impli-cit) theodicies and embracing a thoroughly antitheodicist approach to the problem of evil and suffering.[21]

---

[20] I won't here dwell on the details of James's antitheodicism already explored in Kivistö and Pihlström 2016, chapter 5, as well as Pihlström 2013, 2014a, and 2020a.

[21] In a highly sophisticated recent study, Lauri Snellman (2020) argues, however, that ethical anti-theodicies require a more fundamental conceptual antitheodicism critically refuting (through what he labels a "grammatical metacritique") the metaphysical background assumptions of theodicism.

The antitheodicist, in the sense in which I am using this concept (cf. again Kivistö and Pihlström 2016; Pihlström 2020a), not only rejects all theodicies – that is, all attempts to justify apparently meaningless suffering from an imagined divine perspective yielding ultimate harmony and reconciliation – but abandons the very pursuit of theodicy by refusing to examine the problem of evil and suffering in a context defined by the normative expectation that a theodicy (or a secular proxy) ought to be delivered in the first place. According to (ethical) antitheodicism, there is something profoundly wrong in that context itself, not merely in the specific theodicies that might be provided in order to "justify the ways of God to man". If we even ask the question of how to justify the suffering of, say, the victims of the Holocaust, we already fail to acknowledge those victims and their suffering in an adequate ethical sense. We are guilty of such non-acknowledgment by merely entertaining the *possibility* that their suffering might conceivably be (theodicistically) justified.[22]

It remains to be investigated, however, whether an ethically motivated antitheodicist rethinking of religious and theological ideas, such as Jonas's – or James's – postulation of a finite divinity, amounts to something like a *theodicy by other means*. Furthermore, the same question can in principle be asked regarding any other antitheodicist project as well. Indeed, I have here referred to Jonas and James only in the interest of providing an obvious example. The issue that needs to be raised in their case is whether the revision of our metaphysics of God ultimately serves the "temptation" of theodicy (see Bernstein 2002), that is, our need (which is itself an understandable and natural human need) to render suffering a meaningful element of our world-picture, albeit at a meta-level? My worry, in brief, is that an antitheodicy such as Jonas's or James's may in the end yield a meta-level theodicy, and that this "dialectics of antitheodicism", as we may call it, cannot be easily avoided. The meaninglessness of unspeakable yet concretely real suffering challenges any imagined theodicist harmony, but acknowledging *this* – for example, by acknowledging the need to revise our concept of the divinity as a response – may at the end of the day amount to imagining a meta-level harmony, after the theodicist

---

[22] Note the analogy to the problem of even entertaining the possibility that, say, racism might be true (see Chapter 5). Varieties of this kind of ethical antitheodicism abound. As I have tried to show (see again Kivistö and Pihlström 2016), there is a tradition of "Kantian antitheodicy" seeking to avoid theodicies as violations of the very conditions for the possibility of a moral perspective on the world. In contemporary philosophy, this framework contains various Jewish (e.g., Levinasian), Wittgensteinian, and pragmatist antitheodicies, and as we argue in our 2016 book, there are also remarkable literary analogies to these philosophical ideas. For theodicies and antitheodicies, see also several essays in Rydenfelt et al. 2019, especially Proudfoot 2019.

confusions (including the concept of God they may have presupposed) will have been cleared away. We might thus speak of the dialectics of all attempts at an ethical antitheodicist "enlightenment": arguably, theodicies tend to return as soon as we had believed to have left them behind. Such a meta-level pursuit of harmony and reconciliation may, but need not, take the form of a "finite divinity" theory.

The "return" of theodicies in purportedly antitheodicist contexts may take a number of different forms in different philosophical frameworks. In Emmanuel Levinas's vocabulary, the "temptation" of theodicy in our philosophical thinking is thus multifaceted.[23] As this book only tangentially touches upon the vexing issues of theodicy vs. antitheodicy, let me just briefly take up only a few examples of attempts to respond to extreme evil and irreconcilable suffering in antitheodicist terms, yet (arguably) inviting an implicit theodicy.

Kant himself, the arch-antitheodicist, may be argued to have postulated a theodicy by other means in his doctrine of the *summum bonum*, viz., more precisely, his account of our legitimate hope that the harmony of moral duty or virtue and happiness will ultimately be secured by God through an "infinite progression" of our existence. This postulation of God's existence and the immortality of the soul is of course "practical" rather than "theoretical", as we can know nothing whatsoever about the reality of these Kantian postulates of practical reason. However, the ethical need to postulate God and an immortal soul is unavoidable for us, something that our very commitment to morality – which our reason in its practical use itself requires – entails.[24] While Kant firmly rejected Leibnizian and in principle any possible theoretical, speculative, rationalizing theodicies, he may thus be argued to bring theodicies back to his overall picture through his practical philosophy.[25]

---

[23] For reflections on what Levinas means by this "temptation", see also Bernstein 2002, especially the chapter, "Levinas: Evil and the Temptation of Theodicy". (Bernstein's volume also contains an insightful discussion of Jonas's approach to evil and God.) In his seminal essay, "Useless Suffering", Levinas (2006 [1996]) heavily criticizes both the explicit and the implicit theodicies of Western philosophy by emphasizing the utter uselessness and meaninglessness of suffering; clearly, what I mean by "theodicy by other means" has a lot to do with Levinas's conception of *implicit* theodicy and its role in our philosophical tradition. However, this chapter is by no means a study on Levinas's views on evil and suffering.

[24] See again the discussion of the "postulates of practical reason" in Kant's Second Critique (Kant 1983a [1788]); cf. Chapter 3.

[25] For Kant's rejection of theodicies, see his famous "Theodicy Essay" (Kant 1983b [1791]); cf. Kivistö and Pihlström 2016, chapter 2. See also Chapter 3. I am *not* saying that this is my reading of Kant. On the contrary, I am fully committed to the picture of Kant as the starting point of antitheodicism in Western philosophy of religion (see also Pihlström 2020a). What I am saying is that there is a *worry* that even the Kantian antitheodicy, as compelling as it is, might slide into a theodicy by other means, and this is something that I feel has not been adequately discussed previously, at least not in

One of the most important antitheodicists in the early twentieth century, James, in my view shares the same problem of being unable to completely avoid theodicism. He certainly successfully frames his entire discussion of pragmatism, pluralism, as well as individual diversity and sincerity (cf. Chapter 2) by taking seriously the problem of evil and suffering and rejecting both Leibnizian and Hegelian theodicies (see James 1975 [1907], Lectures I and VIII; see especially 19–22, 138–140), but this does not prevent him from at least occasionally lapsing into a kind of mysticism that ultimately does not have to worry about the concrete reality of evil. While I am not generally a follower of Richard Gale's (1999) controversial interpretation, according to which James had a "divided self" – a division between the "Promethean" pragmatist self and the religiously "mysticist" one – the potential return of theodicies in James's tendencies toward religious mysticism (or at least his embracing such a possibility) is something that could, in my view, be analyzed in terms of Gale's perhaps otherwise simplifying distinction. Even James seems to be willing to grant us the right to believe that everything will ultimately – at a mystical total level – end up in harmony, although on the other hand his "official" pragmatist position seems to be that no such "moral holiday" is possible for us and that we can only afford, instead of any cosmic or religious optimism, a healthy pragmatic meliorism, always seeking to make things better without any final guarantee about our succeeding in that challenge.[26] James's WB (cf. Chapter 4) arguably licenses a belief to mystical ultimate harmony, should that be a genuine option for the believer.

So-called Wittgensteinian antitheodicism, based on the Wittgenstein-inspired approaches in both ethics and the philosophy of religion, might

---

my own earlier contributions. In any case, the postulates of practical reason only remain something we can, according to Kant, legitimately hope for, not anything that we could know to be real, and this is one significant difference between Kant's position and actual theodicies.

[26] On James's antitheodicist rejection of "moral holidays", see Pihlström 2013 and 2014a, as well as Kivistö and Pihlström 2016, chapter 5. The main source of James's views on mysticism is, of course, *The Varieties of Religious Experience* (James 1958 [1902]), but also many of his other works exhibit a temptation toward mysticism. On meliorism as a middle ground between optimism and pessimism, see James 1975 [1907], Lecture VIII (and see again Chapter 3). Furthermore, it could be suggested that insofar as the pragmatic meliorist position is James's final considered view – ultimately rejecting mysticism and moral holidays – then it is precisely the conception of a "finite God" that James, analogously to Jonas, offers as his proxy for theodicies. Instead of being an absolute harmonizer, God is merely a superhuman power that may assist us in realizing a better world – but *this* reconciliatory position may now yield a meta-level theodicy. The same can be said about the role James grants to the concept of *hope* in his meliorism: even when things are going badly, we do retain the right to hope they will turn better. (Perhaps James remains an "optimist" at a meta-level precisely in this sense: meliorism, in contrast to pessimism, seems to remain an option, no matter how badly things are going.) James (1975 [1907], Lecture I) definitely speaks of pragmatism as a "philosophy of hope"; see also Pihlström 2008a, 2009.

seem to be free of the problem of the return of theodicies, due to Wittgensteinian philosophers' (e.g., Phillips 2004) uncompromising rejection of theodicies as confusions of moral and religious language-use coming close to blasphemy. However, insofar as Wittgensteinian antitheodicists genuinely take their departure from Wittgenstein's own writings, they cannot ignore the fundamental role played by the pursuit of a certain kind of ethical, metaphysical, and/or transcendental *harmony* in our relation to the world, especially in the early Wittgenstein. For the Wittgenstein of the *Tractatus* and the pre-Tractarian *Notebooks* (Wittgenstein 1961, 1974 [1921]), happiness consists in a mystical kind of harmony with the world (see Pihlström 2020a, chapter 5, for further analysis). While we may, convinced by antitheodicist arguments, be committed to viewing the world "rightly"[27] in the sense of taking seriously the meaninglessness and irreconcilability of the suffering people have to undergo around us – suffering that cannot be brought into any harmony or eventual reconciliation – it is precisely this world-viewing itself that may at the meta-level be taken to yield a reconciliation with the world that is ultimately harmonious in its ability to take disharmony seriously. The world of the "happy man" is, according to Wittgenstein, different from the world of an unhappy one, and even an antitheodicist can be "happy" about having found a "right" way of viewing the world – thus inviting theodicism back simply by entertaining the idea of a harmonious total perspective.

Even post-Holocaust Jewish moral philosophers such as Levinas or Jonas may bring theodicism back through a side door. Jonas's (1996) "limited" God, as already suggested, is a case in point. Because we cannot harmonize our world-picture by any explicit theodicy "after Auschwitz", we have to satisfy our need for harmony by revising the picture of the divinity (something that, as noted above, takes place in James, too). We cannot reconcile ourselves with the suffering of the Holocaust simply by revising our picture of God, but doing so may be a vital step on the way to seeing the world – in a historical situation after the Holocaust – "rightly" and thus to arriving at a harmonizing reconciliation, again at a meta-level.[28]

Whether something analogous takes place even in Levinas's approach cannot be settled here. Levinas might in fact be one of the very few ethical thinkers who succeed in avoiding all temptations of theodicy – but then

---

[27] The phrase, "viewing the world rightly", obviously alludes to the penultimate proposition of the *Tractatus* (Wittgenstein 1974 [1921], §6.54).

[28] See also Bernstein's (2002) chapter on Jonas ("A New Ethic of Responsibility"). Again, I am certainly not claiming that Jonas is just a closet theodicist. On the contrary, he is certainly sincerely committed to the task of thinking beyond theodicies after the Holocaust. I am again just suggesting that we should perceive a *potential* return of theodicies in his rethinking maneuver.

again even in his case the nagging question might return: is our taking seriously the other's suffering in its horrible "excess", its naked meaninglessness and human bodily vulnerability, a way of ultimately (harmoniously) seeing the world "rightly" in its inescapable ethical dimensions? If we sincerely commit ourselves to viewing the world and our place in it in terms of the fundamental Levinasian ethical relation to the other, especially the other's face, is everything *then* all right – have we then succeeded in finding a meta-level reconciliatory relation to the ethical challenge of being in the world? In this context, our taking seriously what I have elsewhere called "transcendental guilt" (Pihlström 2011a) may be a meta-level defensive move which hides our humanly natural tendency to let our sense of moral guilt become corrupted. If we emphasize our inescapable human predicament of always falling short from the moral duty (at least in Levinas's uncompromising and infinitely demanding terms),[29] will we *then* have arrived at a meta-level reconciliation all over again? At least we ought to be constantly worried about this possibility (to which I will return below).[30]

I have in my earlier work on antitheodicism tried to acknowledge the possibility of ending up with a meta-level picture of harmonious meaningfulness by examining the full reality of meaningless suffering (see, e.g., Kivistö and Pihlström 2016, 283–284). In brief, the key question is whether the antitheodicist can ultimately coherently escape theodicist tendencies and assumptions. While theodicism certainly operates with the idea of a harmonious overall picture – a kind of imagined condition of ultimate happiness in which the sorrows and sufferings that seem to define human life would eventually have been overcome or reconciled – the antitheodicist may be argued to seek a totalizing picture of their own, too. Antitheodicism itself pursues a kind of reconciliation with the absurd world of suffering and pain even when claiming to reject all reconciliatory attempts – indeed, precisely in making this claim itself.[31]

---

[29] By "transcendental guilt", we may roughly mean the idea that we remain morally (and, hence, metaphysically) guilty due to our inevitable failure to adequately respond to the ethical duty posed by the other, no matter which particular contingent actions or omissions we factually commit. This guilt is "transcendental" precisely in being a necessary condition for the possibility of adopting an ethical stance in the first place.

[30] Examples like this could be multiplied. For instance, Albert Camus can with good reason be regarded as an antitheodicist not only blaming Christian theology for injustice but also perceptively analyzing the ways in which secular ideologies tend to lead to violence (see Sharpe 2019, 165–168), but his own views on "universal culpability", our being all evil (172), may reinvoke theodicism by reintroducing the commitment to an ultimately harmonious understanding of the general human tendency to evil. (This is comparable to "transcendental guilt".)

[31] This observation may be compared to the suggestion made by some Holocaust (and Holocaust literature) scholars who have maintained that there is an unbridgeable gap between any attempt at

It may, then, be necessary to acknowledge the impossibility of ever driving through any fully antitheodicist argument. While there is a sense in which "everything changes" – we see the world and human life in a completely different light – as soon as we adopt antitheodicism instead of theodicism,[32] and while I am still fully convinced that antitheodicism is pragmatically, even vitally, needed for us to be able to see the world "rightly" in its dimensions of human finitude, vulnerability, and radical contingency, the problem is that *this* antitheodicist standpoint will then be recommended as *the* correct one, the one and only ultimately true (or ethically acceptable) standpoint from which human suffering ought to be viewed. We may then end up raising antitheodicism to the status of a "totalistic" and ultimately harmonious worldview while only allegedly recognizing pluralism and diversity. At least the antitheodicist should be constantly aware of this problem and should therefore self-critically acknowledge the threatening impossibility of ever finally or completely acknowledging the sheer meaninglessness of others' suffering and of really being able to avoid rendering it meaningful by incorporating it into some coherent meaning-making narrative.

Accordingly, isn't the antitheodicist who reminds us that disharmony will forever be with us to stay also still attempting to offer a meta-level harmonious total picture, albeit an antitheodicist one? That is, isn't s/he recommending her/his own (only different) version of how to see the world rightly and how to live rightly, and perhaps even to be "happy" in the transcendental Wittgensteinian sense according to which the "happy man's" world is different from the unhappy one's? Doesn't antitheodicy, thus, lead to the very same predicament that it (with good reason) found theodicism guilty of, the self-deceptive pretension of happiness and harmony, only at the meta-level?[33]

---

understanding and what really happened; it has been argued that any attempt to understand is inevitably obscene, as it fails to appreciate the ineffability or unspeakability of Holocaust suffering, thus exhibiting a lack of piety. (See Adams 2016 [2014], 308, 317, 328; as well as Patterson 2018.) On the other hand, it could be claimed that explaining or understanding should never be confused with excusing or forgiving. Even so, no matter how deeply we understand what happened in the Holocaust, it is, I think, a legitimate concern that claiming to understand might to a certain degree be a way of non-acknowledging the victims. (But so could, conversely, our not caring to understand, or to understand ever more deeply.) This may, again, be regarded as analogous to the return of theodicism to the antitheodicist discourse claiming to acknowledge meaningless suffering.

[32] I like to compare this to a Kuhnian paradigm shift (cf. Kuhn 1970 [1962]).

[33] Admittedly, theodicies typically seek harmony *in* the world. A Wittgensteinian refusal to find harmony *in* the world while still seeking to find it in one's transcendental attitude to the world as a whole might thus, despite its pursuit of harmony, be compatible with antitheodicy and its insistence on recognizing worldly disharmony. However, the worry here is that even the meta-level pursuit of harmony might in the end indirectly contribute to the theodicist project – or at least the antitheodicist ought to be aware of this potential risk.

There is no easy answer to such a self-reflective worry. In pursuing a truthful relation to ourselves and our fellow humans, we just have to keep asking these questions, given that we are committed to the project of antitheodicist acknowledgment of others' suffering. *This* is part of our never-ending concern with living rightly – and also with happiness and harmony as subordinated to that concern. A world in which we were able to finally and conclusively resolve this matter would indeed be too harmonious for us. One key problem is, then, whether every explicitly developed philosophical antitheodicist move ultimately results in a betrayal of the antitheodicist pursuit of taking evil and meaningless suffering ethically seriously and of recognizing the suffering other. This question returns, preventing any full, complete harmony. We can, eventually, only approach it as Jamesian "sick souls" never finding a stable harmony.

In terms of the distinction between meaningfulness and meaninglessness, a self-critically reflexive antitheodicist also needs to ask whether the antitheodicist argumentation s/he invokes in the interest of acknowledging experiences of meaningless suffering in the end constitutes a problematic pursuit of meaning, after all. Is there a self-reflective ethical vulnerability at the very core of the attempt of viewing the world rightly, even if that attempt is structured in terms of antitheodicism? The question arises whether we will eventually move the horizon of meaninglessness out of our sight when engaging in such philosophical construals of meta-level meaningfulness. This, once again, is one of those questions that self-critical philosophical reflection on ethically appropriate responses to suffering can never avoid. In other words, the problem (or at least *a* problem) here is that we may lack the critical resources needed to counter the WB argumentation of a would-be theodicist who "wills to believe" in meaningfulness despite the meaninglessness around us. It is insufficient to merely cite evil and suffering as evidence against meaningfulness here, insofar as the matter cannot be evidentially resolved. We thus need an active WB courage to *counter* theodicies in our own lives, no matter how live options they might be for some of us.

These critical questions may, furthermore, be intensified by taking a look at how a certain kind of theodicism may seem to return in the context of our attempting to "learn" something from an event as extreme as the Holocaust – or even from our acknowledging the inability to draw any meaningful moral "lesson" from it. It may be self-deceptive to continue to utter, "Never again", as we know that history has unpleasant ways of surprising us and that the only thing the Holocaust really taught us is that something unimaginable could happen (see Patterson 2018).

Possibly, an even more disturbing conclusion seems to follow from our taking seriously Primo Levi's – one of the most perceptive analysts of the Holocaust – ruthless investigation of what he regards as blasphemous prayer. The case of the two prisoners, named Kuhn and Beppo, as analyzed by Levi (1996 [1958]), is famous: it constitutes an utter failure to acknowledge another human being and their purposeless suffering to thank God for one's own survival – for one's not having been selected to be murdered in today's horrible *Selektion* – while the other person, one's neighbor, *has* been selected to go to the gas chamber.[34] Now, the "lesson" of this case narrated by Levi might even be extrapolated to an ethical problematizing of *any* gratitude we are tempted to feel regarding our own fortunate situation – also outside the extreme circumstances of Auschwitz, in quite ordinary human life, religious and secular life included. If we seriously entertain the idea that *our* fortunate situation (in comparison to our less fortunate fellow human beings), whether in terms of health, wealth, social relations, professional success, or whatever, is in some sense an indication of divine grace that falls upon us rather than some others (or, again, any secular proxy thereof), are we not in a sense acting like Kuhn in Levi's description? Are we not thanking God (or the world, or life, or fate, or history, or pure chance) aloud and thereby disregarding, non-acknowledging, the suffering other? Is even silent gratitude by definition theodicist by implicitly accepting the immoral and unjust logic of a world – divinely or secularly structured – that lets some of us flourish while crushing others?[35]

The problem, in other words, is that even mere gratitude, as purely positive and virtuous as it might be taken to be, may in the end seem to wear a theodicy on its sleeve. It might seem like a morally virtuous attitude to acknowledge one's own privileged position as something that one has not deserved by one's own deeds but has somehow fallen upon one, but even if this acknowledgment is sincerely antitheodicistically intended, it may be implicitly committed to the temptation of theodicy, as it may (like Kuhn's prayer) inadvertently endorse a theodicist logic of how goods and ills befall upon innocent human beings.

---

[34] The case, briefly paraphrased, is this: A prisoner called Kuhn had, at Auschwitz, avoided death (this time) and thanked God by praying aloud, while another (considerably younger) one, Beppo, was lying in the next bunk in the same barrack, knowing he had been chosen to be murdered. Levi's moral condemnation of Kuhn's attitude is harsh: "Does Kuhn not understand that what happened today is an abomination, which no propitiatory prayer, no pardon, no expiation by the guilty – nothing at all in the power of man to do – can ever heal?" And he adds: "If I was God, I would spit at Kuhn's prayer." (Levi 1996 [1958], 129–130) See also the discussion (with further references to both primary and secondary literature) in Pihlström 2020a, chapter 6.
[35] Compare this to the brief comments on silence and translation in Chapter 2.

I have no proper response to offer to this worry that we may end up with upon reading Levi's compelling work (and I am not implying that Levi himself would have intended his writings to be interpreted in such an extreme manner, viz., as problematizing the very idea of being grateful for undeserved good things in one's life). In any case, the mere possibility of extrapolating the concern with blasphemous prayer in this way perhaps shows how central the responsibility for acknowledging another human being within the context of a shared human life is for Levi, and how vitally important his analysis of the destruction of such responsibility in the Holocaust is for all of us.[36] More generally, we should note that any attempt to "learn a lesson" from suffering as extreme and absurd as the Holocaust may be faced with a similar extrapolation. We end up in a blasphemous non-acknowledgment of the other when trying to suggest that now we (finally) know that this should happen "never again" (as if we had failed to "know" that earlier). We thereby tend to raise ourselves above the history of suffering, and such *hubris* may in the end crush us.

The self-deceptive obscenity of the mere claim to understand returns here, to the extent that repeating the slogan, "never again", might in the end yield a (theodicist) form of "Holocaust impiety" (cf. Adams 2016 [2014], 308–309).[37] Our (understandable) attempt to learn a lesson from the catastrophe of the Holocaust – or comparable catastrophes in history and the present – may thus unwittingly turn into a secular theodicy, even though the original aim may have been to acknowledge the victims' horrible suffering in an antitheodicist context. My next task is to explain why I believe the kind of pragmatic agnosticism introduced earlier in this chapter might help us in living with this unwelcome *aporia*.

6.7   Sincerity and Self-Deception Again

Different varieties of antitheodicism, we have seen, run the risk of bringing theodicism back. What this reinforces is the need for continuous critical self-reflection that is (fortunately, one might suggest) built into the very concept of antitheodicism all the way from the start. We

---

[36] Compare this to the brief references to Nazism as eliminating the normativity of the human form of life in Chapter 5. The duty to acknowledge other human beings in this context must already take place within a practice that is irreducibly normative.

[37] Note, however, that neither Adams (2016 [2014]) nor other Holocaust (or Holocaust literature) scholars would typically use the vocabulary of theodicism vs. antitheodicism. The relation between theodicism and the problem known as Holocaust (im)piety, or the "obscenity" of understanding, would clearly deserve a much more detailed elaboration. Cf. again also Patterson 2018.

have to understand antitheodicism as an ethical *process*, rather than any sort of final theory. Accordingly, it could be suggested that *antitheodicism* will never collapse into theodicism, even though specific *antitheodicies* may very well collapse into theodicies ("by other means"). This also entails that antitheodicism will never be ready but will always have to be continuously rethought, revised, and rearticulated – also in changing historical circumstances. In terms of "transcendental guilt" (Pihlström 2011a), this further means that whenever (re)thinking our guilty human condition, we must do so by *never* letting our sense of universal human culpability liberate us from our own unique guilt. We are, indeed, transcendentally guilty for being unable to avoid the corruption of *our own* guilt for others' suffering. This is, I submit, a fundamental insight in the Jamesian analysis of the instinctive "blindness" in us (cf. Chapters 2 and 3).

Now, again at the meta-level, my worry is the following. Does this reflexive and processual meta-level antitheodicism, or its Jamesian pragmatist version, itself collapse into theodicism all over again? Such a collapse may happen if we are even for a moment *satisfied* with the antitheodicist account we have arrived at. The processual antitheodicism sketched here thus entails that we must never rest satisfied with our account of evil and suffering.[38] We can never reach final happiness in or harmony with our way of thinking about these matters, or in our way of approaching them philosophically, ethically, or theologically. Our antitheodicism must always be understood as incomplete and inadequate. Like ethics itself, it is a task in which we always inevitably fail; antitheodicism is an infinite project – as infinite as the Levinasian responsibility for the other. We must approach our commitment to formulating our antitheodicism itself via a "negative" philosophical method, focusing on our unavoidable failures and incompleteness, in the context of a Kantian-cum-Jamesian pessimism about the human condition that was discussed in Chapter 3.

The very project of antitheodicism begins from the observation that theodicies can, and should, be criticized for a certain kind of lack of sincerity, or a collapse to insincerity – as has been done in the antitheodicist tradition starting from Kant's (1983b [1791]) Theodicy Essay and its focus on Job's sincerity (*Aufrichtigkeit*), in contrast to his pseudo-consoling friends' insincerity (see again Kivistö and Pihlström 2016, Chapter 2).

---

[38] We might label this duty to avoid even momentary satisfaction in the pursuit of antitheodicism a "Faustian" form of antitheodicism – perhaps also thus acknowledging our temptation of (always again) entering into a contract with the devil.

There is a certain kind of pretense or even Sartrean-like "bad faith" in theodicies.[39] In Jamesian terms, theodicies constitute failures of truthfulness – and thus failures of pursuing *truth* in the pragmatist sense.[40] However, what is crucial now is that the antitheodicist must perceive their own temptation toward such self-deceptive bad faith even within their own quest for sincerity. Antitheodicists should not simply blame others – theodicists – for insincerity but should focus their critical analysis of insincerity on their own thought patterns and assumptions.

For this purpose, we may utilize the concept of "transcendental self-deception", especially its close connection with transcendental guilt (see Pihlström 2007, 2011a; see also, again, Chapter 3). Self-deception is something that we should all, theodicists and antitheodicists (as well as pragmatists and non-pragmatists) alike, be seriously concerned with.[41] If we so much as entertain the idea that by having formulated an antitheodicist approach to the problem of evil and suffering we would be somehow protected from insincerity and an (itself evil) instrumentalization of others' suffering in the service of some imagined ultimate harmony, we are already sliding down a slippery slope back to theodicism. This is the general pattern of what I have above called "theodicy by other means" or the "dialectics of antitheodicism".

Not only philosophical formulations of antitheodicism but artistic and literary ones as well might be examined critically from this perspective. For instance, Holocaust literature could be studied by asking the question (as difficult as it is to even pose such a question in such a context) of whether the very attempt to describe and interpret the meaninglessness of suffering as experienced by Holocaust victims in antitheodicist terms inadvertently yields a meta-level picture of harmony and meaningfulness. This could, again, be comparable to the above-mentioned popular tendency to repeat the words, "never again", in the context of responding to the Holocaust – as if we had "learned a lesson" or as if something positive had come out of that unimaginable yet concretely real horror. Even a Holocaust writer as firmly antitheodicist as Levi (see above) has been claimed to have rendered his own Holocaust experience "meaningful" in terms of his testimony – and somehow this may be the tragic fate of all such moral testimonies. The

---

[39] See also the brief comments on this, in response to a point raised by Steven Crowell, in Pihlström 2020a, chapter 4.

[40] James's use of the word "true" in this context (see James 1975 [1907], Lecture I) ought to be taken seriously, as analyzed in Pihlström 2020a.

[41] For an intriguing analysis of the way in which self-deception relates to Kant's conception of our being radically evil, see Madore 2011 (and the discussion in Chapter 3).

moral witness (cf. Margalit 2002) cannot avoid witnessing, but they must at the same time be fully aware of the impossibility of ever fully witnessing (see also Agamben 2002 [1999]).

What I have elsewhere (Pihlström 2007) labeled "transcendental self-deception" is, I believe, directly relevant to this situation. In the Kantian context, we may understand our temptation to arrive at rationalizing metaphysics – due to the natural tendencies of human reason, as analyzed in the Transcendental Dialectic of the First Critique – as a kind of self-deception of the transcendental self whose cognitive structures are constitutive of the world insofar as it is experienceable by us but who cannot legitimately transgress its cognitive limits. Extending this notion beyond the dialectical transcendental illusions of metaphysics, it may be argued that we engage in transcendental ethical self-deception insofar as we forget the human condition presupposed by our being *selves* in the first place, always already structured by moral responsibility and the ineliminable possibility of our being morally guilty.[42] If we lack full understanding of our necessarily (constitutively) being potentially guilty – if, that is, we remain blind to our own blindness to others, in Jamesian terms – we are in the grip of transcendental ethical self-deception. And this is precisely the kind of self-deception at work in our hubristic belief that we have learned a moral lesson from the Holocaust, a lesson that we could ever appreciate with adequate "piety". Transcendental self-deception is, we might say, at the same time metaphysical and ethical – just like the pragmatic pursuit of truth(fulness), or our failing in such a pursuit, is. It results from our misunderstanding our own place in the world and leads to an ethical mis- or non-acknowledgment of others' perspectives, especially their experiences of meaningless, non-reconcilable suffering.

Let me supplement the rather extreme Holocaust example by a somewhat more mundane, albeit certainly not trivial, one. In the context of the COVID-19 pandemic raging through the globe in 2020–2021 (at the time of this writing), the antitheodicist ethical thinker presumably finds it necessary to take very seriously all the protective measures and restrictions that many countries have introduced in order to prevent the spread of the virus, because otherwise the health care system would be overburdened and a great number of innocent people would catch the infection and some of them (especially the elderly and people in certain risk groups) might develop a serious disease and even die. Following the general logic of antitheodicism,

---

[42] This is thus yet another analogy of Kantian transcendental illusion in our pragmatist discussion of the pursuit of truth (see also Chapters 3 and 5, in particular).

this line of thinking avoids instrumentalizing other human beings' suffering in the service of some overall good, such as the economy. None of the potential individual victims of the virus can be sacrificed for the benefit of the totality. Thus, we cannot, for example, just let some people die in order to prevent the collapse of the economic system – we cannot use those people as means even to protect the (later) victims of that collapse (some of whom will perhaps eventually get sick and die, too, from causes at least indirectly related to such a collapse). However, in the absence (at the early stages of the pandemic) of any effective medical cure or vaccine, there is a sense in which we, precisely by being careful to avoid catching the virus and thereby spreading it further, might have been acting in ways practically equivalent to *trying to let other people catch it first*, hoping that only after the virus had infected a certain (relatively large) number of people would the population as a whole be better protected from the disease. It has been rightly pointed out that a crisis such as the COVID-19 pandemic touches different individuals very unfairly: by ordering everything online, working from our home offices, and avoiding public transportation we privileged people push others to the front line in dealing with the virus. Shouldn't, for example, the Levinasian ethical antitheodicist, firmly rejecting even the *slightest* temptation of using other people as instruments for her/his own benefit, rather volunteer to be among the first to be infected? But this, of course, would not help, because s/he would then also easily run the risk of spreading the infection to others, those s/he wishes to protect.[43] Wouldn't, moreover, *any* attempt at an antitheodicist acknowledgment of others' suffering as something that ought not to take place similarly run the risk of using the others as means ("by other means")? The risk of quasi-theodicist self-deception cannot be fully eliminated from any serious response to a moral crisis such as the COVID-19 pandemic.

The antitheodicist must, then, be constantly wary of the continuous threat of transcendental self-deception – a self-deception going to the very heart of our existing as individual subjects sharing a world with others – right at the center of their (our) antitheodicist project itself. Such insecurity and incompleteness, as a kind of meta-level disharmony, *define* the project of antitheodicy; they are constitutive of the very possibility of adopting an antitheodicist perspective. Antitheodicism must never be *easy* for us. Indeed, it *cannot* be easy and remain genuinely antitheodicist at the same

---

[43] Furthermore, such an apparently ethical volunteering could also be motivated by selfish reasons: the earlier one catches the infection, the better resources will there still be left in the health care system for one's possibly demanding hospital care. On the other hand, treatments might have improved, if one caught the infection later.

time. A sincere antitheodicism must avoid the kind of insincerity that would make things easier for us by self-deceptively claiming that we have moved "beyond" the agonizing meaninglessness of suffering by having found the "right" antitheodicist approach to it. A sincere antitheodicism admits, among other things, that there is no proper lesson to be learned from the Holocaust: the slogan, "Never again", is naïve insofar as it claims to have left the horror behind. So is any attempt to just "rethink God after Auschwitz", unless it acknowledges a kind of impossibility of such rethinking analogous to the impossibility of ever truly witnessing (cf. Agamben 2002 [1999]; Patterson 2018).

Indeed, the sincere antitheodicist should acknowledge our impossibility of never leaving behind – never truly recovering from – the Holocaust, or any horrible suffering our fellow human beings have had to go through. Such suffering is irrevocable, and acknowledging this is part of our antitheodicist challenge. But then again we must acknowledge this irrevocability not in the easy way of insincerely claiming to have moved beyond the horror by means of such an act of acknowledgment. We should, rather, sincerely acknowledge our own inability to be sincere, to avoid the self-deception of theodicism even when developing antitheodicism. This meta-level sincerity is, I would like to think, a fundamental element of the Jamesian pragmatist account of sincerity in its transcendental rearticulation that I have pursued in this book, and therefore in an important sense my elaboration of the Jamesian conception of truth, truthfulness, and individual existential commitment culminate in these worries about our proper relation to the suffering other within our normative practices.

It might be suggested – and I am now finally arriving at the reason why this lengthy treatment of antitheodicism was needed in the present context in the first place – that the dialectics of theodicism and antitheodicism I have sketched here yields a specific form of agnosticism, viz., a humanistic form of agnosticism as (again) distinguished from the kind of agnosticism that would be standardly available in the theism vs. atheism debate within natural theology and its alternatives. This application of agnosticism focuses on our philosophical resources for dealing with others' suffering in a humane manner, on our chances of ever truly embracing a form of antitheodicism that would not run the risk of instrumentalizing such suffering into serving some alleged overall goods, such as the (antitheodicist) attempt to see the world "rightly" and meaningfully. Due to our almost unavoidable tendency to slide into theodicism, it may be advisable to adopt an agnostic view on our ability to develop a sustainable form of antitheodicism, no matter how sincerely we hope to acknowledge others' suffering. Even when formulating a transcendental argument in favor of antitheodicism conceived of as a necessary condition for the possibility of maintaining a truly ethical stance to the suffering of other human beings, we may have inadvertently resorted to a theodicist temptation to construe meaning into our own lives rendering our use of these philosophical (or theological) concepts existentially significant to us. In contrast to this temptation, we should understand the possibility of meaninglessness as a necessary condition for the possibility of ethical seriousness.

We may therefore also suggest that something like Jamesian WB is needed for us to sincerely embrace an antitheodicist attitude to others' suffering in a dialectical situation seeming to make any argument in favor of antitheodicism desperately inconclusive. While James argued, as explained in Chapter 4, that we have the pragmatic right to adopt "the religious hypothesis" at our own risk insofar as it is a "genuine option" for us and the matter cannot be decided on purely evidential grounds, a Jamesian pragmatist might analogously argue that we have a similar right to stick to antitheodicism even in the argumentatively inconclusive dialectical situation we have seen to arise.[44] This insecurity or ground-lessness may itself, at a meta-level, be considered part of the human predicament. Our antitheodicism rests on such a thin ice that we need to put our pragmatic energies into action in order to maintain it, in some version, in our attempts to view the world "rightly". This may be painful, but it is, of course, not even nearly as painful as the real suffering that antitheodicism is designed to acknowledge.

Antitheodicism must, therefore, not only acknowledge others' suffering but make *us* suffer – in Levinasian terms, suffer for the suffering of others (cf. Levinas 2006 [1996]) – but even then the problem remains that such antitheodicism, possibly backed up by a quasi-Jamesian WB, may yet again recreate meaning into our experience of responding to suffering, yielding a kind of "meta-theodicy" by other means. I can see no easy way out of this dialectic constitutive of our uneasy human condition, and admitting *this* is, we may conclude, itself a constitutive feature of any thoroughgoing

---

[44] The problem with employing WB here is that the theodicist could reason similarly. For example, Viktor Frankl's (1969) "will to meaning" could be construed as an analogy to WB seeking to render even extreme suffering such as the Holocaust meaningful. (The contrast between Frankl and, e.g., Levi 1988 [1986] could not be sharper.) WB alone cannot therefore settle the issue. Rather, this case highlights the need to develop and evaluate our WB commitments holistically in the context of our doxastic, ethical, and existential lives understood as "seamless webs" of normative commitments along the lines of White's holistic pragmatism (as discussed in Chapters 4–5).

antitheodicism. But then again, possibly even *this* is, at the meta-level, too harmonious a picture – and so it goes, potentially *ad infinitum*.[45]

6.8 Transcendental Agnosticism

Agnosticism in its meta-level form should, as already hinted above (and this is no surprise at this stage of our inquiry), be seen as a chapter of Kantian-inspired critical philosophy. It is, arguably, transcendental in the sense of addressing and exploring the necessary conditions for the possibility – and therefore also the limits – of religious language-use. Analogously, the humanism that meta-level agnosticism endorses may itself be regarded as transcendental in the Kantian sense: it is only within humanism that we can make sense of our human predicament, as already argued in Chapter 5 and implicitly throughout this book.

An even more thoroughgoing transcendental agnostic might claim that *only* a meta-level meaning agnosticism enables our engagement in religious thought and language-use, because religious discourse is, *qua* religious, constitutively troubled by its sense, or by its own ability to make sense. It would, according to such agnosticism, be pseudo-religious (cf. Pihlström 2013) to simply presuppose with full confidence that religious language makes sense, or is "truth-apt", in a cognitivist and realist manner.[46] An ineliminable unclarity about the ability of religious discourse to make cognitive sense would then be regarded as a constitutive feature of such a discourse as the kind of discourse it is. Thus understood, meta-level transcendental meaning agnosticism would come close not only to certain Wittgensteinian developments in the philosophy of religion but also some "postmodern" views that reject philosophical theism as an adequate account of religious faith.[47]

---

[45] The agnosticism formulated and defended here can be seen as an elaboration of the Kantian-cum-Jamesian pessimism discussed in Chapter 3. Sincerity is both necessary and impossible for us; hence, we must remain agnostic about our existential situation and our ability to live up to its ethical (and, possibly, religious) demands. This type of agnosticism also supports a kind of (sincere) individualism: we should not impose our theodicism or antitheodicism upon others who might view their own suffering differently from us. However, it may be asked whether the same holds, again, at a meta-level: can I impose on others *this* "do not impose your view on others" principle? From a holistic pragmatist standpoint, all my engagements and commitments are all the time ethically at stake. There is no safe meta-level, nor any protected privacy of one's individual commitments (no matter how sincere) that could be immune to criticism. Critical self-examination extends through all our practices, at all levels.

[46] From a pragmatist perspective, it is of course another question what exactly it means to regard religious discourse as "truth-apt"; this would have to be construed in terms of something like James's pragmatist account of truth, as outlined in Chapters 1 and 2.

[47] For example, Kearney's (2010) "anatheism" might be an interesting relative of meaning agnosticism.

Agnosticism, in this meta-level shape focusing on the conditions of meaning, is thus also transcendentally entangled with pragmatic humanism. Continuous puzzlement at the *limits* of religious meaningfulness – of our capacities of engaging in meaningful discourse within a religious form of life – could be taken to characterize the human condition, at least for believers who are critically self-reflective about their faith. Moreover, even the non-religious can be deeply puzzled about human language and its limits of sense more or less in the same sense; Wittgenstein's famous metaphor of language as a "cage" easily comes to mind here.[48]

However, when speaking about, and even defending, a meta-level form of meaning agnosticism, or transcendental agnosticism, I am not assuming that the distinction between "first-order" epistemic agnosticism and "second-order" or meta-level agnosticism would always be crystal clear. Some philosophers might suggest that it makes little sense to speak about agnosticism at the meta-level: from a Carnapian point of view, for instance, questions concerning the choice of a linguistic framework, as distinguished from existence questions within such a framework, are not cognitive questions at all. Thus, for someone like Rudolf Carnap it would hardly make sense to be agnostic about religious meaning: questions of meaning must be settled first as, ultimately, matters of pragmatic choice, and only then can cognitive issues concerning our postulation of entities within a chosen framework arise (cf. Carnap 1950).

However, my proposal in this chapter is "post-Quinean"[49] in the sense that I admit that our way of drawing the distinction between the different levels – the "first-order" level of epistemic concerns and the meta-level concerning meaning – is itself contextualized in terms of our previous and on-going ways of drawing such distinctions and operating within the contexts defined by them. Our conception of what we can and cannot meaningfully say depends on what we take the world to be like – and this, of course, could also be regarded as one of the insights of the later Wittgenstein.[50] The semantic thus partly depends on the epistemic, and vice versa, to the extent that we may (borrowing a phrase sometimes used in Quinean contexts) talk about a "reciprocal containment" of epistemic agnosticism and (meta-level) linguistic meaning agnosticism. Our meta-level agnosticism about religious language may thus also partly depend on

---

[48] See Wittgenstein's 1929 "Lecture on Ethics" (in Wittgenstein 1993); on Wittgenstein and the limits of language, see the essays in Appelqvist 2020.

[49] Of course, it is not only post-Quinean but also holistically pragmatist in White's sense (see Chapters 2, 4, and 5), even though White's holism has not been explicitly utilized in this chapter.

[50] Wittgenstein's *On Certainty* (1969), in particular, would be the key source here.

our *metaphysical* puzzlement about the world we take ourselves to be living in, including puzzlement about evil, suffering, and God.

Let me note, however, that I am not claiming that the meta-level meaning agnostic has to employ the Kantian transcendental vocabulary in articulating their agnosticism. This vocabulary is (we should again observe) optional and subject to pragmatic considerations, as I tried to briefly explain in Chapter 3 when comparing Kant's and James's central ideas and in Chapter 5 when investigating normativity transcendentally. Even so, the focus of agnosticism on questions concerning the conditions and limits of meaning is strongly emphasized in the kind of meta-level agnosticism I have formulated. A pragmatist version of agnosticism can very well leave it an open issue how exactly, or indeed whether, to construe agnosticism in relation to Kantian transcendental philosophy. My argument in this chapter only suggests that such a construal very well fits the overall Kantian pragmatism this book has defended. It is certainly an example of a possible pragmatist development of transcendental reflection on conditions making our lives and discourses human.

Nor is my proposed agnosticism necessarily restricted to the meaningfulness and truth-aptness (or lack thereof) of religious discourses; more broadly, by analogy to religious inclusivism (cf. Chapter 2), the pragmatist meta-level agnostic may argue that metaethically exclusivist, arrogant claims to possess the one and only correct ethical theory are quite as problematic as religious exclusivism is. Pragmatic pluralism extends from the philosophy of religion to (meta)ethics, too. What we need here is a thoroughly ethical acknowledgment, at the meta-level, of our being unable to arrive at an exclusively correct theory (whether ethical or theological); we (may) pragmatically need many different theories, including, for example, Kantian deontology, consequentialism, and virtue ethics, to make sense of our ethically demanding human condition. We may also pragmatically need the rival insights of both moral realism (cognitivism) and expressivism (non-cognitivism), thus remaining agnostic about making any final choice in this regard.

Acknowledging the significance of inclusivism in its various forms is to maintain a thoroughly fallibilist conception of our own philosophical claims. However, if we do so, then we must attribute some concept of truth to those claims themselves. For example, if we remain meta-level fallibilists about moral realism, being undecided about the truth-aptness of moral discourse, we must, by agnostically suspending judgment about whether moral discourse is truth-apt, assume that both moral realism claiming that it is and expressivism claiming that it isn't might be true (or correct). At least we must be able to be philosophically wrong or mistaken, even if there could (in the inclusivist sense) be more than one true philosophical account of a given subject-matter. Our genuine ability to fail in our philosophical endeavors is a necessary (transcendental) condition for the possibility of adopting an ethically sincere attitude to our own pursuit of philosophical truth. This in a sense limits agnosticism "from within".

6.9   Agnostic Humanism, Hope, and Truth

I have in this chapter only discussed selected examples of meta-level agnosticism – both agnosticism about religious meaning and agnosticism about the resolvability of the theodicism vs. antitheodicism controversy concerning the problem of evil and suffering. I have also suggested that this kind of agnosticism is humanistic in the sense of seeking a plausible philosophical account of the human condition. These are clearly central and relevant examples in the philosophy of religion, but here they have primarily served as, indeed, mere examples. The main point of my investigation is the proposal that the concept of agnosticism deserves to be articulated and further developed considerably beyond its initial and obvious epistemic context of employment. By so doing we may put this concept into the service of a pragmatist account of what it means for us to be normatively and sincerely committed to pursuing the truth about our human condition, both in general and in its individual existential variability. This covers not just religion but ethics and philosophy generally.

Even in the epistemic context there would still be much further reflection to do. For example, it might be interesting to examine in what sense exactly the agnostic may still *hope* that God exists. Hope in this sense might be adequate as a religious attitude weaker than full belief, as has been proposed by, for example, Simo Knuuttila.[51] At a step higher meta-level, it could be investigated whether it would be sufficient for a religious agnostic to merely *hope to be able to believe* that God exists. Such an agnostic would not believe that God exists, nor necessarily even hope that He does, but they could hope to be able to so believe (or, of course, to so hope). In principle, an indefinite number of nested doxastic operators could be added to account for ever more complex cases of iterated states of belief and hope. Furthermore, a Jamesian pragmatist might ask whether one's

---

[51] Knuuttila, as far as I know, has defended this view only in some of his publications in Finnish. In brief, the main idea is that for a religious person it is sufficient to hope that God exists; it is not necessary for one's religious attitude to believe that he does. Thus, an agnostic could clearly be a religious person in Knuuttila's sense, if they merely hope that God exists. In principle, even an atheist could be "religious" in this sense, if they hope, despite disbelieving, that God exists.

hope to be able to believe might actually – at least in some special cases of human life – yield an active *will* to believe.[52] In principle, one might remain agnostic about whether one has good reasons to hope that God exists, or, again, to hope (or will) to be able to believe that God exists. Such an agnosticism about hope could express a deeply human puzzlement about what one's proper religious (or non-religious) response to, say, evil and suffering ought to be. For example, one might maintain that given the irresolvability of the problem of evil and suffering, it would be immoral not only to believe in God's existence but even to hope that God exists.

When this intuitively rather straightforward analysis of the relation between belief and hope is brought up to the meta-level investigated in this chapter, the relevant kind of hope will focus on our abilities to make sense (in the factual and/or cognitive sense) of our religious expressions. One might thus hope to be able to utter cognitively meaningful and determinately true or false sentences when engaging in religious discourse – or, conversely, one might hope to be able to avoid making literal sense by using such expressions.

I should like to re-emphasize here the idea that agnosticism – especially in my meta-level sense – is (as already suggested) a form of humanism. Far from being a manifestation of intellectual cowardice or disregard for truth, as its opponents might claim, it is an active attitude of investigating what it means to be human in our complex contexts of belief, disbelief, hope, and despair. Agnosticism actually is a way of *caring* for truth, and hence for our lives and souls, because it is an attempt to walk the thin line between making a commitment to a truth-claim and avoiding such a commitment – always for a definite reason in a context defined by the critical attitude of sincere inquiry. This caring for truth is a key not only to "first-order" epistemic agnosticism about God's existence but also to the meta-level meaning agnosticism analyzed above. The latter critically avoids taking a firm stand to the question concerning the truth-aptness of religious discourse – for various reasons, arguably also including the tendency of realism and cognitivism to entail ethically problematic views such as exclusivism and theodicism.[53] We should not too easily assume that the discourse we engage in is truth-apt (and we might even end up maintaining that a serious commitment to religious discourse transcendentally necessitates our not making such an assumption), but

---

[52] One could also, for example, will to believe to be able to hope – and so it goes, with potentially an indefinite number of added doxastic or volitional operators (cf. Hare 2015).

[53] As analyzed in Pihlström 2020a and in Chapter 2.

we should continue critically inquiring into the pros and cons of the assumption that it is. Agnosticism in this sense is, indeed, a form of sincerity (cf. Chapters 1 and 2).

This kind of continuous inquiry into the truth-aptness of religious discourse must itself be organized along the lines of holistic pragmatism. That is, our very ability of being committed to pursuing the truth within our practices (religious or non-religious) is itself a holistically and pragmatically evaluable matter. This evaluation cannot remain within a merely linguistic analysis (as in logical empiricism à la Braithwaite) but must include epistemic, metaphysical, and ethical elements.[54]

Moreover, if we take seriously the iteration of doxastic (and volitional) attitudes, it is clear that one may also be an agnostic about agnosticism itself. The agnostic, when reflexively self-conscious, need not believe agnosticism to be "true" – whatever that exactly means in this case. They might avoid taking a firm stand even here. Agnosticism might then be defended as a tentative standpoint for critical inquiry, more like an hypothesis that will be further tested than a proposition to be believed to be true. At the meta-level, the agnostic need not believe that it is true that we cannot know whether or not religious discourse is truth-apt. They may remain agnostic about our being able to possess, or come up with, such knowledge. While we ought to resist any straightforward identification of agnosticism with skepticism, there is a certain resemblance between this view and the Pyrrhonic form of skepticism familiar from antiquity. However, such a historical comparison remains beyond the scope of my inquiry in this chapter, or this book.

Agnosticism, then, is designed to acknowledge our intellectually and existentially fragile human condition and its limits, analogously to the way in which Kant in his critical philosophy sought to acknowledge those limits, criticizing various "inhuman" (especially transcendentally realist) attempts to overstep or neglect such conditions and limits. This humanistic sense of agnosticism can, in my view, be most vigorously affirmed and defended insofar as we engage in a pragmatist rearticulation and possibly transformation of agnosticism. It is through (meta-level) agnosticism that we may then pragmatically create and recreate our relation to whatever philosophy of religion is about, be it God, religious language, or evil and suffering. In particular, when transcendentally developed (and conjoined with the Jamesian WB prospects), agnosticism creates an open space

---

[54] The inextricable intertwinement of metaphysics, epistemology, semantics, and ethics is, indeed, crucial in the kind of holistic pragmatism advanced in this book; this I take as a further indication of the value of holistic pragmatism.

rendering both religious commitment and the rejection of religion equally live options.[55] The *possibility* of making an existential WB commitment to a religious worldview emerges, we may suggest, as a *necessary* condition for the *possibility* of a genuinely religious form of life – and this complex modal structure is what the openness of agnosticism consists in.

Finally, this same openness indicates that agnosticism should not be defended – especially not by the pragmatist – as any sort of final or closed position regarding religious meaning. As was strongly emphasized in the early chapters of this book, in particular, pragmatism is also an inherently pluralistic approach to religious (and other) matters. Therefore, instead of simply saying that religious discourse cannot be known to make sense, the pragmatic pluralist should phrase their agnosticism *from within* their (possible, optional) commitment to religious discourse by saying that we are incapable of knowing for sure whether we can make sense by our religious use of words and that this constitutes a reason for acknowledging a plurality of other – in many cases very different – religious or theological, as well as secular, "voices" that could make sense from their own perspectives better than ours (but that might also fail to do so). In this sense, far from signaling any failure of pragmatism,[56] meaning agnosticism could be regarded as a path toward a truly pragmatic recognition of a diversity of sincere, yet inevitably fragile, attempts to make sense.

---

[55] Recall again that agnosticism could be designed to function in other areas of life as well, even though this chapter has primarily focused (albeit at a meta-level) on its significance in pragmatist philosophy of religion. As briefly suggested above, we might remain "meaning agnostics" about our ability to make sense within other discourses as well, including, for instance, ethical or aesthetic ones. An agnostic in (pragmatist) aesthetics might propose to analyze, for example, contemporary conceptual art in terms of its verging on meaninglessness. This may be a somewhat unexplored territory for pragmatist aesthetics, as well as (meta)ethics, calling for further investigation.

[56] In an insightful critical comment, an anonymous reviewer asked why, if pragmatism is primarily a theory of meaning (roughly in the Peircean sense also inherited by James), wouldn't it signal a failure of pragmatism to agnostically maintain that there are statements about which we cannot find out whether they are meaningful or not. It might indeed sound like pragmatism would be inadequate as a theory of meaning if the relation between agnosticism and pragmatism were phrased in this way. My brief (and presumably inevitably inadequate) response is that meta-level meaning agnosticism might actually emerge as an outcome of a pragmatic investigation – such as the one tentatively undertaken here – of the distinctive ways in which religious discourses "make sense" as the specific kinds of discourse they are, that is, by *not* making sense in any ordinary sense of the word. Agnosticism would then be a way of recognizing the plurality of different discourses and practices, not all of which fall into the same framework of meaning-bestowing norms. A certain degree of agnosticism might thus be needed for us to be pluralists in the relevant pragmatist sense. We might have to be meta-level meaning agnostics in order to realize that different religious discourses or practices might make sense in ways that *our* discourse does not recognize as sense-making – and hence in order to be pluralists. However, I do acknowledge that further discussion of this problem is needed.

Conclusion
Pragmatic Transcendental Humanism

This book has argued, within an overall pragmatist context, for an inseparable link between the concept of *truth* and the ethical concept of
truthfulness, essentially intertwined with the concept of *sincerity* understood (here) as involving an ethically and existentially grounded individual
commitment to pursuing the truth. In Kantian-pragmatist terms, we may
say that this intertwinement of the notions of truth, truthfulness, and
sincerity in our practices of inquiry is transcendental, constitutively defining the ways in which these concepts and the practices normatively
structured by them are available to us and thus necessarily conditioning
their employment in our conceptualizations of and engagements with the
ways the world is. Furthermore, in pragmatist terms, there is little we can
do with our concept of truth (no matter how carefully we define it in, e.g.,
a Tarskian semantic framework, or how carefully we specify its role in
scientific theory-formation),[1] if we do not already *acknowledge*, and hence
genuinely *value*, the sincere commitment to seeking the truth. Even if
someone like Trump – or Orwell's O'Brien, for that matter – contingently
happens to say something true, it is worthless in the context of their utter
disregard for truth, that is, their failure to organize their lives and practices
in terms of the norm of truthfulness.

Truth, then, needs a pragmatic context of ethical valuation in order to
thrive. It necessarily (in the sense of presuppositional necessity investigated
by means of transcendental reflection) needs a practice of sincere truth-
seeking within a richly normative human form of life that provides a context
for both individual existential concerns and communal attempts to secure
objectivity or at least intersubjectivity in our inquiries. The main line of
argument of this book has sought to demonstrate that pragmatism, primarily

---

[1] For a Tarskian specification of the correspondence theory of truth connected with a Peircean project
of accounting for the progress of science toward the truth in terms of the increasing "truthlikeness" of
theories within the overall position of scientific realism, see Niiniluoto 1999.

in its Jamesian pluralistic and individualistic version recognizing our endless diversity as human beings as well as our "blindness" in ever adequately acknowledging that diversity, is a plausible philosophical approach for examining this constitutive entanglement of truth, truthfulness, and sincerity. This brand of pragmatism should, however, be interpreted and developed as a non-reductively naturalized form of transcendental inquiry into the constitutive features defining our human condition in its historically contextual and changing manifestations.[2]

Elaborating on this basic picture, I have thus investigated, in addition to the explicit discussion of truth and pragmatic pluralism in Chapters 1 and 2, the sincerity issue in relation to transcendental pragmatism entangling Jamesian pragmatism with Kantian critical philosophy, especially with regard to these two philosophers' shared pessimism about the both epistemically and ethically limited and fragile human condition (Chapter 3), the Jamesian "will to believe" strategy characterized in terms of holistic pragmatism (Chapter 4), and the normativity of the human form of life more generally, pragmatically and transcendentally analyzed within an overall culturalist philosophical anthropology (Chapter 5). However, I eventually arrived at a mild tension between my pragmatist account of the (pragmatically conceptualized) truth-aptness of (for example) religious and other existential and/or *weltanschaulichen* language-uses and discourses, on the one hand, and a meta-level agnosticism about such truth-aptness (Chapter 6). This acknowledgment of an irreducible tension should be understood as an encouragement for reflexive meta-level sincerity in continuing our inquiries into truth and sincerity themselves. It is not a failure of pragmatism but indicates the need for further pragmatist reflection on these notions.

All of these diverse themes – truth(fulness), sincerity, individualism, normativity, diversity, pragmatic pluralism, and the contingency and fragility of the human condition highlighted by agnosticism – can finally be brought under the unifying perspective of transcendental humanism, again pragmatically articulated. While it is not necessary for the (Jamesian) pragmatist to employ the transcendental vocabulary I have recommended, our being committed to humanism is *not* optional in the same way. We cannot just neutrally choose between humanism and, say, "antihumanism", "posthumanism", or

---

[2] As one of my anonymous reviewers formulated it, I have in this volume tried to make a (both historical and philosophical) case for the view that James, as one of the most important public intellectuals of the early twentieth century, remains a socially significant philosopher for us even today, helping us to make sense of, and possibly critically overcome, the "post-truth" era we are now witnessing.

"transhumanism". These are subordinate to a more comprehensive humanism that only makes them possible as critical reflections on how humanism
ought to be developed further in our times of deepening environmental
anxiety and massive global injustice.[3]

It might be claimed that my pragmatist transcendental humanism is
eventually a form of pragmatist *metaphysics* insisting that we live in a human
world whose ontological structures are necessarily shaped by our human
practices and their interest-driven categorizations. It would, thus, be
a metaphysical account of the necessary features of this humanly constituted
reality, of the world as it is possible for us as an object of conceptualization and
inquiry. Certainly I agree that there is no pragmatist humanism without
a pragmatist metaphysics of the human world; my version of humanism
does *not* amount to the Rortyan thoroughly anti-metaphysical and antirepresentationalist humanism.[4] Let me therefore – even though metaphysics has
not been an explicit target of the present inquiry – close this book by briefly
responding to very important points raised by one of my long-time pragmatist
discussion partners, David Hildebrand, who devotes a recent paper to
a critical examination of what I have (in my earlier work) meant by pragmatist
metaphysics and its entanglement with transcendental philosophy.[5]
Hildebrand and I have always agreed about the need – especially for the
pragmatist – to adopt a "living perspective" in philosophizing (Hildebrand
2019, 213).[6] The proper starting point for pragmatist metaphysics, too, is the

---

[3] Note, again, also that my version of humanism is certainly not reducible to what is known as secular
humanism. It *is* definitely secular – investigating the possibility of religious commitment in the
context of human forms of life rather than proposing to make, or defend, any such commitments –
and in this sense it is, ultimately, a form of philosophical anthropology. It refuses to take any religious
or anti-religious stand but remains, as explained in Chapter 6, agnostic. In this sense, the (qualified)
defense of agnosticism in the last main chapter above is an essential part of my overall argument. For
pragmatist reflections on humanism in relation to both naturalism and secularism, see the very
interesting recent contributions by Honnacker 2018 and Jung 2019.

[4] See Višňovský 2020 for a comprehensive examination of Rorty's humanism. While I agree with
Rorty that we should emphasize our answerability to other human beings (instead of a transcendent
World or Truth), Rorty's humanism remains inadequate due to its tendency to reduce the normative
level of representationality to mere causal clashes of vocabularies. Humanism is also representationalism; human beings are world-representing animals.

[5] The fact that Hildebrand's (2019) essay is subtitled "Transcendence and Meliorism" may sound
slightly surprising, given that I have always insisted on pragmatism (and pragmatist metaphysics) as
being "transcendental" in a sense derived from Kant, rather than "transcendent" (cf. Chapter 3). The
distinction between the transcendental and the transcendent is a fundamentally important one, and
too often neglected by many philosophers, even by many pragmatists (including James and Dewey
themselves). On the other hand, employing a "transcendental method" in pragmatist metaphysics
might lead us to discussions concerning the metaphysical status of transcendence (cf. Hildebrand
2019, 214), especially in the context of pragmatist philosophy of religion (see, e.g., Pihlström 2013).

[6] See again also Gunnarsson's (2020) investigation of the "true human being" as the locus of
philosophical theorization, discussed in Chapter 4.

practical – and humanistic – one amidst our human form(s) of life (with the proper caveat concerning the need to avoid any sharp dichotomy between practice and intellect). I suppose one of our few disagreements concerns the need to bring Kant into this picture in the first place, and I can easily understand that readers of this book may have asked the same question: why Kant? Hildebrand carefully notes the various qualifications I have felt necessary to add (e.g., in Pihlström 2003, 2009, and 2013) to the claim that we should understand pragmatism as a form of transcendental philosophy. He then asks – and this is a fair critical question to ask – why we need to go back to Kant at all: "what is the Kantian remainder" and why is it important (Hildebrand 2019, 222)? Indeed, as good pragmatists we do have to ask, "what does this actually *do* for us?" (Hildebrand 2019, 224), and certainly critics like Hildebrand succeed in reminding us that it is not obvious that the pragmatist has much to "gain" from the transcendental method.

Hildebrand is right to suggest that my stubborn insistence on the need for, or the pragmatic usefulness of, the transcendental method is based on the desire to accommodate a kind of necessity (the presuppositional necessity of practice-laden transcendental conditions) into the thoroughly contingent and always reinterpretable practices within which our lives take place. He is also right to note that it is not always easy to see "what [I am] after" (Hildebrand 2019, 225), given all the reservations I have had to add to these formulations in order to have my cake and eat it too, that is, to remain both Kantian and pragmatist. I have no easy or obvious response here, and it may be difficult, at this stage, not only for my (potential) readers but even for myself to get clear about what exactly I have been "after" in this book as well. However, I suppose this is partly a temperamental issue, to echo James; some of us, given their individual philosophical trajectories, may be temperamentally more inclined than some others to try to bring the pragmatist focus on contingency and the Kantian focus on transcendental necessity together. A more philosophical reason for the "need" to invoke Kant might be that only a pragmatist form of transcendental idealism can make sense of pragmatic realism (as I have emphasized in some earlier work, e.g., Pihlström 2009, 2020a, and briefly also here).

I tried to summarize in Chapter 3 why I think pragmatist and transcendental approaches ought to be integrated. I am not sure if I have at all been able to address the obviously legitimate worry that any transcendental necessity attached to our contingent and historically reinterpretable practices would be in tension with the basic idea of holistic pragmatism, that is, that there is a "seamless web" of logical, empirical, and ethical statements to be tested in conjunction.[7] I did try to suggest in Chapter 3, and indeed throughout the book, that there is a kind of pluralism pertaining to the transcendental conditions themselves: transcendental necessity is itself a family-resemblance matter. Different conditions may function as transcendental in different contexts open to transcendental investigation in a variety of ways, and this is compatible with the historical mutability and reinterpretability of the contexts within which we find ourselves. While holistic pragmatists like White have not considered their own view transcendental, I believe it is plausible to suggest that the entire structure of the holistic web itself plays a transcendental role, comparable to the grammar of language-games in a Wittgensteinian context. The pragmatist could, perhaps, prefer to speak about the general traits of our habits, for instance (across a range of practices within which we engage in habitual action), as a pragmatic version of transcendentally necessary structures of our cognitive apparatus. Everything here is contingent, but not everything is contingent at the same time and in the same way. Even the very fact that our human form(s) of life is (are) normatively structured at all (cf. Chapter 5) is, precisely, a *fact* – a "transcendental fact" about our contingent human condition always realized in its historical contexts, yet playing (precisely as such a "fact") a transcendental role in enabling our epistemic and ethical inquiries and deliberations.[8]

It is also extremely important to perceive that the transcendental articulation of pragmatism is itself part of the holistic pragmatist view that may, at least in principle, be tested against recalcitrant experience. From our pragmatist point of view, even the transcendental account of pragmatism must pragmatically function. It must "work". If it doesn't, then it won't survive the pragmatic test it must be constantly subjected to. This is also an element of the pragmatist's humanism: philosophical ideas, pragmatist as well as transcendental, must in the end serve our need to understand more deeply our human condition – and to contribute to ameliorating it. If this is a form of humanistic "metaphysics", then so be it.

---

[7] This problem was raised by one of the anonymous reviewers of the book manuscript.

[8] The obvious worry at this point is that by acknowledging such contingency of all the conditions defining our humanity we end up with the factualization criticized in Chapter 5. In order to block *that* slippery slope, the notion of a transcendental fact should be taken seriously. Even when historically contingent, the human condition at its most general level – the shape our practices take in their normative structures – must be understood as making it possible for us to conceptualize the world we live in in the first place, including our contingent conditions themselves. For this type of oscillation between the transcendental and the naturalistic perspectives (arguably made sense only in terms of pragmatism), see Pihlström 2003, 2016.

This book, then, is my way of submitting *a* version of transcendental pragmatism to a holistic and humanistic assessment, in order to look and see how this particular form of pragmatism survives the challenge of philosophically accounting for our commitment to pursuing the truth, to individual sincerity, and to an appreciation of practice-laden normativity – and even the test of being aware of our unavoidable difficulty in being invariably able to attach cognitive meaningfulness to our discourses, especially religious or other highly personal existential ones.

I am certainly not saying that all pragmatists should turn Kantians (nor, of course, vice versa), but I do hope to have been able to offer some reasons (layered with many qualifications) for why at least some of them, given the kinds of temperamentally emerging philosophical concerns they have, might. Returning to Hildebrand's criticism, perhaps this is one instance of an attempt to take seriously the "personal and perspectival approach to philosophy" (Hildebrand 2019, 225), the pragmatic approach Hildebrand has also himself defended at least since his exemplary early book on Dewey (Hildebrand 2003). If so, then the always recurring tension between the universal and necessary (in transcendental philosophy) and the contingent and changing (in pragmatism) needs to be faced by the (Jamesian) pragmatist.

This is something that I have, again, aspired to do in this book. I hope my investigation of pragmatism as a form of critical philosophy particularly in the pursuit of truth and sincerity has in its own way contributed to the pragmatic project of overcoming a number of unfruitful philosophical dichotomies – not only the one between the (transcendentally) necessary and the contingent but also those between individual diversity and intersubjectively binding normativity, between (empirical) realism and (transcendental) pragmatism, between epistemology and ethics, and between the natural and the normative. A critical synthesis of these apparently mutually opposed philosophical ideas and concepts is a fundamental challenge for our pragmatic pursuit of truth, which itself entangles the concepts of truth and truthfulness with each other. It is a challenge that pragmatism can meet better than any other philosophical framework I am familiar with. No matter how our "post-truth" age develops, we need, I have tried to argue, a pragmatic form of transcendental humanism as a philosophical context within which our commitment to both individual and social sincerity may flourish.

The reader of this book may have felt that the variety of issues touched upon – truth, religion, pluralism, individualism, sincerity, normativity, agnosticism, and pessimism (vs. meliorism) about the human condition – may not have been as systematically related to each other as I have claimed. However, the argument I have tried to develop in these chapters has aimed at showing that they are in fact profoundly, even constitutively, entangled. We cannot form an adequate picture of the metaphysical and epistemic issues concerning the structure of reality and our knowledge about it – our pursuit of truth in the standard sense of inquiring into the way the world is – without seeking to understand what it pragmatically means for us to be engaged, in our distinctive individual ways, in our normatively structured practices, and moreover, what it means to do so in an ethically (as well as epistemically) sincere manner. A philosophical investigation of our project of pursuing the truth can thus never be purely epistemic; it needs to be ethical as well, and this very fact makes it necessary for us to take seriously the various existential contexts within which we seek to know the world around us, including religious contexts. The intertwinement of the issues of "theoretical" and "practical" philosophy is, in my favorite terms, transcendental and constitutive in the sense that the former would be impossible without the latter, and vice versa.

Some readers might also feel that I have in the end arrived at a relatively obvious position: we should take seriously the concept of truth, seek to pursue truth in a sincere manner, and also appreciate individuals' deeply personal existential commitments within our normative practices of inquiry. This hardly sounds like a particularly surprising philosophical view to defend. However, my main purpose has been to indicate *how* we can maintain this view on truth, sincerity, and normativity. Transcendental inquiries primarily address "how" questions concerning the necessary conditions for the possibility of phenomena that are regarded as actual and even obvious in our lives. Kant needed his massive machinery of critical philosophy and transcendental idealism to arrive at a theory on how cognitive experience of objects is possible. In a much more modest context of philosophical inquiry, I have tried to indicate that there are important resources in the pragmatist tradition for examining the "how" question about our normative entitlement to the (perhaps more or less obvious) picture of truth and truth-seeking we should maintain in our practices. Thus, the Kantian and Jamesian path we have walked toward securing our possibly somewhat unsurprising view on truth has, I hope, been worth walking. This path also indicates the way in which a transcendental "how" question takes the shape of a pragmatic "how" question investigating the necessary conditions for the possibility of the "given" features of our practices in terms of our practical commitments to pursuing our humanly natural interests and needs of inquiry.

The philosophical relevance of the obvious ultimately resides in a kind of reflexivity. The pragmatic value of pragmatism lies to a large extent in its ability to take seriously the inevitable context-embeddedness of our inquiries while encouraging us to on-going critical reflection transcending any single finite, always revisable and reinterpretable context. Our practices of viewing the world critically themselves need to be critically examined in all their pragmatic dimensions, and to continue to do so even in a potentially dystopic cultural situation that might lead to a collapse of the concept of truth itself is to remain, in the spirit of Kantian pessimism yet pragmatist meliorism, committed to ameliorating our ways of viewing the world – including our ways of viewing ourselves.

References

Adams, J. (ed.) (2016 [2014]), *The Bloomsbury Companion to Holocaust Literature*. London and New York: Bloomsbury.

Agamben, G. (2002 [1999]), *Remnants of Auschwitz: The Witness and the Archive*. Trans. D. Heller-Roazen. New York: Zone Books.

Aikin, S. F. and Talisse, R. B. (2018), *Pragmatism, Pluralism, and the Nature of Philosophy*. New York and London: Routledge.

Allison, H. E. (2004 [1983]), *Kant's Transcendental Idealism – An Interpretation and Defense: A Revised and Enlarged Edition*. New Haven, CT and London: Yale University Press.

Appelqvist, H. (ed.) (2020), *Wittgenstein and the Limits of Language*. London and New York: Routledge.

Arendt, H. (1958), *The Human Condition*. Chicago: The University of Chicago Press.

Arendt, H. (1976 [1951]), *The Origins of Totalitarianism*. New ed. San Diego, CA: Harcourt.

Arendt, H. (2003), *The Portable Hannah Arendt*. P. Baehr (ed.). New York: Penguin.

Atkins, R. (2016), *Peirce and the Conduct of Life: Sentiment and Instinct in Ethics and Religion*. Cambridge: Cambridge University Press.

Axtell, G. (2013), "Possibility and Permission? Intellectual Character, Inquiry, and the Ethics of Belief." In H. Rydenfelt and S. Pihlström (eds.), *William James on Religion*. Basingstoke: Palgrave Macmillan, 165–198.

Axtell, G. (2019), *Problems of Religious Luck: Assessing the Limits of Reasonable Religious Disagreement*. Lanham, MD: Lexington Books.

Bagger, M. (ed.) (2018), *Pragmatism and Naturalism: Scientific and Social Inquiry after Representationalism*. New York: Columbia University Press.

Bergman, M. (2019), "Pragmatic Aims and Changing Habits." In Rydenfelt et al. (eds.), 57–68.

Bernstein, R. J. (2002), *Radical Evil: A Philosophical Interrogation*. Cambridge: Polity Press.

Bernstein, R. J. (2010), *The Pragmatic Turn*. Cambridge: Polity Press.

Bernstein, R. J. (2017), "Epilogue: Engaged Pragmatic Pluralism." In M. Craig and M. Morgan (eds.), *Richard J. Bernstein and the Expansion of American Philosophy: Thinking the Plural*. Lanham, MD: Lexington Books, 215–228.

Bernstein, R. J. (2018), *Why Read Hannah Arendt Now*. Cambridge: Polity Press.

Bird, G. (1986), *William James*, London: Routledge and Kegan Paul.

Braithwaite, R. B. (ed.) (1955), "An Empiricist's View of the Nature of Religious Belief." In *Theory of Games as a Tool for the Moral Philosopher and An Empiricist's View of the Nature of Religious Belief*. Bristol: Thoemmes Press, 1994, 1-35.

Brune, J.-P., Stern, R., and Micha, W. H. (eds.) (2017), *Transcendental Arguments in Moral Theory*. Berlin: De Gruyter.

Burke, F. T. (2013), *What Pragmatism Was*. Bloomington and Indianapolis: Indiana University Press.

Calcaterra, R. M. (1999), "W. James' Defence of Free Will: A Step toward a Paradigm Shift." In R. Egidi (ed.), *In Search of a New Humanism: The Philosophy of Georg Henrik von Wright*. Dordrecht: Kluwer, 139–146.

Calcaterra, R. M. (2017), "William James's Naturalism within the Common Project of Pragmatist Philosophy." *Rivista di storia della filosofia* 3, 475–491.

Campbell, J. (2017), *Experiencing William James: Belief in a Pluralistic World*. Charlottesville and London: University of Virginia Press.

Capps, J. (2017), "A Pragmatic Argument for a Pragmatic Theory of Truth." *Contemporary Pragmatism* 14, 135–156.

Capps, J. (2018), "Did Dewey Have a Theory of Truth?" *Transactions of the Charles S. Peirce Society* 54, 39–63.

Capps, J. (2019), "The Pragmatic Theory of Truth." In E. N. Zalta (ed.), *The Stanford Encyclopedia of Philosophy (Summer 2019 Edition)*. Available online: https://plato.stanford.edu/archives/sum2019/entries/truth-pragmatic/.

Carlson, T. L. (1997), "James in the Kantian Tradition." In R. A. Putnam (ed.), *The Cambridge Companion to William James*. Cambridge: Cambridge University Press, 363–384.

Carnap, R. (1950), "Empiricism, Semantics and Ontology." *Revue Internationale de Philosophie* 4, 20–40.

Carr, D. (1999), *The Paradox of Subjectivity: The Self in the Transcendental Tradition*. Oxford: Oxford University Press.

Cavarero, A. (2018), "'Destroy Your Sight with a New Gorgon': Mass Atrocity and the Phenomenology of Horror." In T. Brudholm and J. Lang (eds.), *Emotions and Mass Atrocity: Philosophical and Theoretical Explorations*. Cambridge: Cambridge University Press, 123–141.

Cavell, S. (1979), *The Claim of Reason: Wittgenstein, Skepticism, Morality, and Tragedy*. New York: Oxford University Press.

Clifford, W. K. (1877), "The Ethics of Belief." Available online: http://people.brandeis.edu/~teuber/Clifford_ethics.pdf.

Conant, J. (2000), "Freedom, Cruelty, and Truth: Rorty versus Orwell." In R. B. Brandom (ed.), *Rorty and His Critics*. Oxford and Cambridge, MA: Blackwell, 268–342.

Cooke, E. (2006), *Peirce's Pragmatic Theory of Inquiry*. London: Continuum.

Corbin, A. (2018 [2016]), *A History of Silence: From the Renaissance to the Present Day*. Trans. J. Birrell. Cambridge: Polity Press.

Cormier, H. (2001), *The Truth Is What Works: William James, Pragmatism, and the Seed of Death*. Lanham, MD: Rowman & Littlefield.

Craig, M. and Morgan, M. (eds.) (2017), *Richard J. Bernstein and the Expansion of American Philosophy: Thinking the Plural*. Lanham, MD: Lexington Books.

Darby, D. (2009), *Rights, Race, and Recognition*. Cambridge: Cambridge University Press.

Dewey, J. (1986 [1929]), *Experience and Nature*. Chicago: Open Court. (1st ed. 1925; 2nd ed. 1929).

Dianda, A. (2018), "William James and the 'Wilfulness' of Belief." *European Journal of Philosophy* 26, 647–662.

Draper, P. (2001), "Seeking but Not Believing: Confessions of a Practicing Agnostic." In D. Howard-Snyder and P. Moser (eds.), *Divine Hiddenness: New Essays*. Cambridge: Cambridge University Press, 197–214.

Draper, P. (2017), "Atheism and Agnosticism." In E. Zalta (ed.), *Stanford Encyclopedia of Philosophy*. Available online: https://plato.stanford.edu/entries/atheism-agnosticism/#DefiAgno.

Forstenzer, J. (2018), "Something Has Cracked: Post-Truth Politics and Richard Rorty's Postmodernist Bourgeois Liberalism." *Ash Center Occasional Papers*. Cambridge, MA: Ash Center for Democratic Governance and Innovation, Harvard Kennedy School.

Frankfurt, H. G. (2005), *On Bullshit*. Princeton, NJ: Princeton University Press.

Frankl, V. (1969), *The Will to Meaning: Foundations and Applications of Logotherapy*. New York: The American Library.

Gale, R. (1999), *The Divided Self of William James*. Cambridge: Cambridge University Press.

Gavin, W. J. (1980), "Peirce and 'The Will to Believe'." *The Monist* 63, 342–350.

Glock, H.-J. (ed.) (2003), *Strawson and Kant*. Oxford: Clarendon Press.

Goodman, N. (1954), *Fact, Fiction, and Forecast*. Cambridge, MA: Harvard University Press.

Goodson, J. L. (ed.) (2018), *William James, Moral Philosophy, and the Ethical Life*. Lanham, MD: Lexington Books.

Green, J. M. (2014), "Bernstein's Deployment of Jamesian Democratic Pluralism: The Pragmatic Turn and the Future of Philosophy." In Green (ed.), *Richard J. Bernstein and the Pragmatist Turn in Contemporary Philosophy: Rekindling Pragmatism's Fire*. Basingstoke: Palgrave Macmillan, 78–94.

Griffiths, P. J. (2001), *Problems of Religious Diversity*. Oxford and Malden, MA: Blackwell.

Grube, D. M. (2019), "Comparing Pragmatism with Neo-Pragmatism on Realism and Naturalism." In Rydenfelt et al. (eds.), 87–98.

Grube, D. M. and Van Herck, W. (eds.) (2017), *Philosophical Perspectives on Religious Diversity*. London: Routledge.

Gunnarsson, L. (2020), *Vernunft und Temperament: Eine Philosophie der Philosophie*. Leiden: Brill / Mentis.

Gustafsson, M. (2019), "Blind Obedience." In Rydenfelt et al. (eds.), 183–192.

Haack, S. (1995), "Vulgar Pragmatism: An Unedifying Prospect." In H. J. Saatkamp (ed.), *Rorty and Pragmatism*. Nashville, TN: Vanderbilt University Press, 126–147.

Haack, S. (1998), *Manifesto of a Passionate Moderate: Unfashionable Essays*. Chicago and London: University of Chicago Press.

Haack, S. (2019), "Post 'Post-Truth': Are We There Yet?" *Theoria* 85, 258–275.

Hardcastle, G. L. and Reisch, G. A. (eds.) (2006), *Bullshit and Philosophy*. Chicago: Open Court.

Hare, P. (2015), *Pragmatism with Purpose: Selected Writings*. J. Palencik, D. R. Anderson, and S. A. Miller (eds.). New York: Fordham University Press.

Hasker, W. (2005), "Analytic Philosophy of Religion." In W. J. Wainwright (ed.), *The Oxford Handbook of the Philosophy of Religion*. Oxford: Oxford University Press, 421–446.

Hildebrand, D. (2003), *Beyond Realism and Antirealism: Dewey and the Neopragmatists*. Nashville, TN: Vanderbilt University Press.

Hildebrand, D. (2019), "Pihlström's Pragmatist Metaphysics: Transcendence and Meliorism." In Rydenfelt et al. (eds.), 213–227.

Hintikka, J. (1996), *Lingua Universalis vs. Calculus Ratiocinator – An Ultimate Presupposition of Twentieth-Century Philosophy: Selected Papers 2*. Dordrecht: Kluwer.

Honenberger, P. (ed.) (2016), *Naturalism and Philosophical Anthropology: Nature, Life, and the Human between Empirical and Transcendental Perspectives*. Basingstoke: Palgrave Macmillan.

Honnacker, A. (2018), *Pragmatic Humanism Revisited: An Essay on Making the World a Home*. Basingstoke: Palgrave Macmillan.

Honneth, A. (2005 [1992]), *Kampf um Anerkennung*. 2nd ed. Frankfurt: Suhrkamp.

Hook, S. (1974), *Pragmatism and the Tragic Sense of Life*. New York: Basic Books.

Hookway, C. (2000), *Truth, Rationality, and Pragmatism: Themes from Peirce*. Oxford: Oxford University Press.

Hookway, C. (2011), "James's Epistemology and the Will to Believe." *European Journal of Pragmatism and American Philosophy* 3:1. Available online: https://journals.openedition.org/ejpap/865.

Jackman, H. (1999), "Prudential Arguments, Naturalized Epistemology, and the Will to Believe." *Transactions of the Charles S. Peirce Society* 35, 1–37.

James, W. (1962 [1899]). "On a Certain Blindness in Human Beings." In James, *Talks to Teachers on Psychology and to Students on Some of Life's Ideals*. New York: Dover, 2015.

James, W. (1958 [1902]), *The Varieties of Religious Experience: A Study in Human Nature*. New York: New American Library.

James, W. (1975–1988), *The Works of William James*. 19 vols. F. H. Burkhardt, F. Bowers, and I. K. Skrupskelis (eds.). Cambridge, MA and London: Harvard University Press. Contains, for example, *The Principles of Psychology* (1981 [1890]), *The Will to Believe and Other Essays in Popular Philosophy* (1979 [1897]), *The Varieties of Religious Experience* (1985 [1902]), *Pragmatism: A New Name for Some Old Ways of Thinking* (1975 [1907]), *The Meaning of Truth:*

A Sequel to Pragmatism (1978 [1909]), *A Pluralistic Universe* (1979 [1909]), *Some Problems of Philosophy* (1977 [1911]), *Essays in Radical Empiricism* (1977 [1912]), *Essays in Religion and Morality* (1982), and *Talks to Teachers on Psychology and to Students on Some of Life's Ideals* (1983 [1899]).

Joas, H. (2017), *Die Macht des Heiligen: Eine Alternative zur Geschichte von der Entzauberung*. Frankfurt am Main: Suhrkamp.

Jonas, H. (1996), *Mortality and Morality: A Search for the Good after Auschwitz*. L. Vogel (ed.), Evanston, IL: Northwestern University Press.

Jonkers, P. and Wiertz, O. J. (eds.) (2019), *Religious Truth and Identity in an Age of Plurality*. London and New York: Routledge.

Jung, M. (2019), *Science, Humanism, and Religion: The Quest for Orientation*. Basingstoke: Palgrave Macmillan.

Kahlos, M., Koskinen, H. J. and Palmén, R. (eds.) (2019), *Recognition and Religion*. London and New York: Routledge.

Kaila, E. (2014 [1939]), *Human Knowledge*. Trans. A. Korhonen. Chicago: Open Court.

Kannisto, H. (1984), "Filosofisen antropologian mahdollisuudesta" [On the Possibility of Philosophical Anthropology]. *Ajatus* 41 (Yearbook of the Philosophical Society of Finland), 217–235.

Kant, I. (1990 [1781/1787]), *Kritik der reinen Vernunft*. R. Schmidt (ed.). Hamburg: Felix Meiner.

Kant, I. (1983a [1788]), *Kritik der praktischen Vernunft*. In W. Weischedel (ed.), *Immanuel Kant: Werke in zehn Bänden*, vol. 5. Darmstadt: Wissenschaftliche Buchgesellschaft.

Kant, I. (1983b [1791]), "Über das Misslingen aller philosophischen Versuche in der Theodicee." In W. Weischedel (ed.), *Immanuel Kant: Werke in zehn Bänden*, vol. 9. Darmstadt: Wissenschaftliche Buchgesellschaft.

Kant, I. (1983c [1793/1794]), *Die Religion innerhalb der Grenzen der blossen Vernunft*. In W. Weischedel (ed.), *Immanuel Kant: Werke in zehn Bänden*, vol. 7. Darmstadt: Wissenschaftliche Buchgesellschaft.

Kearney, R. (2010), *Anatheism*. New York: Columbia University Press.

Kivistö, S. (2018), "Novelty: A History." In Kivistö, *Lucubrationes Neolatinae: Readings of Neo-Latin Dissertations and Satires*. Commentationes Humanarum Litterarum 134. Helsinki: Societas Scientiarum Fennica.

Kivistö, S. and Pihlström, S. (2016), *Kantian Antitheodicy: Philosophical and Literary Varieties*. Basingstoke: Palgrave Macmillan.

Klein, A. (2015), "Science, Religion, and 'The Will to Believe'." *HOPOS* 5, 72–117.

Klein, A. (2018), Review of Aikin and Talisse (2018). *Notre Dame Philosophy Reviews*, May 9, 2018.

Klein, A. (2019), "Between Anarchism and Suicide: On William James's Religious Therapy." *Philosophers' Imprint* 19, 32; www.philosophersimprint.org/019032/.

Knowles, J. (2019), "Pragmatism, Naturalism, and Metaphysics." In Rydenfelt et al. (eds.), 69–86.

Koistinen, T. (2019), "Contemplative Philosophy and the Problem of Relativism." In Rydenfelt et al. (eds.), 163–172.

Koopman, C. (2017), "The Will, the Will to Believe, and William James." *Journal of the History of Philosophy* 55, 491–512.

Korsgaard, C. (1996), *The Sources of Normativity*. Cambridge, MA and London: Harvard University Press.

Koskinen, H. J. (2017), "Mediated Recognition and the Categorial Stance." *Journal of Social Ontology* 3, 67–87.

Koskinen, H. J. (2019), "Mediated and Transitive Recognition: Towards an Articulation." In M. Kahlos, H. J. Koskinen, and R. Palmén (eds.), *Recognition and Religion*. London and New York: Routledge, 34–50.

Koskinen, H. J. (2020), "Mediational Recognition and Metaphysical Power: A Systematic Analysis." *Journal of Social Ontology* 5, 147–168.

Kuhn, T. S. (1970 [1962]), *The Structure of Scientific Revolutions*. 2nd ed. Chicago and London: University of Chicago Press.

Launis, V. (2018), *Ihmisarvo* [Human Dignity]. Tampere: Vastapaino.

Levi, P. (1996 [1958]), *Survival in Auschwitz: The Nazi Assault on Humanity*. Trans. S. Woolf. New York: Touchstone Books.

Levi, P. (1988 [1986]), *The Drowned and the Saved*. Trans. R. Rosenthal. London: Michael Joseph.

Levinas, E. (2006 [1996]), *Entre-Nous: Thinking-of-the-Other*. Trans. M. B. Smith. London: Continuum.

Lewis, C. I. (1923), "A Pragmatic Conception of the *A Priori*." *The Journal of Philosophy* 20, 169–177.

Lynch, M. (2009), *Truth as One and Many*. New York: Oxford University Press.

Madore, J. (2011), *Difficult Freedom and Radical Evil in Kant*. London and New York: Bloomsbury.

Malpas, J. (1997), "The Transcendental Circle." *Australasian Journal of Philosophy* 75, 1–20.

Malpas, J. (ed.) (2003), *From Kant to Davidson: Philosophy and the Idea of the Transcendental*. London and New York: Routledge.

Manne, K. (2017), *Down Girl: The Logic of Misogyny*. Oxford and New York: Oxford University Press.

Marchetti, S. (2015), *Ethics and Philosophical Critique in William James*. Basingstoke: Palgrave Macmillan.

Marchetti, S. (2019), "Jamesian Liberalism and the Self." In Rydenfelt et al. (eds.), 193–202.

Margalit, A. (2002), *The Ethics of Memory*. Cambridge, MA and London: Harvard University Press.

Martin, M. (1990), *Atheism: A Philosophical Justification*. Philadelphia, PA: Temple University Press.

McDowell, J. (1996 [1994]), *Mind and World*. 2nd ed. Cambridge, MA and London: Harvard University Press.

McIntyre, L. (2018), *Post-Truth*. Cambridge, MA and London: The MIT Press.

Medina, J. (2010), "James on Truth and Solidarity: The Epistemology of Diversity and the Politics of Specificity." In J. J. Stuhr (ed.), *100 Years of Pragmatism*. Bloomington: Indiana University Press, 124–143.

Misak, C. (2013), *The American Pragmatists*. Oxford and New York: Oxford University Press.

Mounce, H. O. (1997), *The Two Pragmatists: From Peirce to Rorty*. London and New York: Routledge.

Murphey, M. G. (1968), "Kant's Children: the Cambridge Pragmatists." *Transactions of the Charles S. Peirce Society* 4, 3–33.

Müller, O. F. (2018), "Pacifism as a Perspective: On the Inevitable Entanglement of Facts and Values." *Studies in Christian Ethics* 31, 201–213.

Niiniluoto, I. (1999), *Critical Scientific Realism*. Oxford: Oxford University Press.

Niiniluoto, I. (2018), *Truth-Seeking by Abduction*. Cham: Springer.

Niiniluoto, I. (2019), "Queries about Pragmatic Realism." In Rydenfelt et al. (eds.), 31–44.

Nussbaum, M. (2018), *The Monarchy of Fear: A Philosopher Looks at Our Political Crisis*. New York: Simon & Schuster.

O'Connell, R. J. (1984), *William James and the Courage to Believe*. New York: Fordham University Press.

Pappas, G. F. (1994), "William James' Virtuous Believer." *Transactions of the Charles S. Peirce Society* 30, 77–109.

Patterson, D. (2018). *The Holocaust and the Nonrepresentable: Literary and Photographic Transcendence*. Albany: SUNY Press.

Pawelski, J. (2007), *The Dynamic Individualism of William James*. Albany: SUNY Press.

Peirce, C. S. (1992–1998), *The Essential Peirce*. 2 vols. N. Houser et al. (eds.) (the Peirce Edition Project). Bloomington: Indiana University Press. Contains, for example, "The Fixation of Belief" (1877) and "How to Make Our Ideas Clear" (1878), in vol. 1.

Perry, R. B. (1935), *The Thought and Character of William James*. 2 vols. London: Milford and Oxford University Press.

Perry, R. B. (1964 [1948]), *The Thought and Character of William James: Briefer Version*. New York: Harper & Row.

Phillips, D. Z. (1986), *Belief, Change and Forms of Life*. Basingstoke: Macmillan.

Phillips, D. Z. (2004), *The Problem of Evil and the Problem of God*. London: SCM Publications.

Pihlström, S. (1996), *Structuring the World: The Issue of Realism and the Nature of Ontological Problems in Classical and Contemporary Pragmatism*. Acta Philosophica Fennica 59. Helsinki: The Philosophical Society of Finland.

Pihlström, S. (1998), *Pragmatism and Philosophical Anthropology: Understanding Our Human Life in a Human World*. New York: Peter Lang.

Pihlström, S. (2003), *Naturalizing the Transcendental: A Pragmatic View*. Amherst, NY: Humanity Books.

Pihlström, S. (2004), "Recent Reinterpretations of the Transcendental." *Inquiry* 47, 289–314.

Pihlström, S. (2005), *Pragmatic Moral Realism: A Transcendental Defense*. Amsterdam and New York: Rodopi.

Pihlström, S. (2007), "Transcendental Self-Deception." *Teorema* 26, 177–189.

Pihlström, S. (2008a), *"The Trail of the Human Serpent Is over Everything":* *Jamesian Perspectives on Mind, World, and Religion.* Lanham, MD: University Press of America.

Pihlström, S. (2008b), "How (Not) to Write the History of Pragmatist Philosophy of Science." *Perspectives on Science* 16, 26–69.

Pihlström, S. (2009), *Pragmatist Metaphysics: An Essay on the Ethical Grounds of Ontology.* London and New York: Continuum.

Pihlström, S. (2010a), "Kant and Pragmatism." *Pragmatism Today* 2:1. Available online: www.pragmatismtoday.eu/winter2010/Pihlstrom-Kant_and_Pragmatism.pdf.

Pihlström, S. (2010b), "Toward a Pragmatically Naturalist Metaphysics of the Fact-Value Entanglement: Emergence or Continuity?" *Journal of Philosophical Research* 35, 323–352.

Pihlström, S. (2011a), *Transcendental Guilt: Reflections on Ethical Finitude.* Lanham, MD: Lexington Books.

Pihlström, S. (2011b), "Morton White's Philosophy of Culture: Holistic Pragmatism and Interdisciplinary Inquiry." *Human Affairs* 21, 140–156.

Pihlström, S. (2012a), "A New Look at Wittgenstein and Pragmatism." *European Journal of Pragmatism and American Philosophy* 4:2. Available online: https://journals.openedition.org/ejpap/715.

Pihlström, S. (2012b), "Eino Kaila on Pragmatism and Religion." In I. Niiniluoto and S. Pihlström (eds.), *Reappraisals of Eino Kaila's Philosophy.* Acta Philosophica Fennica 89. Helsinki: The Philosophical Society of Finland.

Pihlström, S. (2013), *Pragmatic Pluralism and the Problem of God.* New York: Fordham University Press.

Pihlström, S. (2014a), *Taking Evil Seriously.* Basingstoke: Palgrave Macmillan.

Pihlström, S. (2014b), "A Pragmatist Dimension in Georg Henrik von Wright's Philosophy." *Acta Baltica Historiae et Philosophiae Scientiarum* 2:1, 5–17.

Pihlström, S. (ed.) (2015), *The Bloomsbury Companion to Pragmatism.* London and New York: Bloomsbury. (1st ed.: *The Continuum Companion to Pragmatism.* London: Continuum, 2011.)

Pihlström, S. (2016), *Death and Finitude: Toward a Pragmatic Transcendental Anthropology of Human Limits and Finitude.* Lanham, MD: Lexington Books.

Pihlström, S. (ed.) (2017), *Pragmatism and Objectivity: Essays Sparked by Nicholas Rescher's Philosophy.* London and New York: Routledge.

Pihlström, S. (2019a), "Applying William James's Pragmatism to Life: Against 'Applied Ethics'." In C. Stagoll and M. Levine (eds.), *Pragmatism Applied: William James and the Challenges of Contemporary Life.* Albany: SUNY Press, 125–148.

Pihlström, S. (2019b), "Pragmatism and the Phenomenology of Suffering." *Phänomenologische Forschungen* 2/2019, 13–30.

Pihlström, S. (2019c), "Truth, Suffering, and Religious Diversity: A Pragmatist Perspective." In Jonkers and Wiertz (eds.), 41–60.

Pihlström, S. (2019d), "Finnish Versions of Pragmatist Humanism: Eino Kaila and Georg Henrik von Wright as Quasi-Pragmatists." *European Journal of Pragmatism and American Philosophy* 11:1. Available online: https://journals.openedition.org/ejpap/1543#text.

Pihlström, S. (2020a), *Pragmatic Realism, Religious Truth, and Antitheodicy: On Viewing the World by Acknowledging the Other*. Helsinki: Helsinki University Press.

Pihlström, S. (2020b), "Pragmatism and Meaning Agnosticism." *Religions* 11:302. Available online: www.mdpi.com/2077-1444/11/6/302.

Pihlström, S. (2020c), "Theodicy by Other Means? Rethinking 'God after Auschwitz' through the Dialectics of Antitheodicism." *Cosmos and History* 16. Available online: www.cosmosandhistory.org/index.php/journal/article/view/868.

Pihlström, S. and Kivistö, S. (2021), *Critical Distance: Ethical and Literary Engagements with Detachment, Isolation, and Otherness*. Manuscript, forthcoming.

Plantinga, A. (2000), *Warranted Christian Belief*. Oxford: Oxford University Press.

Plato, *The Republic*. Trans. B. Jowett. Available online: http://classics.mit.edu/Plato/republic.html.

Price, H. (2011), *Naturalism without Mirrors*. Oxford: Oxford University Press.

Proudfoot, W. (1985), *Religious Experience*. Berkeley: University of California Press.

Proudfoot, W. (2019), "Recognition, Theodicy, and Experience." In Rydenfelt et al. (eds.), 133–142.

Putnam, H. (1981), *Reason, Truth and History*. Cambridge: Cambridge University Press.

Putnam, H. (1983), *Realism and Reason*. Cambridge: Cambridge University Press.

Putnam, H. (1990), *Realism with a Human Face*. J. Conant (ed.). Cambridge, MA and London: Harvard University Press.

Putnam, H. (1992), *Renewing Philosophy*. Cambridge, MA and London: Harvard University Press.

Putnam, H. (1994), *Words and Life*. J. Conant (ed.). Cambridge, MA and London: Harvard University Press.

Putnam, H. (1999), *The Threefold Cord*. New York: Columbia University Press.

Putnam, H. (2002), *The Collapse of the Fact/Value Dichotomy and Other Essays*. Cambridge, MA and London: Harvard University Press.

Putnam, H. (2004), *Ethics without Ontology*. Cambridge, MA and London: Harvard University Press.

Putnam, H. (2016), *Naturalism, Realism, and Normativity*. M. de Caro (ed.). Cambridge, MA and London: Harvard University Press.

Putnam, H. and Putnam, R. A. (2017), *Pragmatism as a Way of Life*. Cambridge, MA and London: The Belknap Press of Harvard University Press.

Quine, W. V. (1980 [1951]), "Two Dogmas of Empiricism." In Quine, *From a Logical Point of View*. Rev. ed. Cambridge, MA and London: Harvard University Press (1st ed. 1953).

Rawls, J. (1971), *A Theory of Justice*. Cambridge, MA: Harvard University Press.

Rorty, R. (1979), *Philosophy and the Mirror of Nature*. Princeton, NJ: Princeton University Press.

Rorty, R. (1989), *Contingency, Irony, and Solidarity*. Cambridge: Cambridge University Press.

Rorty, R. (1991), *Objectivity, Relativism, and Truth*. Cambridge: Cambridge University Press.

Rorty, R. (1998), *Truth and Progress*. Cambridge: Cambridge University Press.

Rorty, R. (2000), "Response to James Conant." In R. B. Brandom (ed.), *Rorty and His Critics*. Cambridge, MA and Oxford: Blackwell, 342–350.

Rorty, R. (2007), *Philosophy as Cultural Politics*. Cambridge: Cambridge University Press.

Russell, B. (1972 [1945]), *A History of Western Philosophy*. New York: Simon & Schuster.

Rydenfelt, H. (2019a), "Realism without Representationalism." *Synthese* 198, 2901–2918.

Rydenfelt, H. (2019b), "Pragmatist Antinomy." In Rydenfelt et al. (eds.), 45–56.

Rydenfelt, H., Koskinen, H. J., and Bergman, M. (eds.) (2019), *Limits of Pragmatism and Challenges of Theodicy*. Acta Philosophica Fennica 95. Helsinki: The Philosophical Society of Finland.

Rydenfelt, H. and Pihlström, S. (eds.) (2013), *William James on Religion*. Basingstoke: Palgrave Macmillan.

Saarinen, R. (2016), *Recognition and Religion: A Historical and Systematic Study*. Oxford and New York: Oxford University Press.

Saito, N. (2019), *American Philosophy in Translation*. Lanham, MD: Rowman & Littlefield.

Sartre, J.-P. (1946), "Existentialism is a Humanism." Available online: https://warwick.ac.uk/fac/cross_fac/complexity/people/students/dtc/students2011/maitland/philosophy/sartre-eih.pdf.

Sharpe, M. (2019), "After the Fall: Camus on Evil." In T. Nys and S. de Wijze (eds.), *The Routledge Handbook of the Philosophy of Evil*. Abingdon and New York: Routledge, 163–174.

Sinclair, R. (2011), "Morton White's Moral Pragmatism." *Cognitio* 12, 143–155.

Sinclair, R. (2014), "Dewey and White on Value, Obligation, and Practical Judgment." *Sats* 15, 39–54.

Skowroński, K. and Pihlström, S. (eds.) (2019), *Pragmatist Kant*. Nordic Studies in Pragmatism 4. Helsinki: Nordic Pragmatism Network. Available online: https://nordprag.org/nordic-studies-in-pragmatism/pragmatist-kant/.

Smith, J. and Sullivan, P. (eds.) (2011), *Transcendental Philosophy and Naturalism*. Oxford: Oxford University Press.

Snellman, L. (2020), *The Problem of Evil and the Problem of Intelligibility: A Grammatical Metacritique of the Problem of Evil*. Diss. Helsinki: University of Helsinki. Available online: https://helda.helsinki.fi/handle/10138/318648.

Snyder, T. (2010), *Bloodlands: Europe between Hitler and Stalin*. London: Vintage.

Snyder, T. (2015), *Black Earth: The Holocaust as History and Warning*. London: Vintage.

Snyder, T. (2018), *The Road to Unfreedom*. New York: Tim Duggan Books.

Sparti, D. (2005), "Let Us Be Human: Primo Levi and Ludwig Wittgenstein." *Philosophy and Literature* 29, 444–459.

Standish, P. and Saito, N. (eds.) (2017), *Stanley Cavell and Philosophy as Translation: The Truth Is Translated*. Lanham, MD: Rowman & Littlefield.

Stern, R. (ed.) (1999), *Transcendental Arguments: Problems and Prospects*. Oxford: Clarendon Press.

Stern, R. (2000), *Transcendental Arguments and Scepticism: Answering the Question of Justification*. Oxford: Clarendon Press.

Strawson, P. F. (1993 [1959]), *Individuals: An Essay in Descriptive Metaphysics*. London: Routledge.

Strawson, P. F. (1966), *The Bounds of Sense*. London: Methuen.

Strawson, P. F. (1985), *Scepticism and Naturalism: Some Varieties*. London: Methuen.

Stroud, B. (1968), "Transcendental Arguments." *The Journal of Philosophy* 65, 241–256.

Stroud, B. (2000), *Understanding Human Knowledge: Philosophical Essays*. Oxford: Oxford University Press.

Stuhr, J. J. (2017), "Redeeming the Wild Universe: William James's *Will to Believe*." In D. H. Evans (ed.), *Understanding James, Understanding Modernism*. New York: Bloomsbury.

Taylor, C. (1989), *Sources of the Self: The Making of Modern Identity*. Cambridge: Cambridge University Press.

Taylor, C. (1995 [1992]), "The Politics of Recognition." In Taylor, *Philosophical Arguments*. Cambridge, MA and London: Harvard University Press.

Taylor, C. (2002), *Varieties of Religion Today: Re-experiencing William James*. Cambridge, MA and London: Harvard University Press.

Unamuno, M. de (1913), *Tragic Sense of Life*. Trans. J. E. Crawford Flitch (1921). New York: Dover (1954). Available online: www.gutenberg.org/files/14636/146 36-h/14636-h.htm.

Vanden Auweele, D. (2019), *Pessimism in Kant's Ethics and Rational Religion*. Lanham, MD: Lexington Books.

Višňovský, E. (2020), "Rorty's Humanism: Making It Explicit." *European Journal of Pragmatism and American Philosophy* 12:1. Available online: https://journals.openedition.org/ejpap/1878.

White, M. (1973 [1949]), "The Analytic and the Synthetic: An Untenable Dualism." In White, *The American Mind*. New York: Oxford University Press.

White, M. (1956), *Toward Reunion in Philosophy*. Cambridge, MA: Harvard University Press.

White, M. (1981), *What Is and What Ought to Be Done*. Oxford: Oxford University Press.

White, M. (2002), *A Philosophy of Culture: The Scope of Holistic Pragmatism*. Princeton, NJ: Princeton University Press.

White, M. (2005), *From a Philosophical Point of View*. Princeton, NJ: Princeton University Press.

Williams, B. (2002), *Truth and Truthfulness*. Princeton, NJ: Princeton University Press.

Wisdom, J. (1944–1945), "Gods." *Proceedings of the Aristotelian Society* 45, 185–206.

Wittgenstein, L. (1974 [1921]), *Tractatus Logico-Philosophicus*. Trans. B. F. McGuinness and D. Pears, London: Routledge and Kegan Paul.

Wittgenstein, L. (1953), *Philosophical Investigations*. Trans. G.E.M. Anscombe. Oxford: Basil Blackwell.

Wittgenstein, L. (1961), *Notebooks 1914–1916*. G. E. M. Anscombe and G. H. von Wright (eds.), Oxford: Basil Blackwell.

Wittgenstein, L. (1966), *Lectures and Conversations on Aesthetics, Psychology, and Religious Belief.* C. Barrett (ed.). Berkeley: University of California Press.

Wittgenstein, L. (1969), *On Certainty*. Trans. G. E. M. Anscombe and D. Paul. Oxford: Basil Blackwell.

Wittgenstein, L. (1980a), *Culture and Value*. Trans. Peter Winch. Oxford: Basil Blackwell.

Wittgenstein, L. (1980b), *Wittgenstein's Lectures, Cambridge 1930–1933*. Oxford: Basil Blackwell.

Wittgenstein, L. (1993), *Philosophical Occasions 1912–1951*. J. Klagge and A. Nordmann (eds.). Indianapolis: Hackett.

von Wright, G. H. (1971), *Explanation and Understanding*, Ithaca, NY and London: Cornell University Press.

von Wright, G. H. (1974), *Causality and Determinism*. New York and London: Columbia University Press.

von Wright, G. H. (1980), *Freedom and Determination*. Acta Philosophica Fennica 31:1. Helsinki: The Philosophical Society of Finland.

von Wright, G. H. (1998), *In the Shadow of Descartes: Essays in the Philosophy of Mind*. Dordrecht: Kluwer.

Yoder, S. D. (2013), "Making Space for Agnosticism: A Response to Dawkins and James." *American Journal of Theology and Philosophy* 34, 135–153.

Zackariasson, U. (2019), "'We Are All Survivors' – Survivor Guilt and Pragmatic Meliorism." In Rydenfelt et al. (eds.), 153–162.

Zimmerman, A. Z. (2018), *Belief: A Pragmatic Picture*. Oxford: Oxford University Press.

Index

Milton Keynes UK
Ingram Content Group UK Ltd.
UKHW051909270324
440086UK00021B/204